The
Martial
Metropolis

The
Martial
Metropolis

U.S. Cities in
War and Peace

Edited by
Roger W. Lotchin

PRAEGER

PRAEGER SPECIAL STUDIES • PRAEGER SCIENTIFIC

New York • Philadelphia • Eastbourne, UK
Toronto • Hong Kong • Tokyo • Sydney

Contents

About the Editor
and Contributors

ROGER W. LOTCHIN is Professor of History at the University of North Carolina, Chapel Hill. His written works include San Francisco, 1846-1856: From Hamlet to City and articles in the Journal of American History, Pacific Historical Review, Journal of the West, Urbanism Past and Present, and Journal für Geschichte.

CARL ABBOTT is Professor of Urban Studies at Portland State University, Portland, Oregon. Until 1978 he was Associate Professor of History at Old Dominion University, Norfolk, Virginia. Dr. Abbott has published widely in the area of urban history including The Evolution of an Urban Neighborhood: Colonial Place, Norfolk, Virginia; Colorado: A History of the Centennial State; and The New Urban America: Growth and Politics in Sunbelt Cities. His articles have appeared in the Journal of American History, Planning, Social Science History, and Indiana Magazine of History.

ROBERT B. FAIRBANKS is Assistant Professor of History at the University of Texas at Arlington. Dr. Fairbanks is the author of a forthcoming book on housing, planning, and the changing conceptions of the metropolis in Cincinnati from 1890 to 1954 and has published articles in Ohio History, American Studies, and the Cincinnati Historical Society Bulletin.

GREGORY FONTENOT, formerly Instructor of History at the United States Military Academy at West Point, is currently a student at the United States Army Command and General Staff College, Fort Leavenworth, Kansas. Mr. Fontenot is the author of "The Modern Major General: Patterns in the Careers of the British Army Major Generals on Active Duty at the Time of the Sarajevo Assassinations," Master's thesis, University of North Carolina, Chapel Hill. His articles have appeared in Infantry Journal and several other journals.

GEORGE W. HOPKINS is Associate Professor of History at the College of Charleston, Charleston, South Carolina, where he is also Coeditor of South Atlantic Urban Studies. Dr. Hopkins is the author of a forthcoming book entitled Miners for Democracy. His articles have appeared in South Atlantic Urban Studies and Essays in Southern Labor History, edited by Gary M. Fink et al.

KENNETH T. JACKSON is Professor of History at Columbia University and Secretary-Treasurer for the Society of American

Historians. Dr. Jackson has written widely in the field of urban history including The Ku Klux Klan in the City, 1915-1930; American Vistas, edited with Leonard Dinnerstein; and Cities in American History, edited with Stanley K. Schultz. His articles have appeared in the Journal of Urban History, Records of the Columbia Historical Society, and Social Education.

DAVID R. JOHNSON is Associate Professor of History at the University of Texas at San Antonio. His books include Policing the Underworld: The Impact of Crime and the Development of the American Police, 1800-1887 and American Law Enforcement: A History. Dr. Johnson's articles have appeared in various scholarly journals.

ZANE L. MILLER is Professor of History and Codirector of the Center for Neighborhood and Community at the University of Cincinnati. Dr. Miller's many published works include Boss Cox's Cincinnati: Urban Politics in the Progressive Era; The Urbanization of Modern America; Cincinnati's Music Hall, with George F. Roth; Urban Professionals and the Future of the Metropolis, with Paula Dubeck; Physician to the West: Selected Writings of Daniel Drake on Science and Society, with Henry Shapiro; The Planning Partnership: Participants' Views of Urban Renewal, edited with Thomas H. Jenkins; and Suburb: Neighborhood and Community in Forest Park, Ohio, 1935-1976. His articles have appeared in the American Historical Review, Urbanism Past and Present, Urban History Yearbook, and Journal of Urban History.

GEOFFREY ROSSANO is Instructor of History at Salisbury School in Salisbury, Connecticut, and Director of the Oral History Research Program at the Nassau County Cradle of Aviation Museum, Mitchell Field, Long Island, New York. Dr. Rossano is coauthor of a forthcoming book on the history of Long Island.

MARTIN J. SCHIESL is Associate Professor of History at California State University at Los Angeles. Dr. Schiesl has written The Politics of Efficiency: Municipal Administration and Reform in America, 1880-1920 and articles in California History, California Historical Quarterly, and The Age of Urban Reform: New Perspectives on the Progressive Era, edited by Michael H. Ebner and Eugene M. Tobin.

CHRISTOPHER SILVER is Assistant Professor of Urban Studies and Planning at Virginia Commonwealth University in Richmond, Virginia. Dr. Silver is the author of Planning and Politics in Twentieth Century Richmond (forthcoming) and has published articles in South Atlantic Urban Studies and Perspectives on the Urban South: Proceedings of the Fourth Annual Conference on the Urban South.

Introduction:
The Martial Metropolis

Roger W. Lotchin

Collaboration between the city and the military is not new to U.S. history, but the martial metropolis is. The city and the sword have had a long and sometimes illustrious partnership stretching back many years. San Francisco was founded in 1776 as a fort and mission, part of a strategic line of Spanish defenses intended to keep the Russians at bay. The cities of the urban frontier in the Ohio River Valley developed around other forts—Pittsburgh at Fort Duquesne-Fort Pitt, Cincinnati at Fort Washington, and Louisville at Fort Nelson. Each of these fledgling settlements derived support from military patronage and protection while suffering some of the inconvenience and even tragedy of war.

Other cities have profited from somewhat different military relationships. The Brooklyn Navy Yard, from its founding in 1801 to its closing in 1955, served as one of the principal economic bases of a rapidly growing borough. During the Civil War, Springfield, Massachusetts, boomed as its U.S. armory turned out supplies for the Union armies. Connecticut cities such as New Haven and Hartford profited similarly on the sale of Colts, Winchesters, and similar weapons before and after that conflict. Richmond, Atlanta, and other Confederate cities felt the hand of war—but in a much less beneficial way. As strategic targets of war these places felt the destructive impact of a fratricidal conflict. At the turn of the century, Tampa and San Francisco boomed as the jumping-off points for the Spanish-American War and the Philippine Insurrection campaigns, respectively. With the advent of the aviation age, Pensacola became very dependent upon its naval air station. Contemporaneously, El Paso served as the command post and dispatching center for the Pershing Expedition into Mexico in search of Pancho Villa, and cities all over the country gained from World War I. Seattle shipyards turned out thousands of tons of shipping; Southern cities wined and dined the army trainees; and San Diego played host to marines, soldiers, and sailors. World War II lengthened the list of cities associated with the phenomenon of war. Places as diverse as Detroit and Los Angeles vied for the title of "arsenal of democracy," and hardly any major city remained untouched by that conflict. With the coming of the nuclear age, cities came to occupy the center of the target and learned to appreciate the role of hostage to guarantee the nation's good behavior.

Many other examples could be cited, but enough have been noted to document that in the United States the city and the sword have had a long and close association. Yet before the twentieth century, much of this partnership was episodic. Richmond was not permanently besieged, nor Atlanta repeatedly burned, nor Tampa endlessly employed in dispatching soldiers to Cuba. Some cities—like Springfield, Massachusetts, or the Connecticut arms towns, or Brooklyn with its navy yard—enjoyed an enduring partnership with the U.S. military; but most U.S. cities did not, and it is doubtful if even the ones that did were overwhelmingly dependent on service patronage. However, with the dawning of the era of global war in the twentieth century, the U.S. military became more prominent, and its impact on U.S. cities became more permanent. Particularly after World War I, and even more so after 1941, the martial metropolis lost its episodic character. Now literally dozens of urban places have developed long-term, institutionalized relationships with the armed forces.

No one disputes the economic importance of this development. Military expenditures have helped to build the Sunbelt and to undermine their competitors in the urban Frostbelt as well. In the process some cities have gained immensely and others have lost, it would almost seem, disastrously. Congressmen, mayors, and senators have battled constantly and even savagely to share the former fate and to avoid the latter. Without a doubt the institutionalization of military spending has significantly affected the process of urbanization.

However, historians, urban or otherwise, have largely ignored this critical development. To a large degree, so have social scientists. The latter have been very interested in several kinds of civilian-military interfaces. Such matters as the so-called military-industrial complex, the economic impact of defense spending, the supposed growth of U.S. militarism, and other topics have attracted social science interest. Generally, however, they have ignored the urban areas where the money has been spent, the militarism has supposedly been generated, and the civilian-service partnerships created. Historians have neglected this matter even more consistently and have only recently looked at the military-industrial complex itself. A few writers, such as Philip Funigiello, George Pearce, James McGovern, and Leonard Arrington, have dealt with the tie between the city and the sword; but few others have undertaken this task for the twentieth century period.

It is the purpose of this book to end this neglect. The twentieth century has witnessed the coming of age of both the American military and the American metropolis, and this convergence explains the temporal setting of the book. The choice of cities has been influenced by a number of considerations, and the availability of authors was obviously one of these. More important, I sought to cover cities that possessed enduring partnerships with the military services. I also tried to include at least one city that has had predominant connections to one of each of the three major services—the army, the navy, and the air force. Moreover, I wanted to consider both urban and suburban military links. And finally, I wanted to include cities from both regions losing and regions gaining military investment. There is obviously no definitive list of martial metropolises because of the great number of urban areas with significant military resources. However, the selection included in this book is broadly representative of the relationships under review.

Because of these assets, this book should contribute to both military and urban history. In particular, it seeks to provide historical perspective on the development of what is termed the military-industrial complex and, by describing the evolution of these relationships over time, to supply a more urban interpretation of the origins of that phenomenon. The military-industrial complex did not simply grow out of the industrial necessities of the United States during and after World War II. It originated from the urban imperatives of the country and well before World War II. It is hoped that an understanding of these origins will contribute to both more scholarly discussions and a better popular understanding of the current and perennial post-World War II welfare-versus-warfare debate.

Still the controversy over guns versus butter is only one concern of this book. The process of urbanization is an even more important one. The question of what is urban and what is a part of the process of urbanization has been frequently argued. Of late, it has been the subject of intense debate with at least some urban historians arguing that urban history has not yet been written in such a way as to illuminate the process of urbanization or the condition of urbanism. Without wishing to prove or disprove the validity of that contention, it is hoped that the various chapters will contribute something to our understanding of the process of urbanization by analyzing one source of economic support for that process. In this context the term urbanization means what Hope Tisdale defined it as some 40 years ago, the still-standard definition among urban historians today: Urbanization "is a process of population concentration" that leads to the growth of cities and the multiplication of city sites. This book is primarily concerned with the first part of this definition, that is, with the growth of cities, especially insofar as that evolution is underpinned by military money, patronage, and prestige. Defense spending has contributed greatly to both the acceleration and deceleration of urban development and, to a lesser extent, to the multiplication of city sites, if we are to include suburbs. The military connection is an especially appropriate way to view the process of urbanization because it allows us to see that process as both a dependent and an independent variable. The martial metropolises have been both shaped by military decisions and molded by their own. The operation of these two factors together have produced a new type of urban form, organized around its partnership with the military services. In a book of this length and nature, it is not possible to claim either comprehensive or definitive coverage of this subject. It is possible, however, to broach the idea of the martial metropolis and to suggest its general interpretive significance.

The suggestions made here may be controversial for some time to come, but it is certainly appropriate after 45 years of large-scale military spending to begin thinking about the implications of that development for U.S. cities.

1

From Naval Pauper to Naval Power: The Development of Charleston's Metropolitan-Military Complex

George W. Hopkins

Thanks to the great publicity given President Dwight D. Eisenhower's Farewell Address and the controversy surrounding U.S. involvement in Vietnam, the phrase <u>military-industrial complex</u> has become a cliché. Nonetheless, the phrase generally has contained a large measure of truth and common sense. The military-industrial complex has been popularly understood as a cold war phenomenon, headquartered in Washington, D.C., and involving the Pentagon, the Department of Defense, Congress, the White House, lobbyists for major contractors, corporations, unions, universities, and think-tanks. What has usually been missing from these analyses is a fuller understanding of the historical relationship between the military and the industrial complexes of various U.S. cities.[1] Analyzing the origins, growth, and development of these "metropolitan-military complexes" can provide new perspectives on each subject; moreover, studying the reciprocal impact of the military and city on each other at the local level can provide additional insights into the processes of militarization and urbanization, forces that have paralleled and reinforced each other in their combined impact on much of twentieth century urban America.[2]

The author gratefully acknowledges the financial assistance provided by the College of Charleston as well as the hospitality and secretarial assistance provided by the Department of History of the University of Georgia during part of my sabbatical leave. Both institutions helped make the research and writing of this chapter possible.

Charleston, South Carolina, is one crucible in which these two processes have intertwined. Located, according to local lore, on the tip of a peninsula formed by the Ashley and Cooper rivers as they merge to create the Atlantic Ocean, Charleston and its surrounding Lowcountry have had a long martial tradition. However, a devastated post-Civil War Charleston continued its prewar decline, falling from its position as the twenty-second largest city in 1860 (population 40,000) to sixty-eighth place in 1900 (55,807). The city's "commercial-civic elite" failed to overcome its own internal divisions as well as external obstacles to economic resurgence. As Don Doyle noted: "A number of new ventures in railroad expansion, phosphate mining, textile manufacturing, and tourism sparked enthusiasm in the old city at various times, but all eventually fell flat for want of sufficient capital and sustained public support."[3] The same reasons accounted for the failure of the city's South Carolina Interstate and West Indian Exposition in 1901/02. Even nature seemed to conspire against Charleston as cyclones, earthquakes, and hurricanes buffeted the Lowcountry in the late nineteenth century. The city's rivals outpaced Charleston. Savannah's port commerce grew as Charleston declined, and discriminatory rates resulted in more South Carolina cottons going by rail to Norfolk for export than through the state's own chief port. By 1903 the city's docks, owned by outside railroad interests, had begun to deteriorate badly. One historian of Charleston declared with only slight exaggeration that as the city entered the twentieth century, "Charleston, so proud of its past, was a stinking, rotten, unhealthy, poverty-stricken, ill-governed town, better known for its vices than its virtues."[4]

Ironically, the federal government and its military forces, which had done so much damage to Charleston, would also do much to aid the city. What one Charleston native described as "the most important economic decision in the modern history of Charleston" occurred in 1901 when the U.S. Navy established a naval shipyard in the Charleston area.[5] That decision was the result of two major factors. The first was the work of the Army Corps of Engineers, which provided Charleston with a modern, deep-water port by clearing the harbor of wrecked vessels, dredging the harbor channels, and building a system of jetties to keep the harbor free from silt and sandbars. These improvements, completed by 1895, were a prerequisite for any naval presence in Charleston.[6] The other major factor was South Carolina Senator "Pitchfork Ben" Tillman's influence as a member of the Senate Naval Affairs Committee. When the navy decided to abandon its problematic naval station at Port Royal, South Carolina, Tillman argued that U.S. interests in the Caribbean required a navy yard south of Norfolk. He persuaded the navy and Congress to transfer the Port Royal facility to the upgraded Charleston Harbor area.

The Charleston Naval Yard would become what Tillman's biographer described as the senator's "greatest pork-barrel triumph."[7]

However, such a triumph was neither automatic nor inevitable. Significantly, the location of the naval complex, seven miles north of the city limits on the west bank of the Cooper River, far from the historic downtown section, largely prevented community conflict over any adverse effects of the yard on the city proper. This in turn allowed the commercial-civic elite to build a genuine community consensus in its support. While city leaders often wrapped their advocacy of the yard in patriotic rhetoric about "duty" and "strategy," they also viewed the naval presence as crucial to the city's economic salvation. To demonstrate its desire for the yard, the city council made substantial park acreage available to the navy and pledged to construct a larger waterworks plant to meet the yard's need.[8]

Such community support was essential because the yard's existence would be precarious more than once. For example, while construction continued on the yard's dry dock, in 1904 a new secretary of the navy, William H. Moody, charged that the navy had been coerced into accepting the inadequate, undesirable Charleston site solely because of Senator Tillman's political clout. When the secretary tried to delete Charleston's funding from a House naval appropriations bill, Charleston Congressman George S. Legaré enumerated the virtues of the city's harbor, reaffirmed the city's commitment to the navy, and rallied his colleagues to block the move. Legaré shrewdly helped plan visits of important Washington officials to Charleston so that the local elite could welcome their guests, show them the city's fine harbor, and enlist their support of the yard.[9]

The combination of hospitality and lobbying soon provided dividends. The Coast Defense Squadron arrived in Charleston in November 1905 and stayed for almost half a year. During that period, the commercial-civic elite continually entertained squadron commander Rear Admiral Francis W. Dickens and his officers while their men spent over a quarter of a million dollars in the area. The experience converted Dickens into a strong advocate for Charleston, lauding the city's strategic location and fine harbor. Meanwhile, in January 1906 the new secretary of the navy, Charles J. Bonaparte, came to the city on board the cruiser Charleston. City officials welcomed their naval namesake and presented its crew with a silver punch bowl and service. According to the city newspaper, the secretary's official visit signified "the resumption of diplomatic relations between the White House and Charleston."[10]

City leaders were disappointed, though, later in 1906 when the navy's General Board decided that Charleston's harbor could not accommodate the new, larger-scale battleships and that further development of the yard would be limited to the repair of torpedo boats. Instead of hosting battleships, Charleston would serve instead as a base for the reserve torpedo flotilla. The decision to limit the yard's development also reflected the administration's philosophical commitment to private shipyard construction, believing that to be more economical and more efficient than public yard construction. Therefore, the navy limited the number of major public yards performing construction and restricted most naval yards to "refitting and repair."[11]

However, the Charleston yard continued to grow slowly in importance and workload. In 1907 Secretary of War William Howard Taft visited the city and linked the Charleston yard to the nation's defense of the Panama Canal. Later that year, the yard's fine dry dock, 575 feet long, was completed at a cost exceeding $7 million. With well over 800 civilian personnel operating the yard's machine shops, powerhouse, piers, and other facilities, by 1910 the yard added over $0.5 million to the local economy each year.[12] Charleston's modest metropolitan-military complex seemed reasonably well established.

Senator Tillman's political influence accounted for the Charleston yard's continued growth. Tillman's biographer did not mince words: the senator "became party to a cabal consisting of the ten members of the Senate Naval Committee in whose states were located navy yards (representing Portsmouth, Boston, New York, Philadelphia, Norfolk, Charleston, New Orleans, Mare Island [California], and Puget Sound). These gentlemen supported the needs of each other's projects."[13] The activities of "the navy-yard junta" did not go unnoticed. Muckraker George Kibbe Turner's article in the February 1909 issue of McClure's Magazine, titled "Our Navy on the Land," denounced the "pork barrel politics," which had resulted in the proliferation of "State's rights navy-yards" along the Atlantic coastline. Turner cited Tillman and the Port Royal-Charleston shift as a classic example of an unnecessary yard foisted on the navy because of political influence. Turner argued that the navy needed no other Atlantic yards than those in New York and Norfolk—and one at Guantánamo, Cuba. Moreover, private shipyards could build navy ships at less cost. The following year Navy Secretary George V. L. Meyer essentially endorsed Turner's views, calling for economy and the closing of at least eight shore stations. Put on the defensive by Progressives in the Senate, Tillman decried Republican hostility toward his Democratic state and Northern sectional prejudice against South Carolina. He reiterated the virtues of Charleston's harbor and its strategic location. However, perhaps in response to critics' charges, in 1911 the navy transferred its machinists' mates school from Norfolk to Charleston to train more skilled craftsmen.[14]

Meanwhile, despite consensus on the Charleston yard, elite dissensus hindered the city's efforts at growth and development. A fierce political struggle emerged between aristocratic, upper-class advocates of "good government" and a limited "business progressivism" on the one hand, and working-class and middle-class partisans of a more democratic form of progressivism focused especially on municipal ownership of utilities, on the other. The mayoral administrations of Robert G. Rhett (1903-11) had accented the former course of action, while the election of Catholic, Irish-American John P. Grace in 1911 signaled a shift toward the urban liberalism more typical of New York City. Nevertheless, the net result of this internecine political conflict was marginal progress in revitalizing the city's docks, securing effective commercial rail service, and boosting city growth generally. An incredibly low property tax assessment procedure required by state law further complicated efforts at expanding and delivering city services. Although several new business and trade associations were formed and the chamber of commerce reorganized itself in 1910, the navy yard continued to be an increasingly vital dimension of Charleston's economic life. [15]

Sensitive to the politics of appropriations and aware of the national controversy over the number of naval yards, Mayor Grace and the city of Charleston staged a gala reception for the week-long visit of the 11 battleships of the Atlantic Fleet during mid-November 1912. The fact that the harbor channels and the Cooper River easily accommodated the big ships belied critics' charges. Again, the city entertained naval personnel with a variety of parties, parades, and other activities. The seven-day affair was a great public relations success for the city. Significantly, though, the city treasury had to absorb most of the $18,000 cost of the festivities because few of the commercial-civic elite contributed as the mayor had requested— another illustration of local political feuding. [16]

But presidential politics brought important advantages for Charleston and its yard: the election of Woodrow Wilson in 1912 put a Democrat, born in Virginia, in the White House. Wilson's choice for secretary of the navy, Josephus Daniels of North Carolina, combined with Democratic control of the Senate, which made Tillman the new head of the Senate Naval Affairs Committee, further enhanced Charleston's political position. The city and its yard benefited from these arrangements almost immediately, winning a $300,000 award for a new torpedo basin, a $125,000 lighthouse in the harbor, and further dredging and channel development in 1913. The impact of Charleston's metropolitan-military complex grew: in 1913 the navy yard employed approximately one tenth of the area's work force and supplied one fifth of the wages and capitalization in the Lowcountry.

Demonstrating additional clout, Tillman persuaded the navy to relocate its clothing factory from the Brooklyn Navy Yard to the Charleston facility in 1914.[17]

While former Navy Secretary Meyer continued his crusade against the "superfluous number of navy-yards distributed along the Atlantic coast" in a 1915 North American Review article that also denounced the "politics and log-rolling" dominating naval appropriations decisions,[18] the "pork-barrel conspiracy" became even more sophisticated. Senate Naval Affairs Chairman Tillman came to an understanding with fellow committee member Claude Swanson of Virginia; the pair agreed to end their rivalry over the claims of Charleston and Norfolk and instead to support each other's bills against Northern opposition. Working in concert with Secretary Daniels, Tillman and Swansom exercised preponderant influence on naval appropriations during the Wilson administration, and their yards benefited noticeably from that situation. The trio also agreed that navy yards should do more than repair and maintenance; public yards should also do more construction. Tillman, Swanson, and Daniels opposed the profiteering steel, armor, and munitions trusts and wanted more public control over naval construction quality and costs. Moreover, their commitment to naval expansion dovetailed with the desires of preparedness advocates and thus won more votes for their projects.[19]

The Charleston Navy Yard soon began constructing smaller craft such as dredges, tugs, and tenders. Once the United States entered the Great War, the yard expanded, building subchasers, a gunboat, and a destroyer as well as repairing and outfitting many vessels. In addition, the yard's clothing factory turned out thousands of garments for naval personnel. Civilian employment at the yard soared to over 5,500 in 1918, adding over $5.75 million to the local economy. Other military facilities in the area were also greatly expanded as Charleston became a port of embarkation for the U.S. Army. The federal government spent over $20 million building quartermaster and ordinance depots and port terminals north of the city.[20]

The war also allowed Tillman's dream of making the Charleston yard second to none begin to come true. The Helm Board, chaired by former Charleston Yard Commandant J. M. Helm, concluded early in 1918 that the "Charleston Harbor most nearly meets the physical requirements of the Navy Department for a first-class Navy Yard" on the Atlantic coast. Armed with the commission's report and Secretary Daniels' support, Tillman won congressional approval of a $1.65 million appropriation for a second dry dock for the Charleston yard, a 1,000-foot facility capable of handling modern battleship construction. Tillman died unexpectedly on July 1, 1918, with his navy yard seemingly assured of priority status.[21]

The war's impact on Charleston was substantial. The population of the city increased by 20 percent to over 80,000 by 1918; a year later over 100,000 people lived in the Lowcountry, almost 60 percent of whom were black. The usual wartime problems of overcrowded housing and schools, severe traffic congestion, inadequate law enforcement and fire protection, and suppression of prostitution and venereal disease were further complicated by an influenza epidemic. Social tensions generated by the war culminated in a race riot that erupted in Charleston on Saturday night, May 10, 1919. Unlike other racial conflicts of that "Red Summer," Charleston's racial violence was not between indigenous whites and blacks but between local blacks and white sailors stationed in Charleston. City police tried to protect black citizens and called on the navy for help in quelling the disorder; marines with fixed bayonets forced the sailors back to their quarters. The casualties were relatively light; blacks suffered 2 dead and 17 wounded, while whites suffered 8 wounded, 1 of whom was a policeman. The toll would have been much higher had the Charleston police not acted quickly to protect black citizens. While white Charleston was undoubtedly racist, the city's racism was paternalistic and hegemonic and prided itself on its ability to rule without the overt use of force—no lynchings had marred Charleston's civic record. The experience of a race riot shocked and saddened many white as well as black Charlestonians.[22]

Soon after the riot, the dramatic 1919 Charleston mayoralty campaign began. Four years earlier, Mayor Grace had been defeated in his reelection bid by conservative banker Tristram Hyde in a bitterly disputed contest. In 1919 Grace opposed Hyde in a rematch. While some of Hyde's supporters questioned Grace's Catholicism, Hyde centered his campaign on Grace's antiwar, unpatriotic, alleged pro-German views, which could possibly result in the closing of the navy yard and disaster for Charleston if Grace were elected. Grace countered by denouncing Hyde's alleged ownership of part of the land that Hyde, while mayor, had sold at an inflated price to the government for the port terminals site. Grace charged that Hyde represented the worst kind of profiteering "paytriot." Grace succeeded in making municipal ownership of the docks the chief issue of the campaign. The progressive booster argued that Charleston's economic future required city control of the mismanaged docks. Winning the close race, Grace arranged for the city to buy the facilities and set up a nonpartisan Port Utilities Commission to oversee waterfront development.[23]

An even more impressive addition to the burgeoning metropolitan-military complex was the city's acquisition of the $20 million port terminals built by the federal government during the war. Especially useful would be the wharves and warehouses of the quartermaster depot. New York engineer and port expert Edwin J. Clapp hailed the transfer: "Suddenly the war hands to Charleston the most modern port terminal in the country, larger than all that Charleston possessed before. . . . It is probably the most magnificent port terminal in the country." With city control of the entire waterfront complex, Charleston's commercial renaissance seemed ensured. But 1921 proved to be the port's best year until 1945. The time and cost of refurbishing the city docks, efforts to equalize discriminatory railroad rates, and the Great Depression all retarded Charleston's port development.[24]

However, the navy particularly seemed to favor Charleston. For two consecutive years, 1920/21, the Atlantic Destroyer Force spent several winter months in Charleston. The city government and the chamber of commerce had jointly solicited the naval presence and entertained the men with parades, receptions, and other activities. Mayor Grace boasted that the 1921 naval visit "was an invaluable advertisement to our city that as the one hundred and ten vessels of this fleet were stretched out in squadrons in our harbor, with all their auxiliary ships and the Flagship of the fleet, there was yet room for ten times that many." Grace also noted the direct economic benefit: several thousand sailors staying several months "poured into the channels of trade in this city, in round numbers, ten million dollars." Grace denounced those "cheap" and "churlish" citizens who "begrudge[d]" the "mere pittance, even if it be several thousand dollars" spent entertaining naval personnel during their stay while the city received so much in return.[25]

But the navy's favors were unreliable and uncertain—as was the future of the yard itself. Postwar cutbacks of construction and repair work led to mass meetings of yard employees and other citizens protesting discharges and layoffs. The 1,000-foot dry dock Tillman had secured was also in jeopardy. Senator Ellison D. "Cotton Ed" Smith testified before the Senate Naval Affairs Committee, citing the Helm Board's endorsement: "The incomparable superiority of the Charleston Navy Yard lies in the fact that not only is it the nearest yard of first-class equipment to the Panama Canal, but it is the only yard south of Norfolk which is impregnable against an attack by sea." Smith also noted that "from Cape Hatteras to Portsmouth, N.H., a distance of about 700 miles sea front or coast line . . . there are 18 dry docks," while "from Hatteras to Galveston, roughly speaking, a distance of 2,000 miles, we have one dry dock of the lesser type at Charleston, and one small floating dock at New Orleans." Smith made the case for a dry dock capable of handling a disabled or damaged battleship from the Caribbean. He also argued that all yards needed periodic dredging and that Charleston yard required less dredging than the Brooklyn yard. Senator N. B. Dial appealed to senatorial courtesy to save the authorization for the dry dock, telling the committee: "I would feel personal humiliation if it were repealed." Nonetheless, construction of the dry dock was postponed and then canceled. Meanwhile, the clothing factory at the yard was closed.[26]

However, worse news was yet to come. The impact of postwar demobilization, the transfer of half the fleet to the Pacific coast, the naval arms limitation treaties negotiated by the Harding administration, and pressures for economy in administration led Acting Secretary of the Navy Theodore Roosevelt to issue General Order no. 87 on July 10, 1922, which directed that the Charleston Navy Yard be closed "as soon as possible." The next day the city council passed a resolution protesting the action and declared that "the closing of the Navy Yard would be a calamity not only to this City but to the country at large." The Young Men's Board of Trade sent a similar resolution.[27]

Obviously, it would take more than resolutions to reverse the navy's decision. Charleston's commercial-civic elite acted quickly and orchestrated an impressive letter-writing campaign in support of the yard. The mayor, the governor, various representatives and senators, numerous chambers of commerce, business interests, labor organizations, civic groups, and clubs, ranging from New Orleans to Chicago, rallied to protest Roosevelt's decision. While most letters and telegrams outlined Charleston's advantages and urged retention of the yard, others denounced this "injustice to the South" and advocated continuance of the yard "as a matter of fairness to [the] Southeastern section of the U.S." But Roosevelt remained adamant while New York politicians wrote the assistant secretary, asking that the Charleston yard's workload be transferred to their Brooklyn yard.[28]

But as the level of sectional protest continued unabated, navy brass decided to bolster their case. On August 12 an internal staff memorandum to Admiral Coontz on "Subject: Strategy of Closing Charleston Navy Yard" suggested that the department secure "from the General Board or War Plans Division, an authoritative statement substantiating the Department's stand" and concluded that the Charleston yard was the most expendable of the East Coast yards. Four days later the General Board made exactly that recommendation to the secretary of the navy.[29]

The Charleston yard finally won a reprieve in September when Secretary of the Navy Edwin Denby ordered a halt to the yard's closing while a board investigated the situation. In a major effort to influence the board's decision, the Navy Yard Committee of the Charleston

Chamber of Commerce published a slickly produced brief summarizing Charleston's strategic, geographical, navigational, economic, and efficiency advantages. The Navy Yard Committee declared that despite "the vilification, misrepresentations and abuse which have been heaped upon the Charleston Navy Yard from time to time by the press and in Congress . . . No Naval Board has ever made an unfavorable report on the Charleston Navy Yard." Excerpts from previous board reports verified the claim. The committee also quoted extensively from the December 7, 1921, report of Rear Admiral E. A. Anderson, commandant of the Charleston Navy Yard, demonstrating that his yard was the most economical and efficient yard on the Atlantic and deserved more work, not less. Moreover, with five yards north of Cape Hatteras and Charleston the only yard south of Hatteras, Charleston should be the least—not most—expendable yard on the Atlantic. The Navy Yard Committee concluded that "the Charleston Navy Yard is essential to the Navy."[30]

The city's campaign succeeded—barely. The navy officially classified the Charleston Navy Yard as a subsidiary base for repairing and supplying small numbers of vessels. Senator Smith and, to a lesser extent, Mayor Grace claimed credit for saving the yard. But Charleston's commercial-civic elite knew the yard's existence was still precarious. As one official put it: "Charleston was anathema to the Navy in 1923." To counteract that attitude, business and political leaders took several steps. On May 1, 1923, the Charleston Chamber of Commerce and the city of Charleston jointly organized the Bureau of Foreign Trade and Port Development. Significantly, the groups selected Roy S. MacElwee, chairman of the State Navy League, as the first bureau commissioner. MacElwee immediately agreed with Nathaniel Barnwell, chairman of the chamber's Navy Yard Committee, who originated the idea of establishing a Navy Day celebration in the city to promote the navy's positive feelings toward Charleston and to help safeguard the yard. Commissioner MacElwee went to Washington, D.C., won official endorsement of the idea, and arranged naval participation in the first Navy Day in Charleston on October 27, 1923. This event, in the view of the elite, "was the entering wedge" that subsequently "create[d] a splendid impression in the Navy Department" toward Charleston. The second Navy Day jubilee in 1924 was even more successful.[31]

The city's courting of the navy began to pay dividends. Repeated pleas by Congressmen W. Turner Logan and James F. Byrnes (the latter born in Charleston but representing a midstate district), Senators Smith and Dial, and Commissioner MacElwee brought marginally more repair and maintenance work to the yard in the mid-1920s. Even so, the Charleston yard remained a naval pauper, the smallest on the Atlantic coast, subsisting on minimal federal funding. But when the Bureau of the Budget recommended closing the yard in 1925, Secretary of the Navy Curtis D. Wilbur wrote Senator Smith that "there need be no fear" of that happening. The following year efforts were made to reduce funds for the yard, but Senator Smith and Low-country Congressman Thomas S. McMillan were able to block those plans. McMillan also testified repeatedly before the House Naval Affairs Committee to defend the annual dredging appropriation for the Charleston yard. Without such dredging, the harbor would fill with silt, make the channels unnavigable, and render the yard useless. Ranking naval personnel often appeared with McMillan to endorse his request.[32]

Further dividends of the Charleston-navy courtship were brought about by the lobbying of Congressman McMillan, Senator Smith, Commissioner MacElwee, and others on his bureau's Scouting Fleet Committee. Their political pressure convinced the navy to transfer the destroyer squadrons of the U.S. Scouting Fleet from their fall base in Guantánamo, Cuba (which did not vote on navy appropriations), to Charleston beginning in 1927 and 1928. Commissioner MacElwee noted that his committee "coordinated the activities of the subcommittees organized to look to the entertainment and comfort of the 9,000 officers and men stationed here during the stay of the fleet." Mayor Stoney also pointed out the obvious economic impact on Charleston: the squadrons brought "to this port city more than $500,000 a month in new money and during the fall season, before there is a tourist movement, the local benefits are apparent."[33]

Yet Charleston always had to be wary of shifting political winds or poor publicity. When business and political leaders asked the navy why the Charleston yard received so little work in comparison to the five yards north of Cape Hatteras, they received evasive replies: "I regret that there is no real satisfactory answer to all of your questions." Navy officials conceded that "there are too many yards on the East Coast. The number cannot be justified on any ground of economy." That matter became a major public issue again when Rear Admiral T. P. Magruder published an article entitled "The Navy and Economy" in the Saturday Evening Post in September 1927. He echoed the charges above and argued that several Atlantic coast yards could be closed with no loss of efficiency to the navy. However, "this extravagance" would continue because of "strong political opposition" to attempted yard closings. Magruder was called before the House Committee on Naval Affairs and grilled about his article. During the extensive questioning, he advocated closing the Charleston, New York, and Portsmouth yards. Committee members defended their installations while excoriating Magruder for "commercializing a criticism of the institution that has nurtured you since you were a boy" and possibly lowering morale and discipline in the navy by

(CWA), and Works Progress Administration (WPA) funds to keep the yard busy building Coast Guard cutters and tugs as well as destroyers. The yard also repaired and overhauled other vessels. By 1938 the yard employed over 1,600 civilians. Public works grants financed other projects at the yard, including a base hospital addition, officers' quarters, a galvanizing plant, a second dry dock, and other repairs and improvements.[40]

Nonetheless, these projects were not automatically awarded to the Charleston Navy Yard. Constant fear of reduced work assignments and redistribution or cancellation of projects kept the yard situation volatile. The extensive correspondence by Byrnes, Smith, McMillan, and Maybank, among others, kept Charleston in the running in the intense competition among yards for the limited appropriations available. As port commerce declined, Maybank noted in 1936 that "the local Navy Yard is our major industry" and declared, "Thanks to the National Administration, since 1933 there has been spent, and pledged in naval construction work, Federal work relief projects, and plant improvements, exclusive of regular payrolls, upward of $15,000,000." Moreover, a new Coast Guard Aviation Base was under construction while Fort Moultrie was utilized "as a processing base for C.C.C. recruits" as well as "designated a district supply base." In 1936 the War Department selected Charleston as a port of embarkation for a substantial number of troops. Combined with other projects that aided the city and county, the New Deal further developed Charleston's metropolitan-military complex.[41]

In 1938, as Congress debated a large naval construction bill, the city's commercial-civic elite lobbied to get Charleston's share of the appropriation. The Maybank administration, the chamber of commerce, local trade unions, and other groups, working through area Congressman McMillan, invited Vice-President John N. Garner, officials of the Navy Department, and members of the naval affairs and appropriations committees and their spouses to visit Charleston for the city's spring Annual Azalea Festival. This week-long celebration, begun in 1934 to promote good relations between the city and the rest of the state while publicizing Charleston as a tourist attraction, was also effectively used by city leaders to cultivate state and federal contracts beneficial to the Lowcountry. In 1938 almost 200 federal guests toured the Charleston Navy Yard "to see at first hand the advantages possessed by Charleston as a strategic military point and naval construction base." By the end of the year, Maybank reported that "the fruits of this visit has [sic] been evidenced in increased appropriations" to the yard, "which during the past several years has grown to be Charleston's largest industry."[42]

With the passage of both 1940 naval appropriations acts, providing for a "two-ocean navy," Charleston's "largest industry" soon grew larger. Authorizations for construction of destroyers ($109 million) were augmented by outlays for rail, dock, and power plant improvements at the yard as well as for housing and hospital additions. Aggregate statistics demonstrated the immense impact of federal spending on the area: while the annual per capita income for South Carolina in 1940 was $301, Charleston County's figure was $457. President Roosevelt, docked at the Charleston Navy Yard in December 1940, told the press the South would play a major role in the defense effort and would benefit economically from that role. Charleston certainly benefited. By mid-1943, total government contracts for military facilities and supplies in the Lowcountry neared $65 million and employed almost 44,000 people; in 1939 the area had produced only $27 million worth of manufactured goods and utilized only 5,400 workers.[43]

Charleston's population grew quickly and dramatically. According to the April 1940 census, the city of Charleston contained 71,275 people; the county of Charleston included over 121,000. By the end of 1942 the city's population had grown by over 54 percent to 110,000, while the county's population had skyrocketed by more than 82 percent to over 220,000. The difference in growth figures reflected the increased activity north of the city limits in and around the navy yard. In addition, thousands of military personnel left through the port of embarkation, while "all army hospital ships operating from the European war zone" debarked their wounded at the same Charleston port terminal for transfer to inland hospitals. A confidential report of the Senate Committee on Wartime Health and Education dated October 7, 1943, accurately declared that "Charleston is one of the first cities in the Southeast to feel the impact of the war effort and it still remains one of our most congested war production centers."[44]

Of all the usual wartime problems, housing quickly became the most pressing. Charleston had lacked adequate housing before the war. The influx of war workers overwhelmed the area's capacity. The Charleston Housing Authority noted, "During 1940, the lack of available living quarters in Charleston became so critical that the Navy Yard was prevented at times from taking on additional needed personnel for the reason that housing facilities were not to be had." The city's downtown elite were especially unhelpful in efforts to ease the situation. The U.S. Housing Authority soon began building war-related public housing projects. The Charleston area's first such development was a 400-unit project for white workers only built near the navy yard and christened "Ben Tillman Homes" in honor of the yard's founder and first protector. By 1944 the Charleston Housing Authority owned or operated over 7,200 racially segregated units for war workers.[45]

    Segregated job classifications and opportunities at the Charles-
ton Navy Yard, however, caused significant problems. In late 1940
in an article titled "It's Our Country, Too," in the Saturday Evening
Post, National Association for the Advancement of Colored People
(NAACP) spokesperson Walter White cited the Charleston Navy Yard
as an example of a government facility that discriminated against
black workers: "Negro employees in the powerhouse are used to teach
white employees. The whites thus are advanced to the engine room,
classified as engineers and given higher pay. The Negro teacher
remains in the fireman's classification." While that practice reflected
managerial policy, it was probably because "the mechanics union bars
Negroes from membership" that "Negroes in the machine shop in
Charleston are not permitted to rise above the position of mechanic's
helper." Yet valuable time was lost training inexperienced whites
while experienced blacks were denied advancement. When the reno-
vating division, "entirely manned by Negroes," received a substantial
pay boost, "immediately all the Negroes were displaced by whites."
Even white janitors were paid $1.36 a day more than black janitors
performing the same work. [46]
    Resentment over these conditions led to a significant degree of
turnover, which hindered productivity. In June 1942, of those employed in shipbuilding in the yard the navy noted that "about 18 percent are Negroes." Of that group of black workers, 3.4 percent held
skilled jobs, 32 percent held semiskilled classifications, and the rest
held unskilled positions. Merl E. Reed explained the navy's solution
to the problem of racial tensions interfering with productivity: "Toward the end of 1943, four shipyards operated segregated ways . . .
[in which blacks] had greater economic opportunity and suffered from
less discrimination." The Charleston Navy Yard was one of the four
yards. [47] Given the racial attitudes involved, that seemed to be the
most pragmatic solution available. Fortunately, racial tensions did
not result in riots or violence as happened at some other yards during
the war.
    Despite various grievances and problems, the Charleston Navy
Yard compiled an impressive record. The yard mainly built destroyers, destroyer escorts, and landing craft for the amphibious assaults.
Yard workers also repaired a wide variety of vessels. In addition,
the yard operated a navy radio school, which trained 862 technicians
in four years. Civilian employment peaked at approximately 26,500
in the summer of 1943, generating a top payroll of about $68 million.
One observer described the yard during this hectic period: "At night
the yard looked like a giant amusement park lit up by neon lights,
welders' arcs, the glow of forges and the sparks of molten metal, as
work continued around the clock." Yet quality was not sacrificed for
quickness; the yard repeatedly won the army-navy "E" award. The

Charleston Navy Yard's major contribution to the war effort consisted of building 209 ships (10 of which were sunk) worth over $300 million.[48]

Well before the war was over, Charleston's commercial-civic elite were concerned with the city's future in peacetime, hoping to avoid the decline that had hurt the city after World War I. City leaders were encouraged by a 1942 study that classified the Charleston area as one that was "adjudged to have superior prospects of retaining wartime growth." Also in 1942, two years after its founding, the Civic Services Committee of the Carolina Arts Association received a $24,000 grant from the Rockefeller Foundation "to further its work in city planning" for the downtown business area when the war ended. In 1943 Mayor Lockwood declared that postwar planning was "second only to the actual war effort itself" in importance. The city's housing authority provided another example of such concern. In its 1944 annual report the authority noted that it "did not undertake the construction of any additional projects during the year" because the group believed previously completed units met current needs and because the authority "trusts that it will avoid the possibility of creating a post-war 'ghost town,' and that at the same time it will have sufficient vacancies to provide housing for returning veterans when the war terminated." Meanwhile, the Charleston Evening Post warned city leaders to be cautious in their postwar planning and not to commit the city to finance large-scale projects such as the railroad and waterfront programs of earlier eras.[49]

Community leaders realized that Charleston's economic future hung in the balance in the postwar period. If the city hesitated or faltered, Charleston would resume its prewar decline. But the city enjoyed several new advantages: Charleston's harbor channels were in excellent condition, the area's industrial plant had been greatly expanded, as had the municipal airport, and the Santee-Cooper hydroelectric plant, South Carolina's "Little TVA" (Tennessee Valley Authority) completed during the war, guaranteed the Lowcountry sufficient electrical power. Moreover, many war workers remained in the area after hostilities terminated. The Civic Services Committee stressed the importance of these factors: "This gave Charleston for the first time in its life a large industrial population composed of excellent material with adequate housing already in existence." Thus "here was the opportunity for industrial progress which for four-score years has passed Charleston by. Here was the chance to set the city on the march again. Would it be seized or neglected?"[50]

Boosters declared their answer to be "unequivocal and emphatic." In 1946 approximately 300 individual and corporate members of the commercial-civic elite founded the Charleston Development Board (CDB) "to hold as much as possible of the gains which we had made during the war period" while improving and expanding those gains. In this endeavor the group had "the full backing, moral and financial, of the city and county administration." As a result of these combined efforts, within three years almost 100 new plants and firms had begun operations.[51] The legacy of the war was increased industrial development, mainly in the North Charleston area.

A more mature phase of the metropolitan-military complex was reflected in the postwar operations of the port of Charleston. During World War II the federal government took over most of the city's port facilities and improved the terminals at the embarkation site. In 1947 the city conveyed the port terminals to the State Ports Authority (SPA) (created in 1942) as part of the state's program of coordinated port development and revitalization in Charleston, Georgetown, and Beaufort. While city leaders stressed the benefits of state operation, they also conceded that the city's Port Utilities Commission had run up "large deficits" during the commercial decline of the 1930s. State financial support for further port development relieved the city of a major burden; conversely, the state obtained upgraded, modernized terminals valued at $20 million at no cost. The effects of the state-funded and -directed port development brought quick results. By 1949 Charleston had doubled the prewar tonnage it handled (to over 5 million tons annually) and recaptured first place among South Atlantic ports.[52] Federal military improvements passed on to the city, and then the state helped stimulate Charleston's maritime economy.

Other government actions aided the port. The state took over the Cooper River Bridge from Charleston County, freeing the area from maintenance costs while ending the tolls charged as a stimulus to truck and tourist travel. More important, the federal interstate highway network begun in the 1950s, authorized in large part as a national defense program, channeled more trade and tourism to Charleston, furthering the metropolitan-military linkage.[53]

The rechristened Charleston Naval Shipyard and (reorganized) Naval Base remained the centerpiece of the metropolitan-military complex. Its future was crucial to the Lowcountry's continued economic revival. If the yard shrank to its post-World War I status, the area's economic forecast would be cloudy indeed. By February 1946 yard employment totaled 12,600—about half of the facility's wartime peak. Deactivating and decommissioning ships, mainly destroyers, became the yard's chief function. Once the ships were secured, the yard held vessels as a reserve fleet for possible future use.[54] The yard's future again appeared to be limited.

However, Congressman Lucius Mendel Rivers had spent the last half decade building his influence. Elected in 1940, Rivers quickly became the protege of House Naval Affairs Committee Chairman Carl Vinson. Rivers's cultivation of Vinson came to fruition in

1946 when the Atlantic Fleet Mine Force was transferred from Norfolk to Charleston, providing more personnel and more work for the yard. Concerned about the results of the 1946 elections, Rivers vowed not to let "any Republican economy program militate against the splendid record of the Charleston Naval Shipyard." True to his words, in 1947 Rivers made sure that the yard was scheduled to receive a steady stream of ships for overhaul as well as regular maintenance work on the destroyers held in reserve. The following year Congressman Rivers and (now) Senator Maybank announced another significant expansion of the yard's activities: overhaul of submarines, which included a major battery-charging facility. The local newspaper exuded confidence that this new program, coupled with the other recent arrangements, guaranteed that the facility would avoid repeating its post-World War I fate as "a virtual naval boneyard."[55]

The proper mix of public and private investment central to the success of the metropolitan-military complex seemed well established in the Lowcountry by 1948. Revival of the Azalea Festival and Navy Day symbolized the union. Charleston area boosters trumpeted the accomplishments of the commercial-civic elite in 1949 with the publication and widespread distribution of a handbook on the city and county significantly titled Charleston Grows. Confronting the popular image of the city, boosters argued that "Charleston is not an anachronistic survival, sleeping through the present, nor a reconstruction of the eighteenth century, preserved as a museum piece." Instead, because of the war, its aftermath, and the energetic activities of community leaders, for Charleston "a prolonged static period has come definitely to an end, and a new dynamic period, more in keeping with the city's true character, has opened."[56]

Statistics supported the rhetoric. In 1940 Charleston's metropolitan population was 99,000 and soared nearly 60 percent to 157,000 by 1944. Instead of the precipitous postwar decline many expected, the Charleston area's 1948 population stood at 145,000; "in other words, Charleston has kept better than 75% of her population growth by providing new peace-time jobs, new housing, new business opportunities." Retail trade figures and the value of manufactured products for Charleston County in 1948 more than tripled the total for 1940. In addition, "the largest single factor in the local business scene," the Charleston Naval Shipyard and Naval Base, "the major industry in the county, both in numbers of workers and in annual payroll," had also kept pace with the private sector. In 1940 the yard's 6,000 workers earned $7 million; wartime peak employment included 26,500 taking home $68 million; and 1948's work force of 7,677 constituted a payroll of $20.273 million, almost triple that of 1940. Boosters noted that "Charleston County has a net effective annual buying income in excess of 219 million dollars, the largest of any county in South Carolina."[57] The metropolitan-military complex had generated and maintained postwar prosperity in the Charleston area.

Significantly, most of this growth took place outside the city limits of Charleston. The city proper consisted of 5.8 square miles on the tip of a peninsula and had not annexed any additional territory for almost a century. The naval yard and base as well as most new plants and businesses were located north of the city. Postwar growth in the area literally widened the distance between the "tourists' Charleston" and "metropolitan-military Charleston." This course of growth gave boosters the best of both worlds: "the old Historic Charleston and the new industrial Charleston are geographically separate and distinct, so that industrial development here can be wholly helpful with none of the disastrous cultural sacrifices which progress of this kind often involves."[58]

While the situation was economically beneficial to both locales, culturally the areas were light-years apart. One Charleston native described the Lowcountry's evolution: "Between 1930 and 1950, Charleston County grew from 101,050 to 164,856, while the city grew very little. Charleston itself, which had been two-thirds of the county in 1910 now became a small part of an Americanized 'metropolitan area.'" While the city retained its genteel, antebellum atmosphere, by 1949 boosters boasted that "North Charleston has become more than just a collection of factory sites and housing developments and has evolved a community approach to its problems and to the problems of the larger Charleston metropolitan area." That approach was institutionalized with the establishment of an elected county council in 1949 to "co-ordinate its planning with city officials" as well as with the state government.[59]

Ironically, just as the metropolitan-military complex seemed to have stabilized the Lowcountry area, 1949 brought another federal economy drive that threatened to close the Charleston naval facilities. Once again the commercial-civic elite rallied its friends in support of the yard and the base. They managed to save the facilities but had to accept a 28 percent cut in civilian personnel. At the end of 1949, the yard's work force had shrunk to 4,614. The onslaught of the Korean conflict in June 1950 changed the situation overnight. Within two years yard employment had more than doubled, while the payroll climbed by over $11 million as the yard reactivated and readied dozens of reserve ships for duty. As hostilities waned, Rivers arranged for additional work at the yard to avoid layoffs.[60]

Domestic racial strife soon supplanted the Korean conflict as the major issue in the area. Congressman Adam Clayton Powell had protested to President Eisenhower that Navy Secretary Robert Anderson was guilty of "insubordination" because he permitted segregated facilities to remain in operation. Anderson's equivocal response and continuing pressure from civil rights groups led the commander in chief to order the "complete elimination" of segregation at the Charleston yard and 42 other naval shore stations. The Charleston yard was desegregated in three phases. On September 14, 1953, separate drinking fountains were done away with without incident. On October 19 the cafeteria was desegregated. However, when black workers, not content with token desegregation, sat at each table, their action triggered a boycott of the facility by most white workers. By November 10 the Charleston yard was the only installation at which partial segregation still existed. On January 11, 1954, the final barrier was eliminated: the yard's restrooms were desegregated. One white worker lamented: "That's one facility we can't boycott." Only after restroom desegregation were machines dispensing "sanitary, doughnut-shaped paper toilet covers" installed in the facilities. One white worker hung a toilet cover around his neck, and the "Eisenhower collar" was briefly in style. In a less humorous vein, the white boycott of the cafeteria continued in varying degrees for over three years. However, an effective affirmative action program begun in the 1960s greatly improved the situation. [61]

As relative calm returned to the yard, Congressman Rivers and newly elected Senator Strom Thurmond used their clout to add new programs and facilities to the yard and base, further strengthening the metropolitan-military complex. The pair helped engineer the transfer of the Naval Mine Warfare School from Yorktown, Virginia, to Charleston in December 1958, which was to be added to the Naval Mine Craft Base already there. The shift of course required additional construction at the yard. Rivers also raided the Norfolk, New London, and Key West bases in arranging for two destroyer squadrons and one attack submarine squadron, including their combined crews of 6,500, to have Charleston assigned as their home port. Nuclear submarines were assigned to Charleston for repair and maintenance. Rivers's influence was equally apparent in the navy's decision to construct a $10 million Naval Weapons Annex at the Charleston base. One vice-admiral dubbed the facility the "Rivers Memorial Annex." The project initiated "the only East Coast facility for the assembly, storage and repair of the missiles carried by the Navy's ballistic missile submarines." The base would handle Polaris and, later, Poseidon and Trident missiles. Once missile production began, it only made sense to add a fleet ballistic missile submarine training center to the Charleston naval complex as well as another dry dock to handle the additional ships arriving there. Charleston was now a major nuclear power. [62]

More personnel increased the need for more housing; in 1963 the navy named its newest housing project in the area "MenRiv Park" for the navy's biggest booster in the area. The following year, when rumors of defense cutbacks seemed to jeopardize the Charleston yard, Rivers and Thurmond not only saved the yard but were also able to have a reduction-in-force order revoked. The Charleston Navy Yard's 1964 payroll totaled $155 million and accounted for almost half the civilian employment at all the state's ports. According to economist David R. Pender, the generative effects of economic multipliers virtually doubled that payroll's impact on South Carolina's economy, totaling almost 6 percent of the net state product. The commercial operations of South Carolina's ports, based in part on the improved federal terminals transfered to the State Ports Authority, also yielded roughly $300 million or another 6 percent of the net state product. Thus "the overall impact is approximately $600 million, and 12 percent of the net state product," one dimension of the metropolitan-military complex by 1964.[63]

The year 1964 was also significant for another reason. Carl Vinson, 81, announced his retirement after 35 years of service on the House Naval Affairs Committee and then, after 1947, on the House Armed Services Committee, having chaired both committees for much of his tenure. After 25 years of service on the same committees, South Carolina's First District congressman, L. Mendel Rivers, succeeded Vinson as chairman. Journalist Marshall Frady declared: "Nowhere in Congress has the Pentagon had a more dogged and unabashed tribune." Such solicitude for the military, combined with Rivers's extremely hawkish views on the escalating Vietnam conflict and his advocacy of tactical nuclear weapons there, made Rivers a controversial figure. Journalists dubbed him "Ol' Man Rivers," "a living symbol of 'the military-industrial complex'" who was "its secretary-general" while also being "congressional godfather to the military."[64] Rivers' outspokenness only increased his notoriety.

That publicity also invited closer scrutiny of the economic benefits he had secured for his district. One profile of Rivers noted that the Charleston "area had become one of the most elaborately fortified patches of geography in the nation," that Rivers had "finally transmogrified Charleston into a microcosm of the military-industrial civilization." Such accounts often listed all the installations in the First Congressional District, sometimes giving Rivers credit for all of them, forgetting, for example, that the Charleston Navy Yard had been authorized in 1901, four years before his birth. Nonetheless, when Rivers surveyed such lists, he conceded: "I brought 90% of it in." Carl Vinson had facetiously warned: "You put anything else down there in your district, Mendel, it's gonna sink." Rivers reportedly replied that he would "have the Federal government drive pilings in order to reinforce the entire area" to prevent that limitation on future growth. During his term in office, Rivers brought at least ten major installations and programs to the Lowcountry, validating his campaign slogan: "Rivers Delivers."[65]

Rivers's influence was also apparent in the private sector. As additional military facilities came to the Charleston area, more industry followed. The trend accelerated once Rivers began chairing the House Armed Services Committee. In his first five years in that post, five major corporations established plants in the area: Lockheed, McDonnell-Douglas, Avco, General Electric, and J. P. Stevens. Observers declared that Rivers "was acknowledged as the Charleston area's chief economic asset." His reputation assumed legendary proportions; one newspaper noted, "There is an old saw that Charleston floats its economy on the Ashley, the Cooper, and the Mendel Rivers." By 1970, estimates that more than a third of the Lowcountry's personal income and almost half of the employment in the area derived from defense-related activities demonstrated Rivers's impact.[66]

When Mendel Rivers died in late 1970, his legacy to the Lowcountry was a mature metropolitan-military complex. The variety of installations that Rivers helped bring to the area resulted in a more diversified military presence, less susceptible to changing political and economic winds. Allied corporate plants also furnished some insurance against economic dislocation. Nevertheless, Charleston's metropolitan-military complex was linked to a larger political and economic system that the Lowcountry's commercial-civic elite could influence but not control. After studying the nation's power centers, journalist Neal R. Peirce concluded, "With the exception of San Antonio, Norfolk, and perhaps San Diego, Charleston has become the most defense-dependent metropolitan area in the country." Social critic Vance Packard went further, arguing that "for sheer impact of U.S. defense spending on a major metropolitan area, Norfolk is surpassed by Charleston, South Carolina." A. J. Marjenhoff's more precise analysis of the impact of military spending on the Charleston area, utilizing a sophisticated economic model, also verified the Lowcountry's high level of defense dependency and the significant correlation between fluctuations in the national and local economies.[67] That dependency was a perverse measure of Rivers's influence.

However, Rivers's accomplishments were only the culmination of decades of effort by previous boosters. From its inception in 1901, the Charleston Navy Yard and Naval Station faced varying degrees of indifference or hostility from various Navy officials and politicians. Several factors enabled this naval nuisance to survive, expand, and become the heart of a substantial metropolitan-military complex crucial to the economic well-being of the Charleston area. Senator Tillman, the "Navy Yard Junta," and the friendly Wilson administration ensured initial success, while World War I brought Charleston modern port terminals. Senator Byrnes and Mayor Maybank aided the yard through New Deal programs. World War II greatly enhanced the entire naval base, while the cold war dramatically expanded the whole martial presence in the area into a mature metropolitan-military complex with nuclear capabilities. In terms of securing federal largess for the Lowcountry, however, Rivers's impact remained unequaled.

Yet the influence of federal officials and major external events was only half the story. The contribution of Charleston's commercial-civic elite was also vital. From Mayor J. Adger Smyth in 1901, who first alerted Senator Tillman to the naval possibilities of Charleston's recently modernized harbor, local politicians and businessmen became tireless boosters for the yard. They demonstrated how the area could serve the navy's interests. Politicians, businessmen, and navy yard commandants continually emphasized Charleston's strategic location, fine harbor, and appreciative community. That coalition of local boosters and federal supporters saved the yard several times and eventually acquired a more diversified complex.

The militarization of the Charleston area has not been without its ironies. Charleston native Robert Rosen succinctly expressed the most fundamental incongruity: "It is ironic that the federal government and the United States Navy have both destroyed and rebuilt Charleston."[68] Moreover, to the extent that Charleston has become "Americanized," that has been due in large part to the degree to which the area has been militarized. Another anomaly has been the effect of the physical separation between the historic district within the city proper and the military facilities several miles north of the city limits: an antique showplace surrounded and protected by the most modern military technology available. A further aspect of that physical separation is reflected in the incredible divergence between the areas. One observer contrasted Charleston's historic downtown district, "a visual delight" of "glorious serene old homes . . . amid trees hanging with moss," with North Charleston's Rivers Avenue, "an avenue of unrelieved visual mayhem—junkyards, three-minute car washes, used car lots," and numerous fast-food joints.[69] Militarization has also helped increase the metropolitan decentralization, which has furthered the separation between the city and the rest of the area. By 1980 the city's population, even after two decades of annexation efforts, totaled less than 70,000. Meanwhile, the metropolitan area had grown enormously. North Charleston, the city the navy yard created, was incorporated in 1972, becoming the most populous of the almost two dozen suburban areas in the Lowcountry.[70]

Yet another irony embraces the entire territory. The Lowcountry generally has been quite conservative politically and socially. That conservatism has been augmented by the large number of retired service personnel in the Charleston area. Another measure has been the high esteem in which the Citadel, the Military College of South Carolina, has been held by many citizens; Citadel alumni have often acquired significant political and economic influence in the Low-country. These factors have only reinforced the area's support of a strong military to protect "the American way of life," especially "the free market, private enterprise system." Yet, ironically, many of those who have opposed federal social welfare programs have often been the most ardent advocates of what could be termed metro-politan-military welfare for the area.[71] Charlestonians rightly fear that real peace would mean the end of military subsidies and the devastation of the Lowcountry economy. An outside consulting firm studying the area warned that "Charleston has been living off its cultural inheritance and the federal government's military budget" and urged greater nonmilitary diversification. While tourism has increased and downtown revitalization efforts have been substantial, South Carolina's First District congressmen, regardless of party affiliation, have continued to sit on the House Armed Services Com-mittee to safeguard the Lowcountry's vested interest in military appropriations.[72]

The evolution of the Charleston area from naval pauper to naval nuclear power presents a representative case study of the growth and development of a metropolitan-military complex. With a fine natural harbor, improved by jetties, and a strategic location, Charleston's commercial-civic elite and other allies nonetheless had to fight to keep, maintain, and expand the area's military installations. Their efforts involved mobilizing the local community, dealing with chal-lenges from rival cities and sites, and courting and lobbying navy officials and national political and corporate leaders—all of which required substantial time, energy, and money to promote the city's cause. Success came not from an impersonal, rational decision by a centralized warfare state bureaucracy but from an aggressive, persistent campaign by the city's business and political leaders, but-tressed by influential allies, fortuitous wars and domestic emergen-cies, the congressional seniority system, and luck. The interplay of the forces of militarization and urbanization resulted in the Charles-ton metropolitan area becoming an integral part of the nation's military-industrial complex.

NOTES

1. See the essays in Carroll W. Pursell, Jr., ed., The Military-Industrial Complex (New York: Harper & Row, 1972). Paul A. C.

Koistinen is one historian who has traced the development of the military-industrial complex throughout U.S. history, although his focus is restricted to the national level. His essays are available in Koistinen, The Military-Industrial Complex: A Historical Perspective (New York: Praeger, 1980). Also see the essays in Benjamin Franklin Cooling, ed., War, Business, and American Society: Historical Perspectives on the Military-Industrial Complex (Port Washington, N.Y.: Kennikat Press, 1977), which cover the last century.

2. Roger Lotchin coined the term metropolitan-military complex. He has developed this concept in several articles: "The City and the Sword: San Francisco and the Rise of the Metropolitan-Military Complex, 1919-1941," Journal of American History 65 (March 1979): 996-1020; "The Metropolitan-Military Complex in Comparative Perspective: San Francisco, Los Angeles, and San Diego, 1919-1941," Journal of the West 18 (July 1979): 19-30. Also see James R. McGovern, The Emergence of a City in the Modern South: Pensacola, 1900-1945 (DeLeon Springs, Fla.: 1977); and George F. Pearce, The U.S. Navy in Pensacola: From Sailing Ships to Naval Aviation (1825-1930) (Pensacola: University Presses of Florida, 1980).

3. For background on Southern cities in the post-Civil War period, see Blaine A. Brownell and David R. Goldfield, eds., The City in Southern History: The Growth of Urban Civilization in the South (Port Washington, N.Y.: Kennikat Press, 1977), pp. 92-191. Brownell coined the term commercial-civic elite and has developed this concept in numerous articles and books.

No full-length scholarly history of Charleston currently exists. See two articles by Don H. Doyle: "Leadership and Decline in Postwar Charleston, 1865-1910," in From the Old South to the New: Essays on the Transitional South, ed. Walter J. Fraser, Jr., and Winfred B. Moore, Jr. (Westport, Conn.: Greenwood Press, 1981), pp. 93-106; and "Urbanization and Southern Culture: Economic Elites in Four New South Cities (Atlanta, Nashville, Charleston, Mobile) c. 1865-1910," in Toward a New South?: Studies in Post-Civil War Southern Communities (Westport, Conn.: Greenwood Press, 1982), pp. 11-36. The quotation is from the latter article, pp. 13-14. Also see Frederic Cople Jaher, The Urban Establishment: Upper Strata in Boston, New York, Charleston, Chicago, and Los Angeles (Urbana: University of Illinois Press, 1982), pp. 317-451.

4. J. C. Hemphill, "A Short Story of the South Carolina Inter-State and West Indian Exposition," in Year Book, 1902, City of Charleston, S.C. (Charleston, S.C.: Walker, Evans & Cogswell, 1903), app., pp. 105-71 (hereafter cited as Year Book); Jamie W. Moore, "The Great South Carolina Inter-State and West Indian Exposition," Sandlapper 11 (July 1978): 11-15; Doyle, "Leadership and

Decline," pp. 102-3; John Joseph Duffy, "Charleston Politics in the Progressive Era" (Ph.D. diss., University of South Carolina, 1963), pp. 1-31. The quotation is from the latter source, p. 31.

5. Robert Rosen, A Short History of Charleston (San Francisco: Lexikos, 1982), p. 128.

6. Jamie W. Moore, The Lowcountry Engineers, Military Missions and Economic Development in the Charleston District, U.S. Army Corps of Engineers (Charleston, S.C.: U.S. Army Corps of Engineers, Charleston District, 1981), pp. 31-39. A summary of his detailed monograph is also available in Moore, "The Lowcountry in Economic Transition: Charleston since 1865," South Carolina Historical Magazine 80 (April 1979): 156-71. Corps of Engineers's Colonel Quincy A. Gillmore had devised the system of jetties; Moore noted that "a fine historical irony was involved; Gillmore had commanded the army that had battered Charleston during the siege"— from "Lowcountry in Economic Transition," p. 158.

7. Efforts to build an adequate dry dock and naval station at Port Royal beginning in 1894 proved unsatisfactory to the navy. Lack of sufficient rail and road connections to the isolated site undercut the appeal of its harbor. Tillman found the Port Royal situation perplexing. Having "pleaded, begged, and quarreled" in order "to get a few crumbs" for his "little orphan of a naval station," Tillman frankly told his colleagues that the naval appropriations bill under debate in 1899 was a pork-barrel measure: "If you are going to steal, I want my share [for Port Royal]." Tillman also denounced sectional prejudice, which tried to deny the South its proper share of federal largess. However, as rumors spread that the navy would abandon Port Royal, Frederick V. Abbott, Gillmore's successor as head of the Corps of Engineers in the Lowcountry, advised Charleston Mayor J. Adger Smyth of the situation. Stressing Charleston's upgraded harbor, Abbott urged Smyth to try to get the Port Royal facility transferred to Charleston. Smyth visited Tillman and won his support for the switch. The pair found a valuable ally in Rear Admiral Mordecai T. Endicott, chief of the Bureau of Yards and Docks, who supported the shift in site. Senate Naval Affairs Committee Chairman Eugene Hale agreed to the proposal. Soon Secretary of the Navy John Long gave his approval. Tillman was not surprised when a naval board recommended to Secretary Long on January 10, 1901, that a naval station and dry dock be built in the Charleston area. "Report of the Hearings before the Senate Committee on Naval Affairs Relative to the Proposed Transfer of the Naval Station from Port Royal, S.C., to Charleston, S.C., 1 and 5 February, 1901," Year Book, 1900, app., pp. 83-205; R. Goodwyn Rhett, "The Charleston Navy Yard: Why the Government Selected the Port of Charleston," Year Book, 1901, app., pp. 89-90; reprint of "A Report of the Board of

Naval Officers Appointed for the Purpose of Examining into the Expediency of Changing the Location of the Naval Station Now at Port Royal, S.C., to Some Point in the State of South Carolina at or near the City of Charleston," Year Book, 1902, app., pp. 42–86; U.S. Congress, Senate, Congressional Record, 55th Cong., 3d sess., 1899, 32, pt. 3 Appendix: 2627–28; ibid., 56th Cong., 1st sess., 1900, 33, pt. 6: 5491; Francis Butler Simkins, Pitchfork Ben Tillman (Baton Rouge: Louisiana State University Press, 1944), pp. 365–66. Port Royal-Beaufort's commercial-civic elite tried in vain to keep the naval station; this point is developed in Lyon Tyler, "The Charleston Naval Base: From 'Red-Headed Stepchild' to 'Deterrent Capital of the World'" (First draft of an unpublished paper kindly provided to the author), pp. 5–8.

8. Charleston News and Courier, August 13, 1901. See Robert R. Dykstra, The Cattle Towns (New York: Atheneum, 1970), pp. 361–83, regarding consensus and conflict among urban elites.

9. Charleston Navy Yard: Speech of Hon. Geo. S. Legaré of South Carolina in the House of Representatives, February 23, 1904, pamphlet, available in South Carolina Collection, University of South Carolina-Columbia. Legaré also cultivated President Theodore Roosevelt, who was a "Big Navy" enthusiast but who was also irked at Charleston because of its outspoken opposition to his appointment of black Republican physician William D. Crum as collector of customs at Charleston in 1904. Legaré's help in passing the 1905 naval appropriations bill soothed the president's feelings and led to the christening of the battleship South Carolina. See Duffy, "Charleston Politics," pp. 14–16, 96–97.

10. J. C. Hemphill, "A Short Story of the Coast Defense Squadron and the Cruiser Charleston," Year Book, 1905, app., pp. 29–56; Charleston News and Courier, January 11, 1906.

11. Tyler, "Charleston Naval Base," pp. 10–11.

12. Charleston News and Courier, January 21, March 17, 1907; Year Book, 1910, p. xvii.

13. Simkins, Tillman, p. 366.

14. George Kibbe Turner, "Our Navy on the Land: The Greatest Waste of National Funds in the History of the United States," McClure's Magazine 32 (February 1909): 397–411; New York Times, December 5, 1910; U.S., Congress, Senate, Congressional Record, 60th Cong., 2d sess., 1909, 43, pt. 3: 2378–79, 2434–36, 2550–53; Simkins, Tillman, pp. 367–68; Tyler, "Charleston Naval Base," pp. 12–13; Gordon Carpenter O'Gara, Theodore Roosevelt and the Rise of the Modern Navy (New York: Greenwood Press, 1943), pp. 28–39.

15. Duffy, "Charleston Politics," pp. 1–341; Doyle Willard Boggs, "John Patrick Grace and the Politics of Reform in South Carolina, 1900–1931" (Ph.D. diss., University of South Carolina,

1977), pp. 1-101. Grace did get the Seaboard Railway to come to Charleston during his first administration, but Seaboard's limited involvement did not significantly change the port's situation; see Edwin J. Clapp, Charleston Port Survey, 1921 (Charleston, S.C.: Walker, Evans & Cogswell, 1921), pp. 107-9.

16. Year Book, 1912, pp. i-iii, xxvii-xxviii; Charleston News and Courier, November 17, 1912.

17. Duffy, "Charleston Politics," pp. 279-80; Simkins, Tillman, pp. 524-25; Charleston News and Courier, April 28, 1914.

18. George V. L. Meyer, "Are Naval Expenditures Wasted?" North American Review 201 (February 1915): 248-52.

19. Henry C. Ferrell, Jr., "Regional Rivalries, Congress, and MIC: The Norfolk and Charleston Navy Yards, 1913-20," in War, Business, and American Society, pp. 59-72; Benjamin Franklin Cooling, Gray Steel and Blue Water Navy: The Formative Years of America's Military-Industrial Complex, 1881-1917 (Hamden, Conn.: Archon Books, 1979), pp. 183-220; Simkins, Tillman, pp. 525-27.

20. Tyler, "Charleston Naval Base," pp. 16-17; Clapp, Charleston Port Survey, pp. 64-67; Moore, "Lowcountry in Economic Transition," p. 167. The Charleston Dry Dock and Machine Company, a private sector firm, served as an adjunct to the Charleston Yard, performing a variety of repair work.

21. U.S., Congress, House, Preliminary Report no. 6 of the Commission on Navy Yards and Naval Stations, January 15, 1918, 64th Cong., 2d sess., 1915-19, H. Rept., pp. 26-28; U.S., Congress, Congressional Record, 65th Cong., 2d sess., 1918, 56:7, pp. 6908-10; Simkins, Tillman, p. 527.

22. Year Book, 1918, pp. 43-44; Duffy, Charleston Politics," pp. 355-56; Boggs, "John Patrick Grace," p. 150; Charleston News and Courier, May 11, 12, 16, 1919; Charleston Evening Post, May 13, 1919; Arthur I. Waskow, From Race Riot to Sit-In, 1919 and the 1960s (Garden City, N.Y.: Doubleday, 1966), pp. 12-16.

23. Boggs, "John Patrick Grace," pp. 135-79; Duffy, "Charleston Politics," pp. 360-76; Year Book, 1921, p. xxi.

24. Clapp, Charleston Port Survey, pp. 65-68; Duffy, "Charleston Politics," pp. 178-79.

25. Ross Hanahan, President of Chamber of Commerce, to Hon. Joseph [sic] Daniels, October 28, 1920, General Correspondence, 1916-26, Secretary of the Navy, Record Group 80, National Archives (hereafter cited as RG 80); press clippings of 1921 visit sent by J. R. Morrison by direction of Commander, Destroyer Squadrons, to Chief of Naval Operations (Division 6), October 19, 1921, ibid.; Year Book, 1921, pp. xxxv-xxxvi.

26. Preamble and Set of Resolutions Unanimously Adopted by the Employees of the U.S. Navy Yard and the Citizens of Charleston

at a Mass Meeting Held July 23, 1919, to Secretary of the Navy, July 23, 1919, General Correspondence, 1916-26, Secretary of the Navy, RG 80; Josephus Daniels to Hon. E. D. Smith, January 8, 1921, ibid.; U.S., Congress, Senate, Committee on Naval Affairs, Hearings on Naval Appropriation Bill, 1922, 66th Cong., 3d sess., 1921, H. Rept. 15975, pp. 203-18.

27. General Order no. 87 and the resolutions are available in General Correspondence, 1916-26, Secretary of the Navy, RG 80.

28. The voluminous correspondence is available in ibid.

29. R. M. Griswold to Admiral Coontz, August 12, 1922, ibid.; W. L. Rodgers to Secretary of the Navy, August 16, 1922, ibid.

30. R. E. Coontz to Honorable Ellison D. Smith, September 18, 1922, ibid.; Brief Submitted by the Navy Yard Committee of the Charleston, S.C., Chamber of Commerce, November 1922, ibid.

31. Year Book, 1923, pp. xxxii, 29, 33; ibid., 1926, p. 227; Daniel W. Hollis, "Cotton Ed Smith: Showman or Statesman?" South Carolina Historical Magazine 71 (October 1970): 246; R. S. MacElwee to J. A. Carey, Assistant to the Secretary of the Navy, July 23, 1923, General Correspondence, 1916-26, Secretary of the Navy, RG 80; Carey to MacElwee, July 30, 1923, ibid.; Year Book, 1928, p. 257, recalled the origins of Charleston's Navy Day.

32. The voluminous exchanges are available in General Correspondence, 1916-26, Secretary of the Navy, RG 80; Curtis D. Wilbur to Hon. E. D. Smith, November 12, 1925, ibid.; U.S., Congress, House, Subcommittee of the House Committee on Appropriations, Navy Department Appropriation Bill for 1927, 69th Cong., 1st sess., 1926, pp. 858-60; idem, Navy Department Appropriation Bill for 1928, 69th Cong., 2d sess., 1926, pp. 799-801. In 1924 Congressman Byrnes also defended Norfolk when some of its facilities were threatened with relocation elsewhere; see Christopher Silver, "Norfolk and the Navy: The Evolution of City-Federal Relations, 1917-46," Chapter 5 in this volume.

33. Year Book, 1927, p. 243; ibid., 1928, pp. 257-58.

34. Curtis D. Wilbur Hon. E. D. Smith, February 11, 1927, General Correspondence, 1926-1940, General Records of the Department of Navy, RG 80; Assistant Secretary of the Navy T. Douglas Robinson to [former mayor] R. G. Rhett, February 12, 1927, ibid.; T. P. Magruder, "The Navy and Economy," Saturday Evening Post, September 24, 1927, pp. 6-7, 148-50; U.S., Congress, House, Committee on Naval Affairs, Hearings on Sundry Legislation Affecting the Naval Establishment, 1927-28, 70th Cong., 1st sess., 1928, pp. 289-91, 523-38; N. A. McNully, Commandant [Charleston Navy Yard], to Secretary of the Navy, March 30, 1928, Secret Correspondence, 1927-1939, General Records of the Secretary of the Navy,

RG 80; "Report of the Bureau of Yards and Docks," Annual Report of the Secretary of the Navy, 1929, p. 2.

35. Blaine A. Brownell, The Urban Ethos in the South, 1920-1930 (Baton Rouge: Louisiana State University Press, 1975), pp. 11-16, 30-32, 117, 161, 166-67, 188, 202, 214; Year Book, 1929, pp. xxiv-xxvii; H. F. Church, "Chronological History of Constructing the Great Cooper River Bridge," Year Book, 1930, pp. xli-li; Rosen, Charleston, 132-33, 140-41.

36. Year Book, 1930, p. 267; the protest letters are available in General Correspondence, 1926-1940, General Records of the Department of the Navy, RG 80.

37. Charleston News and Courier, October 27, 1931.

38. Thomas McMillan to Hon. Charles F. Adams, October 29, 1931, General Correspondence, 1926-1940, General Records of the Department of the Navy, RG 80; James F. Byrnes to Adams, November 9, 1931, ibid.; Adams to McMillan, November 10, 1931, ibid.; Memorandum for Navy Budget Officer, November 10, 1931, ibid.; Charleston News and Courier, November 13, 1931.

39. Charleston News and Courier, May 30, June 22, September 2, 1933; ibid., September 29, 1934; ibid., May 17, 1936; H. L. Roosevelt to Senator Byrnes, June 20, 1933, General Correspondence, 1926-1940, General Records of the Department of the Navy, RG 80.

40. Charleston News and Courier, September 26, 1936; ibid., October 23, December 8, 1937; ibid., July 8, 1938.

41. The voluminous correspondence is available in General Correspondence, 1926-1940, General Records of the Department of the Navy, RG 80; Year Book, 1932-35, pp. 21-22. Several visits by the commander in chief won Charleston's designation as a "Presidential Port," enhancing the city's reputation; see Year Book, 1936, pp. 18, 177-80.

42. Year Book, 1932-35, pp. 22-23; ibid., 1937, p. 14; ibid., 1938, p. 13; W. H. Allen, Commandant [Charleston Navy Yard] to Assistant Secretary of the Navy, March 30, 1938 [regarding arrangements for "guests"], General Correspondence, 1926-1940, General Records of the Department of the Navy, RG 80.

43. Robert Greenhalgh Albion, "The Naval Affairs Committees, 1816-1947," United States Naval Institute Proceedings 78 (November 1952): 1234-35; Charleston News and Courier, April 18, June 9, 28, August 3, 1941; Roosevelt press conference cited in George B. Tindall, The Emergence of the New South, 1913-1945 (Baton Rouge: Louisiana State University Press, 1967), p. 694; also see David R. Goldfield, Cotton Fields and Skyscrapers: Southern City and Region, 1607-1980 (Baton Rouge: Louisiana State University Press, 1982), pp. 182-83; U.S., Congress, Senate, Committee on Wartime Health and Education,

Confidential Report on the Charleston, South Carolina, Area, War Production Board, Region 4, October 7, 1943, Record Group 46, National Archives, Washington, D.C., p. 5 (hereafter cited as RG 46).

44. Year Book, 1942, p. 11; ibid., 1945, p. 12.

45. Year Book, 1940, pp. 185-86; on the downtown elite's attitude, see Enid Ewing, "Charleston Contra Mundum," Nation 157 (November 1943): 579-81; Year Book, 1944, p. 176. Also see Philip J. Funigiello, The Challenge to Urban Liberalism: Federal-City Relations during World War II (Knoxville: University Tennessee Press, 1978), pp. 13, 24-25, 80-119; and Carl Abbott, The New Urban America: Growth and Politics in Sunbelt Cities (Chapel Hill: University of North Carolina Press, 1981), pp. 98-119.

46. Walter White, "It's Our Country, Too," Saturday Evening Post, December 14, 1940, p. 63.

47. Charleston News and Courier, June 8, 1942; Merl E. Reed, "The FEPC, the Black Worker, and the Southern Shipyards," South Atlantic Quarterly 74 (Autumn 1975): 459. White workers also had grievances, especially those who had come from areas of union strength and higher wages. Complaints about "gross waste," theft of government property, misuse and misallocation of workers and equipment, nepotism and favoritism, and other charges kept yard officials busy investigating the allegations; see the letters in the Records of the Special Committee of the Senate to Investigate the National Defense Program, 1941-48, Record Group 46, National Archives, Washington, D.C.

48. Charleston News and Courier, May 30, 1943; ibid., November 24, December 30, 1944; ibid., August 15, 16, 17, November 2, 1945; Tyler, "Charleston Naval Base," p. 27. The Charleston Dry Dock and Machine Company's modest contribution to the war effort rated one brief mention in passing in Frederick C. Lane, Ships for Victory: A History of Shipbuilding under the U.S. Maritime Commission in World War II (Baltimore: Johns Hopkins University Press, 1951), p. 501.

49. Philip M. Hauser, "Wartime Population Changes and Postwar Prospects," Journal of Marketing 8 (January 1944): 242; Civic Services Committee of the Carolina Art Association [hereafter cited as C.S.C.], Charleston Grows (Charleston, S.C.: Walker, Evans & Cogswell, 1949), p. xiii; Year Book, 1943, p. 19; ibid., 1944, p. 176; Charleston Evening Post, November 3, 1943.

50. C.S.C., Charleston Grows, pp. 4-7.

51. Ibid., pp. 7, 27, 39-40; Year Book, 1946, p. 11.

52. C.S.C., Charleston Grows, pp. 62-63; Year Book, 1946, pp. 12-13; ibid., 1947, p. 12.

53. Year Book, 1943, pp. 18-19; Moore, "Lowcountry in Economic Transition," p. 170.

54. Charleston News and Courier, November 30, 1945; Tyler, "Charleston Navy Yard," pp. 29-31.

55. Marshall Frady, "The Sweetest Finger This Side of Midas," Life, February 27, 1970, pp. 56-57; Year Book, 1946, p. 13; Charleston News and Courier, October 27, 31, 1947; ibid., April 7, 8, 1948; Tyler, "Charleston Naval Base," pp. 32-33.

56. Year Book, 1947, p. 13, 162-63; C.S.C., Charleston Grows, pp. xi, 8.

57. C.S.C., Charleston Grows, pp. xii, 40, 44, 129.

58. Ibid., pp. 28, 183; the Historic Charleston Foundation began its preservation work in 1947, ibid., p. 316.

59. Rosen, Charleston, p. 143; C.S.C., Charleston Grows, pp. 30, 175.

60. Charleston News and Courier, February 4, August 12, 17, 1949; ibid., August 11, 1953; Tyler, "Charleston Navy Yard," pp. 33-34.

61. Charleston News and Courier, April 2, August 21, October 21, 27, November 12, 14, December 31, 1953; ibid., January 8, 10, 19, 27, 1954; ibid., April 25, 1957; Charleston Evening Post, September 14, October 20, 1953; ibid., January 11, 154. The "Eisenhower collar" story is in the Charleston News and Courier Navy Files and did not appear in print. Dated January 26, 1954, the editor considered the incident to be in poor taste and marked the report "copy held out." Tyler, "Charleston Navy Yard," p. 35, noted the affirmative action program's impact.

62. Charleston News and Courier, May 30, July 29, November 12, December 26, 1958; ibid., July 26, September 16, 1959; ibid., January 28, March 30, July 18, November 1, 1960; Charleston Evening Post, December 31, 1959.

63. Charleston News and Courier, December 31, 1963; ibid., December 29, 1970; David R. Pender, "South Carolina Ports and the State's Economy," Business and Economic Review 13 (May 1967): 3-7.

64. Frady, "Sweetest Finger," pp. 52B, 57; Charles McCarry, "Ol' Man Rivers," Esquire 74 (October 1970): 168-71, 211-12; Washington Post, December 29, 1970.

65. Frady, "Sweetest Finger," pp. 55-56; Senator William Proxmire, Report from Wasteland: America's Military-Industrial Complex (New York: Praeger, 1970), pp. 103-4. Rivers pragmatically declared: "Anybody who thinks I'm not gonna look out after my own people is crazy." He could sweeten that blunt reply with an ingratiating question: "Where else can you find a more deserving people,

a more patriotic people, a more efficient people, a more conscientious people, a better climate and a better location?" In return Rivers's constituents and beneficiaries lauded their patron by dedicating various facilities to him; see Charleston News and Courier, December 29, 1970; Aiken [S.C.] Standard, December 31, 1970; Frady, "Sweetest Finger," p. 55.

66. Neal R. Peirce, The Deep South States of America (New York: W. W. Norton, 1974), p. 429; Greenville [S.C.] News, December 29, 1970; Columbia State, December 29, 1970; Frady, "Sweetest Finger," p. 55; McCarry, "Ol' Man Rivers," p. 170; also see the profile of Charleston and South Carolina in a report on the military and the South, Southern Exposure 1 (Spring 1973): 83-85.

67. Peirce, Deep South States, p. 429; Vance Packard, A Nation of Strangers (New York: David McKay, 1972), p. 74; August John Marjenhoff, "The Effects of Defense Spending on the Economy of the Charleston, South Carolina, Standard Metropolitan Statistical Area" (Ph.D. diss., Indiana University, 1974).

68. Rosen, Charleston, p. 128.

69. Packard, Nation of Strangers, p. 75.

70. Rosen, Charleston, p. 150.

71. Pat Conroy, "Shadows of the Old South," Geo 3 (May 1981): 64-82, distills most of the perceptive social commentary about contemporary Charleston contained in this Citadel graduate's novel The Lords of Discipline (Boston: Houghton Mifflin, 1980); also see the critique of Albert Goldman, "Charleston! Charleston!" Esquire 87 (June 1977): 110-13, 154-56.

72. Blaine A. Brownell, The Urban South in the Twentieth Century (Saint Charles, Mo.: Forum Press, 1974), p. 20; Ruder & Finn, Incorporated, "Charleston: The Historic City with a Future," May 1967, n.p., pp. 2-3, available in the Charleston County Library.

2

Junction City–Fort Riley: A Case of Symbiosis

Gregory Fontenot

On Interstate 70 about 125 miles west from Kansas City travelers crest a hill overlooking the Kansas River Valley. The view to the left is dominated by an escarpment; to the right the broad plain of the river unfolds, stretching five miles before it ends abruptly in the steep rim-rock formation of the Flint Hills. On the valley floor, cobra gunships and other aircraft are arrayed on the aprons and runways of Marshall Army Airfield. Directly to the north of the airfield are the native limestone barracks, stables, and quarters of Main Post, Fort Riley, looking exactly as they did when they housed frontier cavalry a century ago. Red and white checkered water towers, modern barracks, and tank parks of the First Infantry Division (Mechanized) dot the mesa above Main Post. As this panorama of contrasts fades from view, motorists flit past tiny Grandview Plaza and come to a town whose name is a part of every soldier's vocabulary. Lying at the convergence of the Smokey Hill and Republican rivers, Junction City extends north from I-70 to the Republican River just over two miles away and west, along the interstate, for nearly five miles. The Republican River, useless as a means of transportation, marks the boundary between Junction City and Fort Riley. But the river is narrow, shallow, and well bridged.

Junction City has alternately baked in the Kansas summers and frozen in the Kansas winters since the middle of the nineteenth century. During this time it has missed the notoriety of Abilene or Dodge City, for it was never a cattle town nor the scene of much marketable excitement. It was secure enough that Wild Bill Hickock is supposed to have said that there was "no Sunday west of Junction City."[1] Junction City owes its security to Fort Riley, having thrived on its neighbor for over 100 years. Yet the town is not a parasite; it

is rather a partner of the post in what, thanks to Dwight D. Eisenhower, we now call the "military-industrial complex."

Though the term military-industrial complex is recent, symbi-
otic relationships between civilian communities and army posts are
not. Army posts, naval bases, and, later still, air bases have always
stimulated the growth of nearby towns and cities. Indeed, military
installations have often been the raison d'être of their satellite communities. In The Soldier and the State, Samuel P. Huntington could
not resist the urge to compare one army post and its satellite. Huntington contrasted the values and appearances of West Point and the
village of Highland Falls. According to Huntington, Highland Falls
was "a motley, disconnected collection of frames coincidentally
adjoining each other, lacking a common unity or purpose."[2] Though
Huntington's description is certainly apt for Highland Falls and towns
like Wrightstown in New Jersey, Killeen in Texas, or Junction City
in Kansas, he was mistaken in his assertion that there was no "common unity or purpose." The purpose or unity for these "motley collections of frames" is to serve their garrison and to ensure their
own survival and well-being by ensuring the survival and well-being
of the nearby base.

While it might seem a simple enough proposition, the prospects
for survival, let alone prosperity, have never been good for bases
or their towns. In a nation where a large standing army and military
installations are anathema, bases have opened and closed as short-
term requirements or political arrangements have dictated. The
country is dotted with the remains of posts that have flourished and
died several times over. The vicissitudes of a post can be calamitous
for its town. Towns like Hindsville, near Fort Stewart, Georgia,
and Leesville, near Fort Polk, Louisiana, have endured alternate
periods of boom and bust since World War II. During the course of
World War II, approximately 8 million soldiers trained at what was
then known as Camp Polk. But Polk, first established in 1941, has
never enjoyed any continuity. Troop levels have fluctuated, and Polk
has been inactivated and reactivated several times, as has Fort
Stewart. Each inactivation of Polk has had, in the laconic words of
an army report, "a disastrous impact on the region."[3] Currently,
there is an active army division at a rejuvenated Fort Polk with the
consequence that Vernon Parish has grown from a population of
4,689 to 32,483 by 1980.[4] But there are no guarantees even now.
For residents of Leesville and Vernon Parish, the past history of
Polk will always loom as an unpleasant reminder of just how fleeting
prosperity can be.

The purpose of this essay, however, is not to chronicle the ups
and downs of army towns but rather to examine an army town that—
despite occasional bad times—has prospered when other army towns

have not. Junction City, Kansas, is a success story. It has succeeded in ensuring, often in the face of stiff odds, the continued survival and expansion of Fort Riley—and thus itself. It has done so because the city fathers of Junction City well understand their situation, which Lieutenant General Harvey H. Fischer succinctly describes, noting that, "Junction City would die without a division-size post."[5] The importance of the post to Junction City cannot be exaggerated. Major General George S. Eckhardt, who commanded the Ninth Infantry Division (The Old Reliables) at Fort Riley in 1966, asserts that he knows of "no city so completely dependent on a military post [as is Junction City]."[6]

Junction City's leading citizens have long understood the importance of the post to their well-being and have done whatever they deemed necessary to ensure their continued prosperity. An analysis of their efforts since World War II is the crux of this chapter. The central question is, What attempts has Junction City's leadership made to influence the army or the government to ensure the town's prosperity? Land acquisition and troop assignments to Fort Riley are crucial to the discussion, since it will become apparent that troop assignments to Riley and the acquisition of more land for training kept the post in use. This point is important because other posts, including those with plenty of land like Fort Polk, were being closed. A related question is, To what degree are the survival and growth of Fort Riley and thus Junction City truly attributable to the efforts of its boosters?

The long-standing success of Junction Citians in maintaining their post and the prosperity of their community has been exceptional. In part this has been because the two halves of this community have worked together. Their symbiosis makes the history of Junction City-Fort Riley an excellent case study in civil-military relationships. Moreover, in order to survive, Junction City, like the great cities of the United States, has influenced the formation of national policy at least so far as the assignment of troop units and the expenditure of millions in military construction and land condemnation is concerned. This study then supplements the work of urban historians such as Mark Gelfand who—in A Nation of Cities—examined the efforts of cities in the United States to affect government policy to ensure their survival and growth. The competition among army towns for troops and dollars also bears a striking resemblance to the competition among the towns Robert Dykstra chronicled in The Cattle Towns. The civic leaders of Junction City, like the entrepreneurs of Dykstra's cattle towns, not only had to deal with their rivals but also had to achieve effective cooperation with their chief customer whether they were soldiers or drovers. Finally, determined city boosters in these Kansas towns waged a fierce struggle against men who saw their farmland given over to the trails and railheads of the late nineteenth century cattle towns or to Fort Riley's need for maneuver space and tank gunnery facilities.[7]

Junction City's story is also peopled with colorful and, in contrast with its size, important names in U.S. military history. J. E. B. Stuart helped build one of the churches in town. George A. Custer and his wife lived at Riley as well, and Elizabeth Custer allegedly haunts the set of quarters she shared with the general. Jonathan "Skinny" Wainwright soldiered here as did George S. Patton, Jr. But the real heroes in this piece are Junction Citians like Dr. F. W. O'Donnell and Louis Loeb, who played polo against Patton and Lucian Truscott, and more recently John D. Montgomery, Robert J. Fegan, Fred Bramlage, and Loeb's son, Dan B. Loeb. These gentlemen are the real reason for the success of Junction City and Fort Riley. That is so because they have understood that army towns are, in the words of Dan Loeb, vice-president of the Junction City Chamber of Commerce since 1961, like "competing drugstores."[8]

The Junction City has been in business since shortly after the establishment of Fort Riley in 1853. Although across the river and four years younger, the town's fortunes have paralleled those of the post. In 1867 one of Custer's officers described Junction City as a "beautiful little village . . . where in spite of all precautions some of the recruits managed to get a whiskey."[9] Though Junction City (a small city of 20,000) is now a bit more garish than beautiful, it remains a place where whiskey can be had but also a place where housing and other services required by the current post population of over 59,000 soldiers and their dependents are available.

Yet the transition did not occur overnight. For the first 60 or 70 years of their existences, Junction City and Fort Riley led fairly sedate lives. There was occasional hubbub centered on the comings and goings of the cavalry, including Custer's Seventh and the more controversial "Buffalo Soldiers" of the Tenth Cavalry Regiment. There was also considerable excitement during World War I when Riley served as a training post. A cantonment called Camp Funston, which housed as many as 50,000 troops during the war, went up almost overnight, as did Army City, which was a collection of shops, restaurants, hotels, and the like erected to provide, at a profit, the goods and services desired by the troops. The entrepreneurs of Army City clearly understood the source of their well-being—knowledge that accounts for its location 80 feet from the eastern boundary of Camp Funston. The editor of the Army City Bulletin noted in August 1917 the advantages of the location and urged Army City's merchants to "give them [soldiers] a square deal."[10] Unfortunately for Army City, Funston was torn down after the war, and the 18,000 acres of Fort Riley once again returned to relative peace as home to the army's mounted Service School and as a cavalry post. This long period of relative stability came to an end on the eve of World War II. Since then Riley has grown to over 100,000 acres in two dramatic acquisitions of land. The first, completed in 1939, increased the post to 51,000 acres. In the second, consummated in 1965, the army obtained just over 50,000 acres.[11]

The views of William H. Avery, one-time governor of Kansas, Junction City's congressman, and a long-time resident of nearby Wakefield, Kansas, suggest a model of analysis for the most critical period of the history of Fort Riley-Junction City, which is the period since the 1939 land acquisition. Governor Avery posits three factors as critical to the success of Junction City. The first was good relations with the army; the second was senior officer post support; and the third was good politics. The most important events in the history of the last 40 years at Fort Riley can be analyzed from these perspectives.[12]

Yet none of this would have been possible were it not for the fact that Junction City's leading citizens have long understood their dependence on the army as their chief source of income. As long ago as 1867 the editor of the Junction City Union reckoned that military posts ensured the success of a community. In April of that year he observed, "From the Atlantic westward, the selections by the military of points for their operations have, without exception, been changed to large, populous and important cities and towns."[13] Nor have contemporary Junction Citians forgotten this lesson. If any were inclined to do so, a quick look at the economic contribution of Fort Riley to their town would refresh their memories. The army itself anticipated in fiscal year 1981 that the annual monetary injection into Geary County, of which Junction City is a part, and nearby Riley County would be $170 million, less the effect of "peripheral" monies brought in by the post. The army believed these monies would raise the annual economic impact in Geary and Riley counties to $286 million. John D. Montgomery, the current editor of the Junction City Daily Union, which has been in the family since 1892, places Junction City's understanding of the situation in stark clarity. The situation as he sees it is quite obvious: "It is in the interest of the town to keep its best customer growing."[14]

There is another element besides economic self-interest at work in Junction City, a matter that is part and parcel of being an army town but that is especially important in the case of Junction City because, unlike most other major army posts today, it is not a creature of World War II. The society of Junction City is a meld of civilian, military, and retired military people. In the words of Robert J. Fegan, a prominent Junction City businessman and booster, "The town and the post grew up together. The military and the town are intermarried. This is over and beyond the economic impact."[15] Many of Junction City's leading citizens are soldiers who have taken second careers in the business community of Junction City. Three retired generals are associated with banks in town. A section of the residential area is called the "United Nations," where many military families live. There is also "Generals' Row" and even a "Sergeants' Major Row" in other neighborhoods.[16] There is, then, a sizable military constituency in the community that is supportive of the post not merely for economic reasons but on principle and by inclination as well.

The military constituency in town contributes to what Governor Avery calls the "one hundred-year happy relationship between Junction City and Fort Riley."[17] This happy relationship came about in part because of natural business and social contacts. However, since the turn of the century and especially in the last 40 years, good relations have existed as the result of carefully considered and well-executed schemes designed with that end in mind. Junction City's boosters have shown considerable acumen in extending their efforts to officers outside the "natural" business that the town might have with the post. Certainly, procurement officers and post commanders were not ignored, but neither were young officers who could render no immediate service to Junction City. In short, Junction Citians are convivial hosts.

Governor Avery reports that the theory under which Junction City operated was based on making an investment with the anticipation of a long-range return.

> Every Second Lieutenant out of West Point [later they
> included others as well] should be welcomed to Fort Riley
> because some day by the law of averages some of those
> Second Lieutenants were going to be Generals in the Army.
> They [Junction City] wanted those Generals to have a
> happy, pleasant memory of their tour at Fort Riley.[18]

The Junction City plan has been effective. Governor Avery recalls that during his years in Congress and in the governor's mansion most division or post commanders had served one or more previous tours at Riley and "could never quit talking about what wonderful people lived in Junction City."[19] Lieutenant General Harvey H. Fischer, whose experience with civil-military relations includes Forts Riley and Hood as well as other posts, describes relations between Fort Riley and Junction City as "some of the best in the country." Indeed, General Fischer avows that he could "write pages on this subject; 'locals' take care of their post and its people."[20]

The grand old men who led and lead Junction City as a kind of shadow government created these good relations through a number of different vehicles, which varied from parties for officers to special help and good treatment for young soldiers. Treatment of officers was especially good, and in the 1930s, 1940s, and 1950s, and before the post became quite large, it was all-inclusive down to lieutenants. Old invitation lists for Junction City parties hosted for soldiers give some indication of at least the possibility of making long-term friends. The invitation list for a party given at the Junction City Country Club on the evening of November 29, 1951, included a First Lieutenant Phillip Kaplan, who returned from May 1978 through June 1980 as the commanding general of the First Division at Fort Riley. Parties have been effective in fostering relations with the post down through the years and were extended to include parties in Chicago where the old Fifth Army Headquarters was located. These Chicago festivities were useful as a means of fostering ties with the immediate superior headquarters of Fort Riley, through which requests for additional land had to pass.[21]

In recent years the annual convention of the Association of the United States Army (AUSA), the army's lobbying organization, has been the occasion of a party for present and former friends of the First Division, Fort Riley, and Junction City or just plain important people. There were 239 names on the list for the Junction City Chamber of Commerce reception for the 1980 convention of the AUSA. The group included scores of officers, at least 65 of whom were in the rank of brigadier general or above. Many of those who attended were retired officers, for another rule is that Junction City does not forget its friends. Additionally, the Kansas legislative delegation was invited, as were important Department of Defense and Department of the Army civilians. But the chamber also invited a number of junior officers and enlisted soldiers. Junction City understands the value of loyalty up and down and endeavors to take care of everyone.[22]

Over the years chamber of commerce fund raising to support social functions with Fort Riley or courtesy rooms at AUSA annual meetings has become better and better organized. From 1955 until 1973, funds were raised by subscription for the Fort Riley Fund, which had replaced short-term fund drives of the early 1950s. Since 1973 the Old Trooper Regiment has superseded the Fort Riley Fund as a vehicle for supporting social occasions. The Old Trooper Regiment is supported by subscription at an annual rate of $400. In 1981 there were 37 members. Typical activities of the Old Trooper Regiment in 1980/81 included large dinners, Society of the First Division functions, AUSA cocktail parties, and golf outings. The Old Trooper Regiment is aimed primarily at senior officers stationed at Fort

Riley or senior officers previously stationed there. Essentially, the goal is to create a favorable impression of Junction City in the minds of senior army officers and large and influential political figures in the country as a whole.[23]

Despite their vast numbers, junior officers have not been and are not ignored by Junction City. Indeed, according to Dan B. Loeb of the chamber of commerce, it was "thought advisable [among the members of the chamber] to create a group who would do social functions with junior officers at Fort Riley."[24] Accordingly, the Fort Riley Ambassadors was organized in 1978. The Ambassadors boast 48 members at a $100 annual subscription rate. Five of their members are sons of members of the Old Trooper Regiment, and virtually all are younger members of business organizations represented on the roster of the Old Trooper Regiment. Richard Pinaire, an attorney in Junction City, believes there are several reasons for the creation of the Ambassadors. One reason was to show young officers "that there are good people living in J.C. and that it is a nice place to live," but the Ambassadors were also created to establish "good relationships [with the army] and [to enhance] the reputation of Junction City."[25] Whether the good relations that have resulted from the activities of the old Fort Riley Fund, the more recent Old Trooper Regiment, and the Fort Riley Ambassadors actually produce tangible benefits is arguable. Nonetheless, Junction City's efforts in time and money suggest that they believe there have been results.

Making incoming officers welcome has also been a long-time strong suit of Junction City. In 1964, having received a packet of information and a welcome to the town, one colonel wrote to John Montgomery, who had been the source of the welcome, to say, "We are already forming a very favorable picture of the people and their environments."[26] Nor was this a new phenomenon. Another soldier wrote to the chamber of commerce in 1954, a year after leaving, to say, "No community has ever extended itself to the Army so completely as has Junction City."[27]

Junction City also endeavored to care for the troops in ways other than making whiskey available. In fact Junction Citians worked just as hard to take care of the enlisted soldiers as they did officers, under the assumption that the former were clients as well. Indeed, the army was not above asking for help when it needed it. Robert J. Fegan assessed the Junction City response past and present by asserting that "anything Fort Riley wanted they [the city fathers] would take off to Washington to get it using political influence."[28] But going to the top was not always necessary, as in the case of their saving the (USO) Soldiers' Center from closing for lack of funds in 1953. Junction City raised the money to keep the center open because as Dick Jones, then president of the chamber, observed, "Junction

City [was] under a moral obligation to do so."[29] They also went to
their pocketbooks in 1954 to stage a welcome for the Thirty-seventh
Infantry Division, which moved from Fort Polk to Riley in that year.
This time the chamber, under the leadership of their Fort Riley Personnel Relations Committee, hit the streets to raise $5,000 to use
during the week of June 13-19, 1954, to help their new division settle
in. Noting that a cost of $5,000 represented only 0.0025 of the divi-
sion's monthly payroll, the chamber considered that this welcome
week was "EFFECTIVE LOW COST PROMOTION!"[30] In any case
the division not only enjoyed a week of fun and games but also received much practical help in housing and other problems. More
recently, Junction City helped finance the Waiting Wives Club and
other similar support activities during the Vietnam War.

The spirit of cooperation for economic self-interest certainly
has been a factor in the establishment and continuation of good relations between Junction City and the soldiers, who were later inclined
to be helpful when Junction City needed help. The rules of conduct for
Junction City businessmen, as enumerated by John D. Montgomery—
certainly one of the most successful men in Junction City—are simple
and straightforward. Montgomery listed those rules in notes he prepared for a talk to his fellow businessmen in 1965. Noting that the
growth of Riley had been very useful to Junction City, he added that
it brought "added and greater responsibilities for all of us—(1) fair
dealing; (2) more improvements in [the] city and, (3) more friendly
contacts with our younger people and with young officers."[31] This is
a theme that Montgomery and others like him have played on through
the years with great success.

Yet there is still more to doing what Fegan calls "anything Riley
wants." The army and Fort Riley had, and still have, needs with
which they require help. Civilian support is especially critical in
keeping the facilities required on a post up to date and adequate for
the number of troops and dependents assigned. It is sometimes difficult to marshal that kind of support for activities that tend to compete with the civilian economy. Perhaps the best example is in the
area of housing. Many civilian communities have been and are hostile
to the building of government housing on nearby army posts. Fort
Riley, however, has never had a problem with Junction City in this
regard. In fact, Junction City has a record of supporting not only
housing but the building of other service facilities at Riley. John D.
Montgomery and Bob Fegan and others in Junction City have long
taken the view that opposing such projects would eventually have a
negative impact on the community. Therefore, Junction City not only
supported government housing but on occasion "asked for additional
'On Post' housing." Montgomery accounts for this unusual stance by
saying, "We thought it was correct and we were willing to risk a

temporary slackening of rental requests in order to make Fort Riley larger and more desirable in the future."[32] Despite short-term risks, Junction City has tended to stick to their dictum of doing anything for Fort Riley.

The good feelings army officers have traditionally had about Fort Riley and Junction City stem both from Junction City's efforts to include them and the natural closeness of the two communities as a result of proximity and long-term dependence. In John Montgomery's words, there is "no wall between Junction City and Fort Riley."[33]

Dan Loeb notes that in Junction City "army brats and townies grew up and grew close together."[34] Moreover, the post and the town tended to intermarry, and some of Junction City's young men made the army a career, as did J. C. H. Lee and Bruce Palmer, both of whom became general officers, and the Seitz brothers, who were from nearby. John A. "Andy" Seitz retired as a brigadier general, having served at Riley on two separate tours and in the Fifth Army, which was Fort Riley's next higher headquarters. Richard Seitz retired as a lieutenant general. Both have retired in Junction City and are active in Fort Riley-Junction City activities. Junction City's ties with the army are strong and, having a long history, well rooted.[35]

The third factor in Governor Avery's formula for Junction City's long-term success is politics. The area of politics has been extremely important, especially in the post-World War II era. Competition for troops and facilities, the lifeblood of Junction City, has been keen. According to Dan Loeb, the "civilian effort had to be made to get the Fort Riley position through."[36] The men most responsible for the Junction City effort since the 1950s have been John D. Montgomery, Fred Bramlage, and Robert J. Fegan. On the lower scale, but just as important, Dan B. Loeb and others have also labored long and hard. Junction City has been successful in making its needs known because where Fort Riley is concerned its leadership has been united. Though Montgomery is a Democrat and Fegan and Bramlage have been active Republicans, they have, according to Major General John F. Ruggles, "locked arms when the welfare and future of Ft. Riley was at stake."[37] This bipartisan alliance has been advantageous, since no matter which party was in power, someone from Junction City had access to the Department of the Army and the Congress. Thus the city was ensured a "foot in the door" at the Pentagon and on Capitol Hill, so that Junction City could "make everyone knowledgeable of our needs and at the same time expedite actions that needed to be taken."[38] Junction City makes optimum use of this open door by sending people to Washington to keep the town's needs in the forefront. Since 1972 they have retained a full-time public relations counselor to see that the Junction City position gets represented when the need occurs.[39]

The big three in Junction City have some guidelines they follow very carefully in this chancy business of national politics. First, they are circumspect men who operate behind the scenes. They also understand the political rules. In John Montgomery's words, "You don't ask someone for a favor unless you have done something for him."[40] The development of good connections takes years, according to Montgomery, who is a past associate of Congressman Claude Pepper and his long-time friend. Montgomery himself ran, albeit unsuccessfully, for Congress in 1964. Robert J. Fegan, who felt that much of Junction City's success in land acquisition came about because they were able to avoid floor fights in the Congress, believes that political power is developed by following three rules:

> You don't run for office, but you carry water to the
>   elephant.
> You never ask for anything personal, but you ask for
>   things for Fort Riley.
> You don't use your influence for individuals.[41]

Another political asset that all three made use of was their involvement in veterans' organizations and in the army's pressure group, AUSA. Fegan believes these associations were valuable. He notes that both he and Bramlage were "involved in [American] Legion politics in which Democrats and Republicans mixed; therefore, we had bipartisan support."[42]

The elements of Junction City's success created a system of operation that enabled the town to have advance intelligence on what the requirements of Fort Riley might be. This information was forthcoming because of their close personal relationships with officers at the post or those in positions of authority in the army as a whole. The possession of such intelligence gave them an advantage, since they had, by their efforts, created generally receptive audiences in the higher echelons of both the military and civilian leadership in the Department of the Army. Once the Junction City plan was accepted as the army plan, its leadership could turn to the task of pulling "every angle we could think of without getting into a congressional fight."[43]

At least this is the system in theory. How it worked in practice can best be seen by reviewing a few illustrative cases and exploring one case in detail. The land acquisition of 1940 has been mentioned, but Junction City has accomplished much more.[44] Since World War II the town has captured the First Infantry Division on at least two occasions when it was earmarked for another another post. Junction City has also been extremely helpful in the acquisition of funds for the construction of improved facilities on the post and on-post govern-

ment housing. Finally and most important, Junction City has virtually
ensured the continued utility of Fort Riley as a training site and a
major army installation by leading the fight in Congress for the
acquisition of some 50,000 acres in 1964/65.

Right through World War II the troop population at Riley
remained relatively small and the fortunes of Fort Riley relatively
uncertain. According to Dan Loeb, "The real importance of Fort
Riley came when we caught the First Infantry Division [after World
War II]."[45] The acquisition of a division ensured a large troop population and a large payroll. Yet obtaining a division did not automatically ensure prosperity. A division had to be caught and kept. Keeping it was problematic since during the 1950s the army was unstable
in size and assignments. For example, in 1955 the First Infantry
Division was to rotate from Germany to Fort Riley, while Riley's
Tenth would go to Germany under Operation Gyroscope. But Junction
City learned to their chagrin that the Big Red One would not return
to Fort Riley. According to army informants, the First Division,
scheduled to return to Riley in the fall, was en route to Fort Ord,
California, instead.[46] Thus the summer of 1955 was an unpleasant
one for Junction City businessmen as they contemplated the loss of
the Tenth Division's 15,000-man payroll and no new payroll to take
its place.

Despite their disappointment at losing the division, they refused
to give up. Instead, they sought to determine how this shift had happened. A chamber of commerce file labeled simply "Fort Riley" includes notes on the loss of the division to Ord. The major problem
in the view of an anonymous analyst in the chamber was, "We do not
keep close enough touch with our Wash DC [sic] contacts to know
what is happening in time to take defensive actions."[47] In this same
analysis the disgruntled author concluded that "we should learn what
happened and when and how so we can learn a lesson."[48] They did
better still. In Dan Loeb's words, the First Division was "short-
stopped" on its way to Ord.[49]

Having discovered what was happening to them, the Junction
City leadership mobilized their people and began work in the winter
of 1954/55 to save what they believed was rightfully theirs. Fegan
and Bramlage began a series of pilgrimages to Washington in January,
and in April Montgomery joined them to do "something for the main
post."[50] According to Bob Fegan, "We fanned out to see our friends
and put the heat on [and] we got people from the White House, the
President's Army Aide-de-Camp, to call DA [Department of the
Army] to let them know there was White House interest in the Big
Red One going to Fort Riley."[51] In the end they were successful,
and in September 1955 the First Division returned to Fort Riley,
where it remained until it was deployed to Vietnam in 1965.

But Junction City's triumph in 1955 did not forever ensure its well-being. The really big challenge for Junction City was yet to come, and those who would have to meet it were either ignorant of the forthcoming battle or only dimly aware that yet another fight would have to be won. John Montgomery had an inkling, for General Bruce C. Clarke had warned him. In addition to having played a key role in the defense of St. Vith during the Battle of the Bulge, Clarke had an excellent reputation as a troop trainer and in the 1950s and 1960s commanded at the four-star level at Continental Army Command and Seventh Army in Europe. It was in a conversation in the 1950s, Montgomery recalls, that Clarke had awakened him to the need to anticipate requirements for additional training space at Fort Riley. Clarke, whose views could be relied on, believed that a revolution in tactics was occurring that would necessitate more maneuver space. Clarke believed that those posts that did not grow would be closed down. Accordingly, he warned Montgomery not to let "Fort Riley become obsolete."[52]

But army towns do not, despite their interest, initiate requests for land acquisition; so the initial role of the Junction Citians was to keep an ear close to the ground and be prepared to support any plans that Fort Riley might develop. Keeping well informed and staying alert were activities in which Junction City excelled. Harold P. Reaume, past executive of the chamber of commerce, avows that in his 30 years in Junction City "our program was 50% opportunistic."[53] Soon Junction City's vigilance was rewarded, for indeed Fort Riley needed more land if it was to survive as an active division post. The additional land was required, according to one post commander, because "Riley was not an adequate facility to train a combat division."[54] The training requirements for tactics, artillery, and missiles exceeded the facilities available. Thus in order for the post to be viable for an active division, it had to be expanded. Major General John F. Ruggles, who—as commander from 1961 to 1963—had responsibility for presenting Riley's plan, felt that expansion of the post would inevitably occur. Ruggles notes:

> It was apparent to me that the political grip that had
> brought the First Division to Ft. Riley was durable
> enough to keep the division there over the years to come.
> I therefore considered it desirable to take action to
> expand the reservation, knowing full well the political
> interests that brought the division there would whole-
> heartedly support such action, as it would "nail down"
> Ft. Riley as a Division post for years to come.[55]

General Ruggles did not have to start from scratch, since Fort Riley already had an ambitious plan initiated in the late 1950s. Robert Fegan remembers that the original Fort Riley plan called for the acquisition of 217,000 acres (to the north of Junction City), taking in the towns of Riley and Keats as well as the railroad that ran east-west north of the town of Riley. A state and U.S. highway would be absorbed as well. [56]

The process for acquiring land involved the submission of the Fort Riley plan to Fifth Army at Fort Sheridan, Illinois. But any plan had to survive reviews by the Continental Army Command and the Department of the Army before it would become part of a budget request. Fegan recalled that in 1960 he got a "tip from my personal sources that now was the time to get land."[57] So the acquisition program that was consummated in 1965 really began in 1960. At this point the Junction City boosters had two objectives. First, they had to sell the Fort Riley plan to the army. Second, they had to avoid allowing the issue to be resolved on the floor of the U.S. Congress. In Fegan's words, "We had to be careful not to let the land acquisition fight become a Congressional fight based on delegates."[58] To do so would, of course, put Kansas with a small delegation at a disadvantage vis-à-vis other posts that were candidates for expansion, especially Ord in California but also Leonard Wood in Missouri. [59]

The task of gaining army acceptance required some effort, since the original Fifth Army position favored Fort Leonard Wood and Continental Army Command favored expanding facilities in California. The Junction City team had some help, however. During the deliberations, Brigadier General John A. Seitz, a Kansas native, was chief of staff at Fifth Army. Though Seitz would not directly determine the decision, he could ensure that Fort Riley's plan got a fair hearing despite the original Fifth Army position. More helpful still was a change of command at Fifth Army that ushered in a new commanding general who had a neutral position. These conditions assisted Junction City, but the victory was due, in Fegan's view, to having "close friends in the Army in high places who had love and affection for Fort Riley."[60]

Yet it would be erroneous to conclude that Junction City's confidence in its friends in the army was such that they could passively await developments. In February 1962 the president of the chamber of commerce renewed the chamber's efforts to "have representation in Washington, D.C., at regular intervals."[61] The chamber offered to pay travel expenses and "other" expenses for anyone willing to go to the Capital and act on behalf of Junction City. Additionally, any such trips would include a briefing prior to departure and a report on return. [62] Later in that month, E. D. Jackson, the president and author of the original chamber letter, and Howard Goad, a local businessman and one-time mayor of Junction City, spent three days in Washington. In one day they made their marks with four generals and over a dozen colonels on the Department of the Army staff. These officers were assigned in the secretary of the army's office, the Office of the Chief of Staff, the Public Information Office, and other positions of responsibility. But most important, old acquaintances from Riley got them into the "Real Estate Office," where the file of Fort Riley's land acquisition happened to be at that moment. While in the office, they spoke with both Department of the Army attorneys and the officer responsible for the file and were told there were problems that made the acquisition "a dead issue at this time."[63] Undismayed, they sold the "Chamber of Commerce tradition on our wonderful community and the opportunity here for enlarging the post in the near future as covered under Fort Riley's 1964 budget."[64] They also pointed out that the problems the army had on record "were as of this date disposed of."[65] On the first evening they renewed old acquaintances and brought in some army officers in the Washington area for cocktails. The following day they met with key members of the Kansas delegation, where they received assurance of support. Frank Carlson, the senior senator from Kansas, promised he would "lead the fight."[66] Their report also noted that the Junction City effort after their departure had been taken up by "Bob Fegan and Fred Bramlage."[67]

It is, of course, difficult to ascertain what the direct benefits of such trips were to the eventual acquisition of land for Fort Riley, but the reports leave no doubt that hard intelligence was obtainable and obtained by "visitors" to the Pentagon. Though there is no evidence of substantive help from officers they met with on the trip, Jackson and Goad could report two general officers as "very interested in Fort Riley and real happy to see old friends."[68] There is also considerable evidence of an affirmative response to "information" letters to senior officers. Lieutenant General Harvey Fischer wrote on May 4, 1964, to "express my happiness that you all are about to achieve this dream."[69] This suggests a certain quality of personal diplomacy with the not unnatural friendly response from officers in the Pentagon or elsewhere who felt at home with their Junction City visitors or who were at least sympathetic to the Junction City-Fort Riley bond.

The second objective of obtaining funding without a congressional fight was potentially more difficult than winning army approval. At this stage there were at least three possible dangers to the land acquisition program. First, local opposition was a very real danger, especially since the state had recently acquired land and federal money to build Tuttle Creek Reservoir north of the city of Manhattan, Kansas. The Tuttle Creek acquisition had outraged Riley County farmers, who would now see a second similar-sized chunk of their land taken as well. Moreover, there was an acquisition move in progress to build Milford Reservoir near Junction City. Second, early in the Kennedy administration, economies in defense were de rigueur, so that it was possible that an acquisition plan might clear military channels but die at the Department of the Army or the Department of Defense. Finally, serious congressional opposition would ensure the death of any acquisition scheme, given the small size and thus relative power of the Kansas delegation in Washington.

Junction City applied its not-inconsiderable talents and political acumen to ensure the proper public support at the state level and to circumvent any hostile elements in the Congress. They began with a media blitz on the advantages of expanding the post. John D. Montgomery's Daily Union fired the first shots in December 1963. In that first editorial, "Foresight Pays Off," published on December 16, the Daily Union reviewed the history of the post and the various efforts made to preserve it by expansion and noted that a week previously the Department of Defense had announced plans to close some 26 military installations across the United States. Fort Riley, claimed the Daily Union, would surely be among those destined to close had it not been expanded in 1940. What, wondered the Daily Union, would have been the economic status of Junction City, Manhattan, Chapman, Abilene, Milford, Riley, Dwight, Alta Vista, Enterprise, Herington, Woodbine, White City, and other communities near the post if Fort Riley had not been expanded in the past.[70] Leaving the reader to ponder the catastrophic results of the failure to expand the post, the editor moved on to "recall that the expansion of Fort Riley 25 years ago was not popular with some. . . . But who can maintain that the overall economic gains [did not] offset the economic losses a hundred fold?"[71] The message was clear. Fort Riley must be enlarged at the expense of 500 farm people who lived on the land earmarked for Riley in order that thousands might continue to enjoy the economic benefit of the post.

But local economics was not the only factor introduced. The purchase of land for Fort Riley was also touted as good for the national economy and vital to combat readiness. The Topeka Daily Capital obligingly took up this double-edged ax in an editorial entitled "A Larger Fort Riley," which was published on January 24, 1963. The Topeka paper noted that the costs of moving troops to California to maneuver and fire major weapons systems would offset the $16.5 million price tag for the acquisition of land. The Daily Capital did note with regret that the acquisition "will, of course, have a great effect on the lives of those who must move," adding further that this had come on the heels of the Milford and Tuttle Creek Reservoir projects, which had already resulted in many relocations.[72] But echoing the Daily Union, the Topeka paper concluded, "The public

welfare is involved and while it is regrettable that condemnation proceedings break old ties, there seems to be no alternative."[73]

Support for those potent arguments was nearly universal in the
print media. The continued health of Fort Riley, the seventh largest
"town" in Kansas, seemed demonstrably more important than trouble-
some questions about those who would lose their homes or the fact
that reservations of adequate size lay dormant elsewhere. Even
Manhattan, the county seat of Riley County, which would bear the
burden of the loss in tax base, seemed able to live with the acquisition. The Manhattan Mercury noted on May 29, 1964, as the fact of
acquisition loomed near, "The losses will be more than offset by the
gains coming from enlarging the Fort and upgrading its future role."[74]

Virtually no one, aside from the farmers involved, raised any
protest. The 50,000-acre chunk of land destined for inclusion in the
post lay on its northern border. On that plot 496 men, women, and
children lived on 91 farms, which averaged 550 acres each. Such
opposition as existed came from here. Several farmers elected to
fight the purchase when it became public in 1963. They organized
the Riley-Geary County Survival Association under the leadership of
Lyle Sylvester and two other farmers, one of whom was related to
Sylvester. The opposition came for the obvious reasons, but it was
also marked by the perception that the acquisition was "not an army
push but strictly civilian."[75] The Survival Association was able to
obtain the support of the Kansas Farm Bureau and the Clay Center
Chamber of Commerce, a farming community west of the post.[76]
They made a spirited defense of their position, arguing that the
acquisition was not necessary to military readiness and that it was
"largely spearheaded by certain Junction City businessmen who hope
for personal gain from this expansion."[77]

The fighting, in fact, got a little dirty. At one point Montgomery
and Congressman Avery, who were leading the effort for the land
acquisition in the House of Representatives, learned that their portraits, framed in toilet seats, had been hung from telephone poles
on U.S. Highway 77, which was destined to be swallowed up in the
acquisition.[78] There was considerable name-calling and pressure
exerted from both sides. In a sworn statement before the Senate
Armed Services Committee, the association claimed that the Junction
City leadership told one of its members," We are going to get the
land . . . and if you value your homes and land above national security, that is too damn bad."[79] Despite the impassioned arguments of
the Riley-Geary County Survival Association, no effective public
campaign against the acquisition developed nor were their efforts in
Congress more than a pinprick. Like the farmers in Dykstra's history
of the Kansas cattle towns, Riley County farmers succumbed to the
heavier guns of the town interests. Thus the Kansas delegation in

Congress was able to present a united front, and the Junction City effort could be safely directed toward circumventing opposition in the House and Senate, where base closing and not expansions had been the vogue.

In Fegan's words, "We pulled every angle we could think of without getting into a Congressional fight."[80] Junction City enjoyed one or two advantages in the national legislature, which they put to good use. First, the senatorial delegation had accumulated considerable seniority. Senator Carlson, the senior senator, was by this time also something of an expert on land condemnation, having pioneered the effort to acquire land for water projects in Kansas. He had been at it for 30 years. In fact, the Milford Lake project, which abutted Fort Riley on the west, was in progress at virtually the same time, making it possible to deal with both issues at once. Carlson was also on good terms with the all-powerful Senator Bill Russell. Thus, when the acquisition bill came up from the House, there was "no organized opposition to the land acquisition."[81]

In the House, where conditions were not as favorable, timing and connections seem to have been the key ingredients. Junction City was nothing if not patient, and its leaders had good connections. John Montgomery had worked for Congressman Pepper and for Congressman Sykes of Florida, both of whom enjoyed considerable power. More important, Congressman Avery had achieved a good working relationship with Carl Vinson, a giant in passing military legislation.[82]

By the time the Fort Riley package was prepared for consideration in 1962, the time was not, in Vinson's view, favorable, especially since the Kennedy administration seemed bent on dismantling the peacetime defense establishment. Vinson urged Congressman Avery to bide his time for the present. While waiting, Avery spent some time "working on a few things" with Congressman Vinson. Having followed Vinson's advice, Avery was pleased to note that "a year later [after Vinson advised him to wait on the land acquisition] the money was appropriated."[83]

The evidence suggests that once the plan to increase the size of Fort Riley became part of the army plan, there was very little difficulty in seeing it through. Even though Lyle Sylvester and his compatriots spoke their piece before Senator Stennis's Subcommittee of the Armed Services Committee, there was virtually no congressional opposition. This was so partly because the land acquisition was part of a large military authorization but also because Frank Carlson was well known and experienced in federal land acquisitions. It was also true because of the wide public acclaim for the acquisition in Kansas and the unity of opinion in the neighboring towns of Junction City and Manhattan. Perhaps most important, Bill Avery understood how things got done in the House, and the project enjoyed support in the army from soldiers who would receive no direct return on the investment of their support. Clearly, Junction City's success in ensuring the growth of its post was a result of adherence to a three-part plan. The plan included the creation and maintenance of good relations with the army coupled with good politics at all levels.

Having achieved the doubling of the post and inclusion in the bill that Fort Riley would remain a divisional post, Junction City might have been justified in concluding it was safe and the work complete. Nothing could have been further from the truth. In the summer and fall of 1965 the First Infantry Division deployed to Vietnam, where they remained until 1970. At first Junction City was sanguine that the departure of the troops would not have any considerable effect on the town. In September 1965, after the first brigade left, the Daily Union printed a story headlined: "Troop Shift Has Little Area Effect."[84] But that statement was made when the division had moved only a brigade and was supposed to send no other troops. The army sought to reassure the town. General Harold K. Johnson, then chief of staff, announced that the post would retain "an important role."[85] Junction City felt reassured—but not for long. Retail sales plummeted from nearly $2.8 million in August 1965 to $1.7 million in January 1966. In that month, to the tremendous relief of the business community, the formation at Fort Riley of the Ninth Infantry Division was announced.[86] However, the recovery was temporary and the economic situation at Junction City remained troubled until 1968, when the Twenty-fourth Infantry Division was brought home from Germany and replaced the Ninth, which, like the First, had gone to Vietnam. During this period, Junction City's population dropped from a high of 20,975 in 1965 to a low of 16,849 in 1967 and had returned to only 19,282 by 1980.[87]

Still, during the hardest of times, Junction City kept plugging. It established very good relations with the "transient" Ninth Division. Major General Maurice W. Kendall, then a brigade commander with the Ninth, recalls being genuinely impressed with the friendliness of the Junction City leadership and the degree of interest they took in the post. On his arrival, Kendall, whose troops were located at Camp Forsyth on the Republican Flats immediately adjacent to the town, went to considerable lengths to clean up the cantonment, which had been left in some disarray by the harried and hurried First, which had departed unexpectedly. He recalled that at the first function to which Junction Citians had been invited, they made comments in detail about the improvements he had made.[88]

Junction City also went to the wall in support of the troops in Vietnam. Local merchants were helpful about credit arrangements for the families of the soldiers left behind. This was critical, since many troopers went weeks without pay in the transition from peace-time in Kansas to wartime in Southeast Asia. The chamber of commerce was instrumental in supporting the Waiting Wives Club formed by those left behind by the Big Red One. Junction City also gave moral and financial support to other organizations designed to serve the needs of soldiers and their families.[89] Through it all, Junction City toughed it out and stayed loyal. Not surprisingly, the Big Red One came home to Kansas in May of 1970, thus justifying the faith in adversity that the town had displayed.[90]

But Junction City had learned the lesson all army towns eventually learn: Nothing is forever. Like the smart business people they are, they have since diversified. Nearby Milford Reservoir with some 150 miles of shoreline has helped as have the four lanes of Interstate 70, which pass the southern tip of Junction City. But these were advantages Junction City did little with until the Vietnam era. Junction City made its move to diversify by hiring away from the state of Kansas a man named Jack Lacy, who had proved himself very effective in the State Economic Development Commission.[91] Lacy, who invented "The Land of Enchantment" logo for New Mexico, spent most of the 1970s in Junction City, where he was instrumental in bringing several businesses to the city. But Lacy did not work alone. The rest of the chamber of commerce membership and the standard city boosters played important roles as well.

Junction City has enjoyed considerable success in its efforts to diversify. Now, besides Fort Riley, they have several operations, new since 1965, including Evans Rail Car, Whittaker Cable, North Central Foundry, and Mid-American Machine Corporation. These companies build everything from rail cars to electrical harnesses to castings for Allis-Chalmers. Lastly, Mobile Travelers, founded in 1967, produces a line of campers and vans. These new operations provide employment for roughly 1,100 people. Besides new industry, Junction City has two new major service operations. United Telephone has its state offices in Junction City as does Communication Services, Inc. But the big plum is F. W. Woolworth's regional support center, which employs 400 people in a 30-acre building servicing Woolworth stores in some 13 states. The Woolworth operation is also the largest occupant of the recently created industrial park on the southwest edge of town. Still, Junction City's foray into the private sector remains small. The roughly 2,000 people employed in new, recently acquired industrial and service operations supplement very nicely the 2,300 civilian employees at Riley. Even so, the main source of income for Junction City is still supplying the goods and services for the 20,000 troops and their 30,000 dependents.[92]

The prognosis for the continued health of Junction City despite her increased diversity still rests on the continued good health of the adjacent military community. Junction City is aware of this situation and continues to plan for the future. The town remains well connected with the army. John D. Montgomery and son, John Grey, both are ex-civilian aides to the secretary of the army, as was R. F. Fegan, who died in October 1982. Fred Bramlage, a Republican member of the team, currently serves as an aide. Junction City has friends in the army and remains an earnest friend of army causes. To maintain these good relations, it continues to employ the Old Trooper Regiment and the Fort Riley Ambassadors.

But will the post grow and prosper? After all, stability in the market place is stagnation. Moreover, weapons and tactics have undergone changes since 1965. Tanks move faster and fire farther than ever. Is 101,000-acre Fort Riley big enough to ensure that it will continue to rate a full division? The front page of the Manhattan Mercury for Sunday, February 15, 1981, featured a story headlined "Fort Looking for More Land." This report would seem to answer the question. At that time the army, according to the Mercury, was "reviewing a proposal which would call for the addition of approximately 30,000 acres to the Fort."[93] It is premature to predict whether the army will get its 30,000 acres; but given the evidence of the recent past, farmers on the borders of the post must be nervous. Lyle Sylvester, leader of the ill-fated Riley-Geary County Survival Association, expressed his satisfaction at being well out of harm's way, having moved to a farm east of Wamego, Kansas, some 30 miles from the post.

NOTES

1. Joseph G. Roso, They Called him Wild Bill (Norman: University of Oklahoma Press, 1974).

2. Samual P. Huntington, The Soldier and the State (New York: Vantage Books, 1957), p. 465.

3. Robert G. Muir and Associates, Architects & Planners, Analysis of Existing Facilities, Environmental Assessment Report: Fort Polk, Louisiana (Fort Worth, Tex.: Fort Worth District Engineers, 1980), p. 17.

4. Ibid., p. 11.

5. Letter dated December 15, 1981, Lieutenant General Harvey H. Fischer to the author. General Fischer commanded Fort Riley while also serving as the commanding general of the First Infantry Division (the Big Red One) from December 1958 until January 1960.

6. Letter dated December 10, 1980, Major General George S. Eckardt to the author.

7. Mark J. Gelfand, A Nation of Cities: The Federal Government and Urban America, 1933-1965 (New York: Oxford University Press, 1975). See also Robert R. Dykstra, The Cattle Towns (New York: Atheneum, 1976). On the military-industrial establishment, see Sam C. Sarkesian, ed., The Military Industrial Complex: A Reassessment (Beverly Hills, Calif.: Sage, 1972). See also Paul C. Koistinen, The Military-Industrial Complex: A Historical Perspective (New York: Praeger, 1980).

8. Interview with Dan B. Loeb, Junction City Chamber of Commerce, Junction City, Kansas, June 4, 1981. Dan B. Loeb is the son of Louis B. Loeb, who was an able representative of Junction City in Fort Riley social circles in the years before World War II.

9. Robert M. Utley, Life in Custer's Cavalry (New Haven: Yale University Press, 1977), pp. 17-18.

10. Nyle H. Miller, Edgar Langsdorf, and Robert W. Richmond, eds., Kansas in Newspapers (Topeka: Kansas State Historical Society). See the Army City Bulletin, August 31, 1917 article entitled "Fifteen Thousand Working at Camp Funston!" See also W. F. Pride, The History of Fort Riley (published privately, N.P., 1926), pp. 277-78.

11. Higgenbotham and Associates, Architects & Planners, Analysis of Existing Facilities and Environmental Assessment Report: Fort Riley, Kansas (Kansas City, Mo.: Kansas City District Engineers, March 1977), pp. 3-4.

12. Interview with Governor William H. Avery, June 2, 1981, Wakefield, Kansas.

13. Dykstra, Cattle Towns, p. 32.

14. Interview with John D. Montgomery, Junction City, Kansas, June 11, 1981. Montgomery is a remarkable man who, in addition to publishing 16 Kansas newspapers, has also published or edited papers in Florida, Cuba, and Brazil. He also has banking interests in Junction City. A member of the 1924 Olympic boxing team, he still has considerable energy (he was 79 in June 1981), which has held him in good stead not only in his business interests but in numerous service organizations and in the Democratic party. He has served in several appointed offices at the state and national levels including service as a civilian aide to the secretary of the army.

15. Interview with Robert J. Fegan, First National Bank, Junction City, Kansas, June 8, 1981. The son of R. B. Fegan, who was also an activist in Fort Riley-Junction City, Fegan owned Junction City's independent telephone company until 1968 when it was sold to United Utilities and had banking interests in town. Active in national veterans' organizations, he also served as president of the Fort Riley-Central Kansas Chapter of the Association of the United States

Army. Finally, he was active in state and national politics as a Republican. He died in 1982.

16. Two of the generals, the brothers Seitz, are Kansas natives who were born and raised in the area.

17. Avery interview, June 2, 1981.

18. Ibid.

19. Ibid.

20. Fischer letter, December 15, 1981.

21. On Major General Kaplan, see letter dated November 20, 1951, from the Adjutant General, Fort Riley, Kansas, to All Concerned. Kaplan was the most junior officer on the invitation list. Information on other parties can be obtained only by perusing the chamber files. There was no consistent filing system used, but the files are staggeringly complete right back to the depression era.

22. On the 1980 AUSA reception, see Junction City Chamber of Commerce, "1980 Invitation Guest List, Chamber of Commerce Reception," an undated, unsigned document.

23. Interview with Dan B. Loeb, Junction City Chamber of Commerce, Junction City, Kansas, June 10, 1981. See also the 1980/81 roster of the Old Trooper Regiment.

24. Ibid. See also the 1980/81 roster of the Fort Riley Ambassadors.

25. Interview with Richard Pinaire, Law Firm of Hoover, Schemerhorn, Edwards & Pinaire, Junction City, Kansas, June 10, 1981. Pinaire is a native of Junction City who graduated from Junction City High School in 1967, Kansas State University in Manhattan in 1971, and the Law School of Washburn University in Topeka in 1973. He is active politically in the state and national Democratic parties. All of these credentials make him an excellent ambassador.

26. Letter dated April 3, 1968, Colonel William M. Glasgow, Jr., to John Montgomery.

27. Letter dated July 13, 1955, Lieutenant Colonel Kenneth W. Schlueter to the Junction City Chamber of Commerce.

28. Fegan interview, June 8, 1981.

29. Letter dated March 30, 1953, Dick Jones to members of the Junction City Chamber of Commerce.

30. Open, unsigned letter dated April 3, 1954, Junction City Chamber of Commerce mailing to all chamber members.

31. John D. Montgomery, note cards in personal files dated May 13, 1965.

32. Letter dated January 26, 1981, John D. Montgomery to the author.

33. Montgomery interview, June 11, 1981.

34. Loeb interview, June 3, 1981.

35. Loeb interview, June 4, 1981. See also Pride, History of Fort Riley on the social interactions of Fort Riley-Junction City.

36. Loeb interview, June 4, 1981.

37. Letter dated December 5, 1981, Major General John F. Ruggles to the author.

38. Loeb interview, June 4, 1981.

39. Ibid. The public relations firm Junction City retains is Cocke and Phillips International of Washington, D.C.

40. Interview with John D. Montgomery, Junction City, Kansas, June 4, 1981.

41. Fegan interview, June 8, 1981.

42. Ibid.

43. Ibid.

44. The prewar acquisition of 32,370 acres was designed to make the post suitable for a cavalry brigade and remount depot. Local support for the acquisition was intense. Not surprisingly, nearby Manhattan supported this effort, but so did the property owners. See "Landowners Favor Sale," Junction City Daily Union, December 19, 1939. Harold P. Reaume, who managed the Junction City Chamber of Commerce from August 1, 1926, until November 30, 1957, recalls the acquisition of 1941 began with joint military-civilian "tub-thumping" in 1937. See letter dated August 29, 1981, Harold P. Reaume to the author.

45. Interview with Dan B. Loeb, Junction City, Kansas, June 5, 1981.

46. Dan B. Loeb has indicated that Junction City was "tipped." Fegan recalls that they learned of the change by reading the unit newspaper of the First Division. In any case, they learned of the loss of the First Division by unofficial channels.

47. Junction City Chamber of Commerce, file labeled "Fort Riley," undated, unsigned notes labeled "The Major Factors."

48. Ibid.

49. Loeb interview, June 4, 1981.

50. Junction City Chamber of Commerce file labeled "Fort Riley." This file has a great number of documents listing lobbying efforts in Washington and other efforts to save the First Division for Fort Riley.

51. Fegan interview, June 8, 1981.

52. Montgomery interview, June 11, 1981.

53. Letter dated September 19, 1981, Harold P. Reaume to the author.

54. Interview with General Theodore W. Parker, United States Military Academy, West Point, New York, May 21, 1982.

55. Ruggles letter, December 5, 1981. General Ruggles could not recall who wrote the original expansion study, but he was involved in passing on the post's recommendations.

56. Fegan interview, June 8, 1981.

57. Ibid.

58. Ibid.

59. Ibid.

60. Ibid. See also interview with Brigadier General John A. Seitz, Junction City, Kansas, June 8, 1981.

61. Letter dated February 3, 1962, E. D. Jackson, chamber of commerce president to members of the chamber.

62. Ibid.

63. Letter dated February 11, 12, 13, 1962, E. D. Jackson and Howard Goad to John D. Montgomery, chairman of the Fort Riley Committee. The letter is a four-page report detailing the activities of a lobbying trip to the Capital.

64. Ibid.

65. Ibid.

66. Ibid.

67. Ibid.

68. Ibid.

69. Letter dated May 4, 1963, Lieutenant General Harvey H. Fischer to John D. Montgomery.

70. "Foresight Pays Off," Junction City Daily Union, December 16, 1963.

71. Ibid.

72. "A Larger Fort Riley," Topeka Daily Capital, January 24, 1963.

73. Ibid.

74. Manhattan Mercury, May 29, 1964.

75. Interview with Lyle E. Sylvester, Wamego, Kansas, June 9, 1981.

76. Ibid.

77. Ibid.

78. Both Governor Avery and John D. Montgomery claim they were amused, but the portraits did create an interesting and, at the time, well-publicized demonstration of the farmers' assessment of who was after their homes.

79. U.S., Congress, Senate, Subcommittee of the Committee on Armed Services, Military Construction Authorization Fiscal Year 1965, 88th Cong., 1964, H. Rept. 10300, p. 720.

80. Fegan interview, June 8, 1981.

81. Interview with Senator Frank Carlson, Concordia, Kansas, June 11, 1981.

82. Montgomery interview, June 11, 1981; Avery interview, June 2, 1981.

83. Avery interview, June 2, 1981.

84. "Troop Shift Has Little Area Effect," Junction City Daily Union, September 1, 1965, p. 7.

85. "Gen. Johnson Says Post Will Retain an Important Role," Junction City Daily Union, September 3, 1965, p. 7; Montgomery, Personal File labeled "Fort Riley Growth." Retail sales in the year from October 1964, before the division left, to October 1965, the month the division left, were down 23.7 percent. During the period October 1965 to January 1966, retail sales in both Manhattan and Junction City dropped steadily. November 1966, for example, was 33.9 percent lower than November 1965. On monthly sales tax statistics, see the Kansas Business Review, vols. 18-21, October 1965-August 1968.

86. John D. Montgomery, personal file labeled "Fort Riley Growth Period." Retail sales in the year from October 1964, before the division left, to October 1965, the month the division left, were down 23.7 percent. During the period October 1965 to January 1966, retail sales in both Manhattan and Junction City dropped steadily. November 1966, for example, was 33.9 percent lower than November 1965. On monthly tax statistics, see Kansas Business Review, October 1965, vol. 18, no. 12 through August 1968, vol. 21.

87. 1980 figures provided by Junction City Chamber of Commerce extracted from the 1980 United States Census. For the remainder of Junction City population statistics, see League of Kansas Municipalities, Information for Kansas Officials (1963-67 ed.).

88. Interview with Major General Maurice W. Kendall, West Point, New York, October 1981.

89. The chamber helped fund the Waiting Wives' Club and found space for the club to meet. For its part, the Union covered the activities of the departed troops and maintained a strongly supportive position not merely for the war but for the soldiers themselves. The chamber plan for helping soldiers through the rough times while pay caught up was straightforward. In essence, the city merchants carried soldiers' debts.

90. Some of those interviewed have suggested that the division was originally bound for Fort Benning. Dan Loeb asserts that Junction City averted that disaster thanks to an army officer who warned the town's leadership.

91. Avery interview, June 2, 1981.

92. Interview with Dan B. Loeb, Junction City, Kansas, June 2, 1981. On troop population and Fort Riley employment statistics, see U.S. Army, Fort Riley Average Monthly Data (2d Quarter FY 81) (Fort Riley, Kans.: AFZN-em-2, March 1981). According to this report, the post has a usual economic impact of $170 million per year.

93. "Fort Looking for More Land," Manhattan Mercury, February 15, 1981, p. 1.

3

Suburbia Armed: Nassau County Development and the Rise of the Aerospace Industry, 1909–60

Geoffrey Rossano

OVERVIEW

The explosive growth of Nassau County, New York, during the first 60 years of this century offers a special vantage point for observing the dramatic interplay between two pivotal forces affecting modern metropolitan life: suburbanization and militarization. Important as these developments have been in molding recent America, however, they have rarely been analyzed jointly. Directly adjacent to New York City and home to both urban commuters and giant defense plants, Nassau County presents a convenient test case. Created as a small, rural jurisdiction in 1898, Nassau in the next six decades mushroomed into one of the nation's most populous suburbs. Simultaneously, the county earned a reputation as the archetypical bedroom community, a unidimensional landscape of tract homes and rushing commuters. The most detailed history of the region to date is aptly titled Nassau: Suburbia U.S.A.

Until 1940 this facile characterization seemed completely accurate as hosts of city dwellers relocated to Nassau's open spaces while pursuing careers in the nearby metropolis. The region's suburban, middle-class nature expressed itself most clearly in an anti-industrial, anti-blue-collar bias that persisted for decades. Neither county nor village officials evinced much interest in industrial development, and barely 1 percent of the population worked in local shops and plants. Residents and politicians fully expected their area to remain a green preserve for the mobile middle class.

Yet, surprisingly, by 1960 the stereotype was no longer valid, as the proportion of commuting workers declined dramatically and factory employment skyrocketed. The growth since 1940 of an indigenous military aviation industry provides the key to this shift. After halting efforts dating back to 1909, the period of the 1930s, World War II, and Korea witnessed the rapid development and maturation of a major manufacturing sector, which further evolved in the 1950s into the modern aerospace field.

Military industrialization inevitably altered the urban-suburban relationship and fueled the great 1950s population boom. From near total subservience to New York City, the growth of nationally oriented aerospace firms created a far more autonomous economic base. Militarization of the local economy also altered the priorities of local officials, who finally accepted industry as an ally in the quest for the good life, not an alien to be barred from residence. Without conscious direction, the "Sunrise Homeland" of the dashing commuter was transformed into the home of the Hellcat, the Thunderbolt, and the Lunar Module.

NASSAU BEFORE THE WRIGHT BROTHERS

Nassau County at the dawn of the aviation age covered 275 square miles of rolling hills, broad level plains, tidal marshes, and barrier beaches stretching from Long Island Sound to the Atlantic Ocean, from the New York City line to Suffolk County's western border. Separated politically from Queens County only in 1898, its 1900 population barely exceeded 55,000, a modest increase of 9,500 over the previous decade and 18,000 above the 1880 level. Cropland accounted for 50 percent of the terrain, and nearly 1,700 individual farms furnished the economic base for this essentially rural region. Indeed, urban-rural strains helped precipitate the 1898 split when future Nassau residents refused to join the New York City consolidation.

Sparse settlement patterns were reflected in the limited size of towns and villages dotting the landscape. Hempstead, Nassau's retail and transportation hub, counted only 3,600 residents, while Freeport, a nearby fishing village, supported 2,600 inhabitants, the county's second largest concentration. Remaining population clustered along the south shore in Valley Stream, Lynbrook, Lawrence, Woodmere, and Hewlett. At the very center of the county lay the broad, treeless Hempstead Plains. Though supporting grazing activity since earliest colonial times, most cattle were gone by 1900, replaced with potato and vegetable farms. The small agricultural villages of Farmingdale, Bethpage, Hicksville, and Westbury circled the plains. Where ocean and sound lapped Long Island's shores, baymen fished and clammed, went lobstering, and tongued for oysters.

Although north shore communities Glen Cove and Port Washington exported sand, brick, and starch, manufacturing was sharply limited. The 1900 census listed only 321 industrial establishments with 1,650 workers—small shops generally—supporting local agriculture, carriage and harness makers, coopers, packing houses, and lumber yards. Thus Nassau in 1900 apparently stood apart from its giant urban neighbor, declining participation in political consolidation, supported by agriculture and fishing to the nearly complete exclusion of manufactures.

Yet Nassau was no idyllic garden isolated from the nearby city. Rather, it was overwhelmingly enmeshed in an urban web of trade and travel. The era of the self-sufficient homestead had passed a century and a half before, and Nassau growers depended entirely on the New York market. Dairymen shipped daily in refrigerated rail cars, while vegetable growers utilized special trains carrying produce, wagon, farmer, and all. Baymen and deep-sea fishermen sped their catch to Manhattan's Fulton Market.[1]

Vacationing city folk provided a second important link to the burgeoning metropolis. With scenic ports and beaches, Nassau offered several popular resort attractions. Railroads and steamboats brought thousands of excursioners to north shore villages like Sea Cliff and Oyster Bay or to the great oceanfront hotels at Long Beach and the Rockaways. On a single day in July 1899 the Long Island Railroad carried 1,500 visitors to Freeport. Hundreds of vacation cottages rimmed bays and coves, while other urbanites traveled eastward to picnic on the Hempstead Plains and pick the wild violets that grew there in profusion. Nassau's wide-open spaces also accommodated early automobile competitions, including the world-famous Vanderbilt Cup races.

Many visitors so enjoyed the area that they adopted Nassau as a second home. Wealthy New Yorkers first erected expensive country residences after the Civil War, and by 1900 the northern third of the county was parceled out among urban aristocrats. Vanderbilts, Guggenheims, Phippses, Whitneys, Morgans, and Kahns all created great estates, and their presence shortly earned the name Gold Coast for the entire section, offering a backdrop for F. Scott Fitzgerald's novels.[2]

A few city-bound commuters already resided in Nassau at the turn of the century. During the preceding 20 years (1880-1900) the Long Island Railroad tirelessly promoted the concept of commutation, of working in the city and living in the country. The Nassau County Review in May 1900 noted that the county could accommodate thousands of homes if transportation could be assured.[3] That same year new management of the Long Island Railroad committed itself to develop beach resorts and to provide express trains that would allow commuters to live on Long Island throughout the year.

Daily travel for thousands was not an impractical goal, for by 1898 the local rail system was virtually complete, and in 1900 the Pennsylvania Railroad announced plans to construct a tunnel under the East River (separating Manhattan from Long Island) and a huge terminal on Seventh Avenue. Such projects promised elimination of time-consuming ferry trips from Brooklyn, opening the way for large-scale commutation. Within just a few years the number of daily trains on Nassau's south shore routes increased from 12 to 19 and along the central main line, from 15 to 25.

Even in 1900, then, overwhelmingly rural Nassau was totally dependent on the city economy, and the path to the future appeared clear: growth as a giant bedroom suburb and playground for urban visitors, overlaid on a strongly rural base. With no native industry and limited natural resources, there seemed little to deflect these trends. In fact, economic and social developments in the next 30 years only strengthened such habits.

The commuter's dramatic rise was undoubtedly the most important of these developments. Pennsylvania Station in Manhattan opened in 1910, greatly facilitating uninterrupted travel from anywhere in Nassau County. Another terminal was constructed in Brooklyn, and by 1918 the tracks were electrified as far east as Hempstead. New commuter villages and expanding old ones clustered along the line, sustained by the rushing morning and evening trains. Close-in Great Neck and Port Washington attracted much of the resulting influx. City investors, realtors, and former New York Mayor W. R. Gracie initiated intensive development there; and one Port Washington resident soon noted, "Our population is largely made up of New York businessmen." As late as 1906 the Nassau Boulevard sector near the county's center remained a mile square tract of open fields. A real estate development corporation then stepped in and built streets, parks, and homes, all converging on a new, central commuter railroad station. Two decades later builder William R. Gibson constructed 725 homes in Valley Stream and the need for a station quickly surfaced. For a time the Long Island Railroad proved uncooperative; so in 1929 Gibson constructed one himself at a cost of $55,000 and donated it to the line.

A few statistics hint at the dramatic growth of Nassau's railroad commuter contingent, one that exceeded 30,000 by 1930, as shown in the accompanying table. George LeBoutillier, a senior vice-president of the line, proudly noted in 1925 that good railroad service over a generation was responsible for the remarkable growth of Long Island.

LIRR Station	Number of Commuters		
	1911	1923	1930
Great Neck	132	626	1,306
Port Washington	128	857	1,075
Freeport	425	2,211	n.a.
Rockville Center	589	1,759	3,000+
Floral Park	—	—	2,582

What the railroad could not accomplish in establishing Nassau as a commuter haven, an expanded auto network would. First came increased access to Manhattan via three new East River bridges completed soon after 1900: the Williamsburg (1903), the Manhattan (1909), and the Queensboro (1909). Further east on Long Island, Sunrise Highway, constructed in the 1920s over New York City's old waterline right of way, played a crucial role in opening up southern Nassau communities and furthering the real estate/commuter boom. Work also commenced on Northern and Southern state parkways, designed to speed urban residents to newly developed parks and beaches on Long Island and Nassau commuters to their jobs in Queens, Brooklyn, and Manhattan. A fantastic boom in auto traffic resulted. Nassau registered only 8,766 cars in 1916, then 40,000 in 1922, and over 112,000 by 1930. Significantly, few of the highway improvements designed to speed commuters to the city serviced trucks and commercial vehicles, reflecting both planner Robert Moses's and local residents' opposition to industry and the blue-collar workers who went with it.

Spurred by these real estate and transportation developments, Nassau's population surged from 125,000 in 1920 to over 300,000 in 1930, the greatest percentage increase of any decade in county history. More than 5,000 houses were built in 1923 alone. At the same time, dozens of incorporated villages were chartered, each with restrictive zoning covenants designed to exclude industry and lower-middle-class residents while controlling the pace and tone of development. Interestingly, rapid population growth caused a drastic decline in the percentage of locally employed workers. Creation of large estates and housing tracts by 1930 reduced farm acreage by two thirds, and agricultural employment, long an economic mainstay, fell to 4,000. Alternatively, rapid increases in residential population spurred the retail, home construction, and real estate trades. But Nassau manufacturing stagnated, employing barely 4,000 workers, fewer than the number of real estate agents, and all local employment opportunities combined accommodated but 25 percent of the labor force. Instead, most newcomers continued working in the city. Where farmers and baymen defined the Nassau experience in 1900, the rushing commuters and their supporting cast now held sway.[4]

The county was well on its way to becoming the archetypical "bedroom" community. America's Great Depression slowed, but did not deflect, these trends, and had World War II not intervened a decade later, housing construction might have engulfed all potential industrial sites. But the war did arrive with an unforgettable explosion in December 1941, and with it came the fantastic growth of indigenous, defense-related industry, decisively changing the course of Nassau's development.

THE BIRDMEN COME TO NASSAU

Just as Long Island's emerging commuter economy depended on the neighboring city to sustain it, so, too, the rise of Nassau aviation was first nurtured and supported by the nearby metropolis's industrial strength, financial resources, and public enthusiasm. Only later would these bonds dissolve as Nassau's military aircraft manufacturers shed their reliance on the city that spawned them. In so doing, they cut the county's overwhelming ties to the urban economy, providing a base for more autonomous growth linked instead to events occurring in Washington and overseas.

Aviation first reached New York City through the efforts of the infant New York Aeronautical Society, founded in 1908 and soon renamed the Aero Club of America. Led by energetic Charles Willard, these aviation enthusiasts contracted with Buffalo inventor Glenn Curtiss to purchase a pusher biplane. In June 1909 Curtiss and his rickety machine arrived at Morris Park Racetrack in the Bronx (New York City). Dissatisfied with the terrain, he searched for a more favorable location, soon selecting the broad Hempstead Plains of Nassau County. There in the summer of 1909 he initiated a series of exhibition flights and flying lessons. This decision proved just the start, and the following year witnessed the great international Air Meet at Belmont Park on the Nassau/Queens border. The first big affair of its kind held in the United States, it attracted 25 French, British, and American fliers who competed for $75,000 in prizes. The meet proved a great social event, too; and financier Thomas Ryan, socialite Eleanor Sears, and Lieutenant Governor Woodhull all attended. Huge crowds from Brooklyn, Queens, and Manhattan gathered, and special trains were pressed into service to transport the mass of urban spectators. Later that summer several additional exhibition flights were conducted at Sheepshead Bay Racetrack in Brooklyn. The following January (1911) the Aero Club, now counting over 500 members, held an aviation show in New York City. Soon

thereafter the city-based club established an aerodrome in Nassau
on the edge of the plains, with a 1,000-acre field, a grandstand, and
25 hangars. Though still a novelty, flying rapidly gained notoriety,
and city newspapers enthusiastically printed articles recounting the
adventures of the intrepid birdmen.[5]

A combination of Nassau topography and New York City money
and enthusiasm seemed to bode well for the infant aviation "industry."
Hempstead Plains offered a safe, spacious field, broad enough to
accommodate the largest air fleets. Close to the metropolis, several
roads and rail lines provided rapid access. The city, in turn,
offered all the fledgling industry might need: financial backing, spectators, machine shops, engine manufacturers, skilled workers, and
publicity organs. By 1916 Nassau was the undisputed leader of East
Coast aviation, and hardy urban spectators often ventured into the
county to view pioneer birdmen and perhaps take a lesson or two.

But for all its excitement and allure, aviation in 1916 remained
dangerous and impractical, a pastime for ardent sportsmen and
eccentric inventors. No viable commercial or military market for
airplanes yet existed, and builders in their one- and two-man shops
usually faced discouragement procuring investment capital and sales
orders. Only Glenn Curtiss's plant in far-off Buffalo qualified as a
bona fide factory. Thus early aviation lent color but exerted no
appreciable impact on Nassau's economy or development.

World War I changed all that, transforming aviation into a
practical and deadly science, forever shedding the cloak of amateur-
ism. Large government orders and modern warfare's technological
stimulus compressed decades of experimentation into just a few
years. War also changed, dramatically and permanently, Nassau's
relationship with the emerging industry. Massive production and
training quickly replaced haphazard individual efforts.

Inaugurating large-scale aerial conflict, the "War to End All
Wars" provided a tremendous stimulus to industry. The United States
went to war with fewer than 200 semiobsolete planes on hand or
order. Yet Washington planners promised to equip 400 deadly squadrons for duty on the Western Front. Most domestic manufacturers
realized such enormous requirements could only be met with heavy
government support and firm assurance of large orders justifying
plant investment and expansion. Congress provided the necessary
ingredient in July 1917 by appropriating $640 million for aviation
procurement.[6]

Drawing on New York City's vast manufacturing strength and
variety, a major war industry soon developed. One important builder
was the LWF Corporation, originally founded in 1915 by Edwin Lowe,
Robert Fowler, and pioneer birdman Charles Willard. Reorganized
a year later, control then passed to Joseph Olser, president of the

Fifth Avenue Bond and Mortgage Company, and Albert Flint, a prominent New York railroad executive. They soon moved the company to larger quarters in Queens, a new 250,000-square-foot factory, the first in the country constructed specifically for airplane manufacturing.

Another contractor born during the war years was Chance Vought Corporation, formed by Birdseye Lewis and Chance Vought, who opened a factory and office in Queens. In nearby Nassau, adjacent to the military flying fields, Buffalo's Glenn Curtiss built a large factory specializing in military-related research. The NC flying boats that crossed the Atlantic in 1919 were designed and fabricated there. Many smaller firms also flourished during the war years. General Vehicle Corporation of Queens quickly switched over to aircraft engine production. The Heinreich Brothers Airplane Company of Nassau was organized specifically to supply the army, as were the Huntington Aircraft Company of New York, United Eastern Airplane of Brooklyn, and the Breese factory in Nassau. A local cottage industry seemed to blossom overnight into an important manufacturing sector, recruiting and training thousands of workers.

With its favorable terrain and proximity to New York, Nassau also played a major role in military training efforts. Drawn by open spaces, rapid transportation, and ready access to urban embarkation facilities, the army drilled thousands of Doughboys there, including the famous Forty-second Rainbow Division. On the old aviation exhibition grounds and surrounding farmland, the Signal Corps established the largest flying complex in the eastern United States at what were later named Roosevelt and Mitchell fields.

Hundreds of fliers trained at the Nassau fields. The Air Service also constructed the Aviation Concentration Center nearby where crews and equipment from all across the nation gathered while awaiting shipment overseas. As part of this total aviation effort, the army undertook an extensive building and improvement program, filling and leveling fields and erecting hangars and workshops. Finally, a large Naval Air Station was developed at Rockaway to guard the maritime approaches to New York City. When the war ended, many of the facilities remained, forming the basis for later civilian and military efforts. Roosevelt Field quickly became the premier airport in the metropolitan region, while Mitchell Field was designated the Air Service's primary East Coast base.[7]

Thus within a span of less than two years, Nassau was temporarily thrust to the forefront of military aviation, and the entire region witnessed an explosive increase in productive capacity. For the first time a major industry seemed ready to settle into the Nassau economy, independent of local demand and tied instead to events in Washington and overseas. The overwhelmingly military nature of the program was clear and destined to have far-reaching effects. Aviation previously had been a civilian endeavor, serving a fickle public. Henceforth, the army and navy would dominate the market.

AFTER THE WAR TO END ALL WARS

Despite apparent progress and glittering growth prospects, the end of World War I triggered the near complete collapse of U.S. military aviation. Government contracts valued at $700 million evaporated overnight. Surplus aircraft flooded the market, depressing prices and demand for new production and nearly bankrupting civil air manufacturers. In 1918 the military purchased 13,991 planes. Orders tumbled to 682 in 1919, and by late 1920 over 90 percent of the airframe industry had disappeared. General disorganization prevailed for several years thereafter. Curtiss Company, largest of them all, concluded an expensive agreement with Washington to repurchase airframes and engines in an effort to stabilize the market. They were unsuccessful. With military inventories bloated by wartime purchases, the army faced instead the distasteful task of trimming flying to the bone.

The civilian market offered little relief from the grim sales picture. Wartime designs proved unsuitable for general use, and there remained substantial skepticism that aviation was viable in a peacetime economy. The chief of the Army Air Service gloomily observed in the early 1920s that without government aid, the aircraft industry could not survive on commercial orders. Attempting to provide such aid, aviation visionary General Billy Mitchell lobbied hard for research and design contracts and sponsored trophy racing and several record-breaking flights, including the 1923 Dawn-to-Dusk transcontinental attempt and the 1924 Army Around-the-World expedition. Among surviving Nassau-based firms, the Curtiss factory depended almost exclusively on military contracts.[8]

Unfortunately, sharply limited military support and infrequent civilian orders proved insufficient to ward off economic disaster, and local manufacturers' fortunes mirrored the national chaos. LWF of Queens folded in 1923. The Breese Company of Nassau, which produced several hundred primary trainers from 1917 to 1922 and which persisted in spite of the downturn, eventually closed also, including Cox-Klemin of Queens and Continental Aircraft of Nassau. It seemed inevitable that a promising new industry was about to disappear entirely.

But such was not the case, for a tenuous foothold had been established. Curtiss's wartime plant near Roosevelt Field conducted extensive research and testing and manufactured the record-breaking Pulitzer racers of the early 1920s. Billy Mitchell and Jimmy Doolittle often visited there. After a period of postwar consolidation, nearby Mitchell Field became the army's primary East Coast base owing, in large measure, to its proximity to New York City. The Air Service twice (1920 and 1925) hosted the National Air Races.[9]

City papers, especially the New York Times, enthusiastically reported aviation developments in the region, and one of the most spectacular was the 1919 arrival at Roosevelt Field of the British R-34 dirigible. That same year a U.S. navy crew piloted a Nassau-built flying boat from Rockaway, Long Island, to Plymouth, England, via the Azores and Portugal. Postwar conversion of Roosevelt Field to civilian use provided a superb base for popular operations; and a wide variety of commercial ventures soon commenced, including flight and mechanics' schools, barnstormers, air taxis, and America's first skywriting company. City crowds flocked to Nassau on sunny weekends to watch the daredevils and perhaps experience a thrilling joy ride. Wealthy New Yorkers such as band leader Roger Wolfe Kahn maintained their own planes and hangars. On a more institutional level, New York philanthropist Daniel Guggenheim established a fund to promote aviation, which, among other projects, financed the School of Aeronautics at New York University.

Charles Lindbergh's dramatic solo flight from Nassau to Paris in 1927, an improving national economy, and sustained technological progress went a long way toward finally earning public acceptance of the struggling industry. The number of registered pilots began increasing dramatically, as did passenger traffic volume. A few manufacturers even earned profits on sales of airplanes, and several new entrepreneurs entered the field, including Grover Loening with a factory in Manhattan, Igor Sikorsky in Nassau and Queens, and Sherman Fairchild in Nassau. By 1929/30 sales were booming and the New York metropolitan region was the nation's leading producer of aircraft and equipment, followed closely by southern California. Having barely survived the postwar slump, industry again seemed poised to blossom on Long Island.[10]

These hopes were cruelly shattered by the onset of the Great Depression. Once again aircraft manufacturers experienced declining demand and negative cash flows, and once again Long Island firms began closing their doors or departing for more hospitable locations. High labor costs and a desire to eliminate duplicate facilities were paramount concerns. Sikorsky's factory in Queens removed to Bridgeport, Connecticut, while Curtiss closed his large Nassau plant and consolidated operations in Buffalo. Chance Vought of Queens moved to Hartford, while Fairchild (with 600 Nassau workers in 1928) transferred airframe production to Hagerstown, Maryland.

Times were hard for civilian operators, too. Crowds stayed home, unable to afford the price of a joy ride or a half-hour lesson.

Fliers scraped by as best they could, working at odd jobs during the week, praying for good weather on the weekend. Many joked that the most dangerous aspect of Long Island flying was the risk of starving to death.[11]

Despite New York's industrial and financial advantages, the topographic attractions of nearby Nassau, and a strong aeronautic tradition stretching back two decades, the depression years found the overall impact of aviation on Nassau development still quite limited. In the early 1930s barely 4,000 workers labored in all local industries, and probably fewer than 300 worked in Nassau aviation factories. Rather, city-bound commuters and their attendant retail services dominated the economic landscape. Some further factor was required to alter the course of Nassau's development, to initiate the shift away from bedroom suburb toward a more independent industrial economy.

This as yet unforseen combination of events proved to be the worldwide rearmament of the late 1930s, followed immediately by World War II. Led by two previously unknown companies, Grumman and Republic, industry finally emerged as Nassau's economic leader, helping break the overwhelming ties to the city.

INDUSTRY FINALLY LANDS IN NASSAU

Grumman Corporation, destined to become a U.S. aerospace leader, was incorporated in December 1929 and opened for business in a rented Long Island garage the following June. Founders included Leroy Grumman, Leon (Jake) Swirbul, and William Schwendler, who had been, respectively, general manager, shop manager, and design engineer at the Loening aircraft factory in Manhattan. When Grover Loening sold the firm in 1928 to Keystone Corporation of Pennsylvania, they remained on the payroll as subordinate management but soon chafed under outside direction and opted to strike out on their own. The Loening brothers, their former employers, contributed half of the $65,000 in start-up capital.

Drawing on these same Loening connections, the new firm and its 21 employees began work by repairing Loening flying boats and building replacement parts. Despite the deepening depression, their initiative soon paid off, and in 1931 they received a small U.S. Navy contract to build two floatplane pontoons with retractable landing gear. Washington seemed very pleased with the results and awarded a follow-up order for six more pontoons at $59,000. Increased business encouraged a move out of the garage and into the reserve hangar at Curtiss Aviation Field in Valley Stream, where the team of aggressive aviation entrepreneurs quickly commenced work on an experimental navy fighter designated FF-1. Their gamble again proved successful, and the fleet air office in Washington ordered 27 of them for a total cost of $641,000. In December 1933 Grumman engineers delivered the improved F2F-1 and received still another government contract for 54 fighters worth $996,000. Specializing in carrier aircraft, Grumman's orders during the mid-1930s included advanced fighters and amphibians. By 1938 the company had moved from Curtiss Field to the abandoned Fairchild factory in Farmingdale and soon, with Wall Street backing, into their own new 150,000-square-foot building in Bethpage. Grumman then employed almost 500 workers, held a $3.5 million order backlog, and generated total annual sales of $4.5 million.

The U.S. rearmament program of the late 1930s led to even greater commercial success. President Franklin Roosevelt in January 1939 requested a special congressional appropriation of $321 million for military aviation; and the following year Grumman built 145 planes for the navy, and then 426 more in 1941, including the famous F4F Wildcat, a 330-mile-per-hour fighter destined to play a decisive role in the later Guadalcanal campaign. [12]

Grumman did not rule the local aviation industry unchallenged, however, and their chief rival proved to be Seversky Aircraft Corporation, reorganized in 1939 as Republic Aircraft. The company was a direct outgrowth of Major Alexander DeSeversky's single-minded determination to build the world's fastest, strongest military fighters. Born in Georgia, Russia, in 1894, he attended the Imperial Naval Academy, saw extensive service in World War I, and first visited the United States in 1918. He incorporated his firm in 1931 as a successor to the previously unsuccessful Seversky Aero Corporation. Receiving support from Wall Street and the Pennsylvania and Grand Central railroads, offices soon opened on Lexington Avenue in New York City. They remained there until 1936 when Seversky acquired a 250,000-square-foot plant in Farmingdale, straddling the Nassau-Suffolk border. In the interim his employees worked in rented space and lived from hand to mouth. These were lean years, and Seversky's troubles reflected the generally difficult experiences of the entire industry. Stock issues and private investment capital drawn from New York City's financial establishment, not sales, kept the struggling corporation afloat. Seversky pushed ahead, however, convinced that his vision of air power was nearing reality. His early designs were not commercial successes, but in the hands of aviatrix Jacki Cochran, they competed all across the country and set several speed records.

Commercial progress was first achieved in 1935 when Seversky secured an army contract for 35 training planes. With the order in hand he moved his company into its own industrial space, and the following year the firm captured a further military order for 77 pursuit planes worth over $1.7 million. Despite a severe shortage of working capital, employment soon shot up to the 600 to 750 range, temporarily making Seversky the county's largest industrial employer. Unfortunately, these two army contracts were insufficient to support the enlarged work force and physical plant, and between 1931 and 1939 Seversky sold only 140 airplanes. The generosity and forbearance of investors and creditors finally evaporated and a corporate reorganization followed. The work force contracted to only 150, and Seversky himself was exiled into early retirement.

The approaching winds of war soon revived the beleaguered company's fortunes, however, fulfilling the major's aviation dream. Rapid rearmament in Europe and the United States quickly generated a flood of new business. Sweden ordered several dozen fighters and attack planes, and Republic's overall backlog topped $10 million. The company was also informed in July 1940 that as part of the National Emergency Defense Program it would be expected to produce 827 military aircraft by March 1942. Work on the P-43 Lancer and the soon-to-be legendary P-47 Thunderbolt then rushed ahead. An initial contract for $58 million worth of Thunderbolts was awarded, and in late 1940 Republic's work force mushroomed to 1,500 in two shifts. A $9 million plant expansion began, as did programs to train 8,000 additional workers. [13]

Increasing violence in Europe and the Far East and the United States's own rearmament program thus forced the almost overnight maturation of Nassau's military aircraft industry. The outbreak of war in December 1941 dwarfed even these efforts. Grumman hurried a crash plant construction program and opened a navy-financed $33 million factory. By war's end, available work space had jumped from 150,000 square feet in 1938 to over 2.7 million square feet. In the first four months of 1942 they delivered 334 F4F Wildcats, which soon posted a five-to-one kill ratio versus the Japanese Zero. In August 1942 Grumman initiated production of the 400-mile-per-hour F6F Hellcat, ultimately a Pacific legend. During the first five months of 1944, Hellcat pilots destroyed 770 enemy craft while losing only 70 of their own, and at the "Marianas Turkey Shoot" of June 19, 1944, they downed 353 Japanese aircraft with the loss of only 21 U.S. planes.

An aerial armada of Grumman Wildcats, Hellcats, Bearcats, and Avengers poured forth from Nassau factories as an army of men and women labored in the main plant and subleased space across the county. Total employment reached 6,650 in January 1943, jumped to 19,550 the following year, and peaked at 25,100 in early 1945. Special trains rumbled over the Long Island Railroad tracks, delivering workers from Nassau, Brooklyn, and Queens. Grumman executives also created day-care centers for the hundreds of young mothers flocking to the shop floor. In 45 months of wartime service, this work force built 17,000 airplanes. So efficient did Grumman become that in late 1944 they informed the navy that production would soon top 700 machines per month. Overwhelmed by such numbers, the Pentagon insisted on a 500-per-month schedule. Nevertheless, in March 1945 Grumman built 605 airplanes.[14]

Over at Republic wartime demands also elicited production miracles. The prototype P-47 first flew in 1941 and with its 18-cylinder supercharged engine delivered speeds of 450 miles per hour. Heavily armed and armored Thunderbolts soon blanketed Europe, escorting U.S. bombers and attacking enemy tank and ground formations, earning an overall five-to-one kill ratio. As early as September 1941, Republic employment stood at 3,500, with 100 to 200 new workers added each week. In the next four years, 23,000 Republic employees built 16,000 planes. Government Facilities Agreement loans financed nearly 2 million additional feet of production space.[15]

Grumman and Republic were by no means the only important wartime plants operating in Nassau County. An entire aviation-engine-instrument-equipment industry grew up with them. The most important allied firm was the giant Sperry complex in suburban Great Neck-Lake Success. Searching for additional space to expand operations, the Sperry Gyroscope and Instrument Company of Brooklyn moved to Nassau in 1942, eventually assembling a work force of over 32,000. Nearby Fairchild Camera employed 4,400. All around the county hundreds of subcontractors labored also, and every garage and factory seemed to resound with the chatter of riveting hammers and metal-forming machines. In all, approximately 100,000 workers joined the aviation production effort, and a huge, skilled labor force was trained and many millions of square feet of industrial space was built. For the first time, local industry developed a significant, even dominant, presence in the Nassau economy; and unlike previous flirtations, when this war ended the manufacturing sector did not recede into the background. Despite a temporary postwar dip, newly established patterns persisted and expanded, energizing Nassau's renewed growth, changing forever Long Island's economic character from suburban and agricultural to suburban and industrial. And this time county leaders took notice, admitting that industry did indeed play a vital and desired role in local affairs.

INTO THE POSTWAR ERA

Just as the end of World War I sharply impacted Nassau's infant aviation industry, so too the effects of VE and VJ days were immediate and striking. In less than two weeks in September 1945

Washington canceled contracts for 31,000 aircraft, and 450,000 workers quickly lost their jobs. Grumman watched its $380 million backlog shrink by 80 percent. The company then laid off all its 25,000 employees and hired back a permanent force of only 3,500. Similarly hard hit, by November 1945 Republic employed only 3,700 of its wartime peak of 23,000 workers.

With huge surpluses of military equipment destined to suppress sales, but with tempting prospects for commercial and recreational flight in the offing, Nassau companies began diversifying away from war production by targeting the emerging civilian economy. Grumman developed the Widgeon amphibian plane and the somewhat larger Mallard flying boat. Neither proved very successful, however, and combined sales by June 1948 barely reached 95 craft. Grumman also attempted to apply its metal-working expertise to the production of truck bodies, canoes, and rowboats. Though each venture proved profitable, sales of such nonaviation items comprised only 5 percent of total business volume.

Republic tried to supplement military orders, too, first with its huge RC2 Rainbow transatlantic carrier. With sales of only 20 aircraft, it proved an economic disaster. They then attempted to tap the low-price end of the civilian market with the RC3 Seabee; but production expenses rose dramatically, the expected market failed to materialize, and the whole project was written off with a $6.5 million loss.

Despite disappointments engendered by diversification attempts, Nassau's aviation industry did not repeat the dismal post-World War I experience. Rather, Grumman and Republic returned to their original production lines, military aircraft, and quickly scored a series of successes, especially in the new field of jet planes, which alleviated most postwar gloom.[16]

Jet fighters first appeared in the closing days of World War II. While they failed to affect the war's outcome, the future was clear to all military planners. The sky would soon belong to the jets. Though surplus stockpiles in the United States and the absence of a sharp external threat slowed equipment changeovers, development proceeded steadily. In 1946 Republic Aviation became one of the first U.S. corporations to introduce a successful jet fighter, the XP 84. At 611 miles per hour, the Thunderjet proved the fastest craft in the Air Corps inventory. Duly impressed, the Pentagon ordered 500 new fighters in a contract valued at $55 million, and the plane was in full production by 1947, markedly increasing demand for Nassau workers. That same year Grumman introduced its first jet, the F9F Panther, and the prop-driven AF2 Guardian antisubmarine plane. The navy soon placed large orders for both.[17]

The temporary postwar slump in military production ended completely in 1948 with passage of the Supplemental National Defense Appropriation Act. Based upon recommendations of the President's Temporary Air Policy Board, this legislation quickly tripled the rate of military procurement. The Department of Defense, which had previously purchased over 600 Republic F-84s, awarded contracts for 409 more, while Grumman received orders for 378 new jet and propeller aircraft.

When the Korean War erupted only two summers later, further rapid aviation expansion ensued, providing the driving force in the growing Nassau economy. Republic's F-84 proved a mainstay of the air war, and total local employment expanded to almost 30,000 by 1954, surpassing even the World War II peak. The firm's order backlog climbed to nearly $1 billion, while subcontracting to nearby companies included 2,200 local shops. Before production of the F-84 ended in the mid-1950s, over 4,000 were delivered.[18]

Grumman enjoyed a similar upsurge in orders. The Bethpage-based firm first tried to minimize the volatile personnel expansion and contraction that accompanied wartime production efforts by subcontracting as much work as possible to other Long Island companies. Nevertheless, employment doubled during the war years and navy orders generated a $900 million backlog. The government also agreed to build a $33 million test field and assembly plant in eastern Suffolk County, which added still another 600,000 square feet of production space. Grumman's late Korean War entry, the swept-wing Cougar, proved highly successful and outfought its Soviet-built MIG opponents 15-0, further enhancing the corporation's reputation with military planners.[19]

By 1953/54, Nassau's two airframe manufacturers held order backlogs approaching $2 billion, operated over 5 million square feet of industrial space, and employed 40,000 workers. Over at the Sperry complex in Great Neck-Lake Success, 18,000 employees manufactured a wide range of navigational gear and ordnance. Thousands of other workers labored for smaller contractors and subcontractors and provided the catalyst for the fantastic growth that characterized Nassau's history during the 1950-60 decade. Indeed, by 1955 five large industrial firms dominated the entire local economy: Republic, Grumman, Sperry, Arma, and Fairchild, a dramatic switch from the mid-1930s when manufacturing was almost non-existent.[20]

Nassau's fantastic growth is revealed in census reports. During the 1950-60 decade, population spurted upward from 660,000 to 1.3 million, with the most rapid increases occurring during the Korean War, when local defense plants were hiring hundreds weekly. In both 1950 and 1951, over 95,000 residents settled in Hempstead Township alone, while Oyster Bay received 30,000 annually from 1953 to 1956. Undoubtedly, much of this growth was due to proximity to New York City and the desire of urban dwellers for new residential space. But growth was also a direct response to the expanding labor market created by the defense plants, among the very largest employers in the entire metropolitan area. Several observers and analysts commented on the intimate relationship between defense jobs and Nassau growth. Looking back over recent history, Newsday observed in 1965, "When Long Island's economy was in its prime in the 1940s and 1950s, the base of the boom was high-paying employment at five giant defense contractors."

Clearly the arrival of the aerospace industry was a predominant factor in causing Nassau to become a region of heavily settled urban and suburban areas, supporting a diversified industrial complex. And the economic impact was not limited to the major employers. Military production inevitably fostered much subcontracting, creating a host of satellite industries and job opportunities. Smaller firms in turn subcontracted to a tertiary net of local companies. As several industry analysts have commented, modern scientific, military, and space activities cut across more technical and production fields than any other human endeavor. This statement is certainly true of Nassau's defense contractors as they made the post-Korean War transition from airframe and instrument manufacturers to aerospace innovators.[21]

Throughout the late 1950s and 1960s Grumman continued developing successful military aircraft, including the A-6 Intruder, the E2C Hawkeye, and the F-14 Tomcat. They also initiated a second, and ultimately successful, attempt to diversify their product line, introducing the Gulfstream series of corporate aircraft. Finally, they earned a place as a major National Aeronautics and Space Administration (NASA) contractor, winning a central role in the emerging space industry. Every astronaut who went to the moon traveled aboard a Grumman craft. By 1960 Grumman was the largest employer on Long Island.

Nearby Republic also moved ahead into the aerospace age, replacing its F-84 Thunderjet series with the F-105 Thunderchief and turning to research missiles, target drones, and solar labs. Other employers, like Arma and Fairchild, built advanced jet engines, missile components, and satellite ground stations. Hazeltine shifted from defense contractor to computer innovator. Sperry became a world leader in electronics, radar, guidance systems, and computers, operating 12 separate divisions in Nassau.[22]

THE DEFENSE INDUSTRY AND NASSAU DEVELOPMENT

The impact of the total defense/aerospace industry on local economic and growth patterns was enormous, and the effect of even a single large plant proved immense. According to a study completed in 1958, Republic employed workers drawn from 216 communities and pumped over $1 million in wages into more than a dozen of them. They subcontracted that year with 588 local firms, while 640 other nearby companies received Republic business for everything from office supplies to building maintenance. Over 40,000 Nassau jobs were directly or indirectly dependent on Republic's payroll. A few years later Grumman announced that it subcontracted to over 1,100 Long Island firms.

Several studies of Nassau's economy during this period indicate that 75,000 local defense workers generated an additional 100,000 to 125,000 jobs in related industrial and civilian sectors, especially in the wholesale, retail, and construction trades. Such employment in turn supported 600,000 of Nassau's total 1960 population of 1.3 million, a far cry from the 1920s when just 1 percent of the local population was employed in manufacturing and almost none in military-related industry. [23]

How different Nassau's experience was from other areas of the metropolitan region and how central a role military production played is illustrated by the degree of local dependence on Defense Department orders. In New York City in the late 1950s only 3.5 percent of industrial production was defense related. In neighboring Westchester County the proportion was 4.1 percent, and it was 7.4 percent for the entire state. In Nassau the corresponding figure consistently exceeded 50 percent. Significantly, Westchester County, similarly situated to New York City and of approximately equal size, lagged far behind Nassau in population growth during the 1950s. [24]

Also important is the fact that many of Nassau's nonmilitary workers would never have been employed but for the original military presence. Companies were often attracted to Nassau by the availability of factory space created to house defense production during the 1941–45 and 1950–54 eras as well as the large, skilled labor pool trained during those peak years. Finally, many small companies that began as defense subcontractors realized their vulnerability to the military budget process and diversified into other fields. In 1959 military contracts accounted for 85 percent of all business at Syosett's Fairchild Instrument and Camera. The firm then made active efforts to produce computer components, tape recorders, and home sound movie cameras; and by 1965 military orders provided only 35 percent of total revenues. [25]

All these developments markedly reduced Nassau's dependence on the New York City employment market and stimulated a more autonomous county economy based instead on Washington-generated defense orders. Throughout the 1920s and 1930s as much as 75 percent of Nassau's labor force worked in New York, while those who remained behind filled a host of service industries, especially retail and wholesale trades, real estate, and housing construction. The post-World War II population surge seemed certain to strengthen this pattern. But the wartime success of the aircraft and instrument industry had already set in motion an economic sea change. Development of local industry and the attendant further growth of service occupations created thousands upon thousands of Nassau-based job opportunities. The percentage of commuters began dropping sharply, by 1960 encompassing perhaps 40 percent of the work force. By 1970, despite further population growth, the number of commuters declined by 10,000. Local employment, by contrast, jumped 140,000.

This vast change in economic orientation from commuter to local, from white collar to industry, broke the pattern of suburban homogeneity and led to changes in government and politics. After decades of ignoring industry and scorning industrial workers in favor of homeowner amenities, local officials finally accepted the importance and permanence of manufacturing. Concerned about post-Korean War layoffs, then Governor Averill Harriman asked the Department of Defense to channel more contracts to Long Island, while the state commerce commissioner urged Washington to support local guided missile work. The commissioner, industrial leaders, and the machinists' union also met to develop a master plan for manufacturing development. County Executive Holly Patterson vowed to take up any slack caused by a falloff in orders and began an industrial site research program, which eventually led to construction of several industrial parks specializing in diversified, nondefense, precision manufactures. The 1950s also witnessed, at long last, construction of a modern highway to accommodate truck and other commercial traffic, the (in)famous Long Island Expressway.

Recognizing the importance of military production to his constituents, Nassau Congressman John Wydler in the late 1950s and 1960s took an active role in aerospace deliberations. When Douglas Aircraft in California tried to recruit Long Island workers to the West Coast, Wydler maneuvered in Congress to have Douglas subcontract work to Long Island firms instead. The indifference and hostility that local officials first evidenced toward industrial growth gave way in the 1940s and 1950s to active lobbying in Washington and Albany for aid and contracts.

The local political landscape also reflected economic and demographic changes occurring within the county. Throughout most of

Nassau's modern history its population consisted of Protestant descendants of the original colonial families, augmented in the early 1900s by middle-class commuters relocating from New York City. The Republican party, dominant since the Civil War, identified itself closely with these long-time constituents and the new commuter throng. Local political leadership was exercised by men such as Assemblyman George Wallace, Clerk Thomas Patterson, Senator John Childs, Judge Robert Seabury, and Supervisors Smith Cox, William Jones, and Augustus Denton.

The growth of industry after 1939 attracted a rather different group of residents, often of ethnic Italian, Irish, and Jewish stock. In time, representatives of these new communities rose to prominence, and by the late 1950s they had replaced much of the old-line leadership. Men like Joseph Carlino, Edward Speno, Ralph Caso, Sol Wachtler, and Joseph Margiotta drew much of their support from ethnic and blue-collar constituencies. In so doing they created one of America's few Republican, ethnic machines.[26]

REPRISE: MILITARY AVIATION AND NASSAU DEVELOPMENT

The Nassau County of 1900 had subsisted for generations as an agricultural region supplying New York City with fruit, vegetables, and dairy products and well into the new century remained an amalgam of small farms, large estates, and rapidly growing commuter villages. Local transportation, whether railroad or automobile, funneled goods and individuals into the city and then back home again.

Despite rapid population growth between 1900 and 1940, prewar Nassau remained overwhelmingly rural or suburban, home to thousands of rushing commuters and their support services. Manufacturing, never a part of Nassau's development process, remained decidedly anemic, and the two largest firms in early 1939, Grumman and Republic, employed just 1,200 workers between them. It appeared highly unlikely that Nassau would ever become an industrial region. Public sentiment was largely antimanufacturing, while local officials often proved indifferent. Not until the mid-1950s was a modern highway built to accommodate truck and commercial traffic. Rather, the entire county seemed destined to evolve into a classic bedroom suburb. Even intensive suburban development was opposed by many, most notably through creation of numerous incorporated villages that enforced exclusionary zoning regulations.

Although home to some of aviation's most notable early exploits, local aircraft construction remained very limited until the outbreak of war in 1917. World War I and its resulting production demands then became the first important contributors to Nassau's modern industrial development. Contractors accumulated the requisite capital, plant, personnel, and technology. Their efforts were exclusively military, and the county soon hosted army and navy training establishments, manufacturing plants, and active bases. Despite a sharp postwar slump, the military legacy endured and colored all future production efforts.

Drastic government cutbacks in 1918/19 and the inability to develop a viable civilian market precipitated eight years of intense hardship within the aviation industry, only temporarily alleviated between 1926 and 1929. The depression then cut short any nascent aeronautic revival. After more than 20 years of flight and many spectacular achievements, the new industry exerted little impact on Nassau's economy and did nothing to deflect the growth of commuter suburbia.

Yet like the delicate plant growing between giant boulders, Nassau's aviation industry survived harsh conditions; and when war clouds threatened again in the late 1930s, it rapidly evolved into a formidable engine for local economic growth. Newcomers Grumman and Republic, as well as Sperry after 1942, matured into industrial giants, employing 82,000 workers at war's end. Subcontractors and smaller manufacturers added thousands of additional jobs. In the space of only five years, defense employment leapfrogged to become the growth factor in Nassau.

The close of World War II triggered a slowdown in military procurement, which the civilian economy proved unable to ameliorate. Many thousands of workers lost their jobs. But Nassau's new defense firms were now too large and their relationship with Washington too close to permit recapitulation of earlier dismal experiences. Both military and civilian defense planners realized that the U.S. industrial machine could not be allowed to deteriorate if it were again to provide timely aid in some future conflagration. Additionally, political tensions and technological developments in the postwar world led to a renewed arms buildup. The Korean War, just five years after the close of hostilities with Japan, fueled a boom that provided tens of thousands of jobs and stimulated the fastest growth rate in Nassau history. During these same war years manufacturing payrolls accounted for 40 percent of all county wages. As late as 1964/65 half of the top ten county employers were major aerospace contractors.

Two wars following so closely in succession and markedly higher cold war procurement levels finally cemented the major shift in Nassau's economy. After decades as an orphan child, industry became the mainstay of growth and prosperity, and this industry was tied directly to the military. Huge plants stood on former potato fields and trained tens of thousands of skilled workers. County leaders realized that local economic health was linked to the success of these firms and took active steps to enhance their profitability. Officials also backed measures to attract even more industry to Nassau to counter cyclical military procurement patterns. Once having accepted the integral role of manufacturing, Nassau had to encourage industry continually or face the risk of declining living standards.

With defense contractors as a base, Nassau's invigorated and altered economy matured and diversified, coming more closely to mirror patterns common in the neighboring city, drawing sustenance from the generous wages paid production workers and engineers and the high-tech nature of aerospace methods. Almost despite itself, Suburbia U.S.A. became the home of attack bombers, production lines, and giant factories. Suburbia armed was suburbia transformed.

NOTES

1. Edward J. Smits, Nassau: Suburbia U.S.A. (Garden City, N.Y.: Doubleday, 1974), pp. 1-4, 6, 13-22. See also Paul Bailey, ed., Long Island, A History of Two Great Counties, Nassau and Suffolk (New York: Lewis Historical, 1949), pp. 28-34.

2. Monica Randall, The Mansions of Long Island's Gold Coast (New York: Hastings House, 1979), pp. 11-32; Lisa Sclare and Donald Sclare, Beaux-Arts Estates (New York: Viking Press, 1975), pp. 21-35; Sea Cliff: Diamond Jubilee 1883-1958 (Rockville Center, N.Y.: Kennedy Associates, 1958); Smits, Nassau, pp. 212-16; Jackeline Overton, Long Island's Story (Port Washington, N.Y.: Ira Friedman, 1929), pp. 230-31, 263, 276, 302.

3. The Long Island Railroad was a tireless promoter of Nassau development, and its Passenger and Traffic departments printed dozens of booklets and pamphlets describing Long Island life and attractions in the years from 1876 to 1930. Among the most useful for this study were: "The New York Improvement and Tunnel Extension of the Pennsylvania Railroad" (Philadelphia, 1910); "Long Island Summer Resorts, Guide and Directory" (New York, 1878); "The Beauties of Long Island" (New York, 1895); "Suburban Long Island, The Sunrise Homeland" (New York, 1921/22); and "Long Island, America and Sunrise Land" (New York, 1933). See also Floral Park Golden Anniversary 1908-1958 (Floral Park, 1958); Village of Great Neck Golden Jubilee (Great Neck, 1972); Bailey, Long Island, pp. 421-29, 441; Smits, Nassau, pp. 151-55, 162.

4. Smits, Nassau, pp. 173-87.

5. Ward Baldwin, The Year in Flight (Providence, R.I.: Livermore and Knight, 1911), pp. 58-59; "The International Air Meet," Scientific American 103 (November 1910): 361-62; "New York Aviation

Show," Scientific American 104 (January 1911): 28; Richard Winsche, "Echoes of Belmont Park," Nassau County Historical Journal 25 (Spring 1964): 15-33; Preston Bassett, "Aviation on Long Island," in Bailey, Long Island, p. 413. See also author interviews with Preston Bassett and Clarence DeGiers.

6. Baldwin, Year in Flight, pp. 62-65, 80-93; Henry Arnold, "Building America's Aviation," Scientific American 117 (December 1917): 414; "Aircraft Manufacturers Association Report," New York Times, June 17, 1917, p. 4; Barbara Stubbe, "The Story of Roosevelt Field: Forty Years of Flight, 1911-1951," Nassau County Historical Journal 24 (Summer 1963): 1-11; Smits, Nassau, pp. 86-94; Aero, America's Aviation Weekly, June 1, 1912), p. 218.

7. "Government May Take Aircraft Factories," New York Times, June 2, 1917, p. 6; "Government Takes Factories in Queens," New York Times, December 12, 1917, p. 15; Walter H. Phipps, "The Heinreich Military Tractor Biplane," Aerial Age Weekly, March 29, 1915, pp. 54-68; "Eastern Military Tractor," Aerial Age Weekly, October 30, 1916, p. 172; "Airplanes for 1917," Aviation, February 1, 1917, pp. 38-43; Aircraft Yearbook for 1919 (New York: Aircraft Manufacturers Association, 1920), pp. 176-81. See also "News of the Week" in Aerial Age Weekly for the following editions: March 22, 1915, p. 24; May 24, 1915, p. 233; December 6, 1915, p. 168; May 17, 1916, p. 159; August 7, 1916, p. 655; October 30, 1916, p. 168.

8. William Mitchell, "America in the Air," National Geographic 39 (1921): 339-52; "Aviation in the United States," New York Times, July 21, 1921, p. 14; "How the Fastest Airplane in the World Was Built," Aerial Age Weekly, November 1922, p. 537; "Airplane Contracts," New York Times, November 21, 1918, p. 16; "Curtiss to Discontinue Making Airplanes," New York Times, June 2, 1920, p. 17; The Airplane Industry of the New York Metropolitan District (New York: Merchants Association of New York, 1928), pp. 9, 27. See also author interviews with William Wait and William Stockert, August 1982.

9. "Aircraft Trade Review," Aerial Age Weekly, March 28, 1921, p. 514; "Will Buy Back Planes Valued at $2,700,000," New York Times, April 27, 1919, p. 10; "Some Aviation Economics; What Shall We Do with the Vast Industries When the Sword Is Sheathed?" Scientific American 119 (October 1918): 313, 323, 325; Airplane Industry of the New York Metropolitan District, p. 14; Frederick T. Jane, All the World's Aircraft (London: S. Marston Low, 1920), p. 287. See also author interviews with William Wait and Fred Higginbotham, July and August 1982.

10. "New Field for Curtiss," New York Times, September 17, 1920, p. 5; "Great Growth Shown in Airplane Output," New York

Times, September 3, 1926, p. 12; "The Industry's Progress during 1928," Aviation, January 5, 1919, p. 17; William Kaiser, "The Visit of the R-34," Nassau County Historical Journal 26 (Summer 1965): 49-60; "Airplane Business Brisk," New York Times, November 24, 1927, p. 19; "Commercial Planes Gaining in Favor," New York Times, March 8, 1926, p. 31; "Curtiss Aeroplane Reports Big Gains," New York Times, March 3, 1927, p. 30; "Curtiss Aeroplane Shows Sharp Gain," New York Times, March 14, 1928, p. 35; "Flying Industry Growing Rapidly," New York Times, July 22, 1928, p. 11; "Employment and Production in Airplane Manufacturing," Monthly Labor Review 29 (August 1929): 62-63; Francis Walton, "Aircraft Plants Expanding in Eastern States," New York Herald Tribune, January 18, 1929, p. 12; Howard Mingos, Aircraft Yearbook for 1928 (New York: Lanciar, 1929), p. 75. See also author interviews with "Slim" Henicke, Louis Meier, and "Butch" Micallizzi, June and July 1982.

11. "Curtiss Moves to Buffalo," Aero Digest 16 (May 1931): 54; Francis Walton, "The Infant Industry," Aero Digest 14 (April 1929): 58-59; "The Curtiss-Wright Corporation," Aero Digest 19 (April 1934): 28; "The History of the Fairchild Aviation Company," Aero Digest 19 (January 1934): 35; Francis Walton, "Cities Now Vie for Position as Aviation Capital," New York Herald Tribune, February 2, 1929, p. 9; C. H. Biddlecome, "Lowering Manufacturing Costs by Specialized Production," Aviation, November 3, 1929, p. 1075; Sidney Bowen, "Trends of the Industry during 1930," Aviation, January 10, 1931, p. 15; Edward Jones, "Mergers and Consolidations in the Industry," Aviation, January 25, 1930, pp. 152-53. See also author interviews with William Stockert, August 1982, and Preston Bassett, November 1982.

12. Preston Bassett, "Aviation on Long Island," Long Island Forum 13 (Summer 1949): 20; Mingos, Aircraft Yearbook of 1934, p. 248; idem, Aircraft Yearbook for 1936, p. 267, and idem, Aircraft Yearbook of 1937, p. 290.

13. Minutes of the Board of Directors of the Seversky Aircraft Corporation for April 28, 1931; June 11, 1936; July 19, 1937; December 7, 1938; and December 29, 1938. See also Minutes of the Republic Aviation Corporation for May 18, 1939; July 18, 1940; November 28, 1940; and December 19, 1940. See also Cyrus Caldwell, "Personalities," Aero Digest 23 (July 1933): 28; and idem, "Personalities," Aero Digest 26 (August 1935): 17; Mingos, Aviation Yearbook for 1937, p. 319; idem, Aviation Yearbook for 1938, p. 317; Jane, All the World's Aircraft—1932, pp. 297, 334; "Factory Training in the East," Aviation, October , 1940, p. 34.

14. "Experiment at Republic," Fortune 35 (February 1947): 124; "Happy Days at Grumann," Fortune 37 (June 1948): 115, 180,

185; War Manpower Commission, Defense Employment in Central Long Island (New York: War Manpower Commission, 1943), pp. 38-41, 45-49; United States Military Aircraft Acceptances (Washington, D.C.: Civil Aeronautics Administration, 1945), pp. 35-36; Leonard Levenson, "Wartime Development of the Aircraft Industry," Monthly Labor Review 59 (November 1944): 909-11; Grumman Aircraft Engineering Corporation Annual Report for 1944, p. 8.

15. "Experiment at Republic," p. 124; Mingos, Aircraft Yearbook for 1946, p. 365; "Battle Hymn at Republic," Time, September 15, 1941, pp. 45-47.

16. "Analysis of the United States Airplane Industry," Fortune 35 (Feburary 1947): 127; "Shall We Have Airplanes?" Fortune 37 (January 1948): 77-78; "The Killer Plane," Time, December 29, 1952, p. 60; "Experiment at Republic," pp. 170-72; "Decision at Republic," Fortune 35 (February 1947): 123.

17. "The Wildest Blue Yonder Yet," Fortune 37 (March 1948): 95-97; "Elements of Airpower" (Presentation of the Aircraft Industry before the President's Air Policy Commission, September 1947), pp. 10-12; A. Clausen McLauen, Aircraft Yearbook for 1951 (Washington, D.C.: Lincoln Press, 1952), p. 288.

18. "Air Power Budget at Record High," Aviation Week, April 18, 1948, p. 12; "Congress Forcing Air Funding Boost," Aviation Week, March 29, 1948, pp. 7-8; "Orders Are Coming in for the Aircraft Industry," Aviation Week, April 1948, pp. 9-12; "Big Increases for Aviation Funds Asked by Truman in 1949 Budget," Aviation Week, January 19, 1948, p. 11; "Industry to Double Plane Output," Aviation Week, July 30, 1950, p. 11; "Republic Buildup Yields Planes," Aviation Week, April 14, 1952, p. 41. See also Annual Reports of the Republic Aviation Corporation for 1949, p. 3; 1951, pp. 61-62; and 1953, p. 113.

19. "Grumman Plant Bursting at the Seams," Aviation Week, April 14, 1952, p. 14; "Grumman Cleared for Takeoff," Fortune 42 (September 1950): 66-68; "Grumman Produces New Model Cougar," Aviation Week, May 3, 1954, pp. 17-18. See also Grumman Annual Report for 1953, p. 5.

20. "Record Post-War Spending Predicted," Aviation Week, January 19, 1953, pp. 12-14; "Republic Sales and Profits Double," Aviation Week, October 31, 1955, p. 8; Bart Neess, ed., Long Island Fact Book of Nassau and Suffolk Counties (Garden City, N.Y.: Long Island Association of Commerce and Industry, 1965), pp. 71, 117; Grumman Annual Report for 1956, p. 2; Fred Hamlin, "The Industry," in Aircraft Yearbook for 1954, pp. 106-7. See also idem, Aircraft Yearbook for 1955, pp. 108-10.

21. Newsday, May 29, 1965, p. 5; and "Long Island Looks to Light Industry," New York Times, July 1, 1949, p. 21.

22. Craig Lewis, "Grumman Biplane Probes Spray Market," Aviation Week, November 25, 1957, pp. 32-33; "Defense; The Plum Drops," Newsweek, December 3, 1962, pp. 83-84; Russell Hawkes, "The Cougar Doubles as a Flight Trainer," Aviation Week, January 28, 1956, pp. 66-67; Edward Balbon, "Grumman Transport to Roll Out in 1958," Aviation Week, July 8, 1957, pp. 25-27; "The Lunar Excursion Module," Newsweek, November 19, 1962, p. 76; "Republic Enters Astronautics Field," Aviation Week, August 4, 1959, pp. 33-34; "Republic Launches Space Program," Aviation Week, August 11, 1958, p. 45; "Long Island Looks to the Future," Newsday, February 16, 1965, p. 31; "Thank God for Grumman," Long Island Daily Commercial Review, September 20, 1965, p. 2; "Republic Seeking Diversification to Back up Phase out of F-105," Aviation Week, January 21, 1963, p. 113; "Republic Broadens Space, Missile Fields," Aviation Week, June 21, 1965, p. 21; "Grumman Buys into Hydrofoil Company," Aviation Week, August 27, 1956, p. 28; Michael Getler, "CEM Award Caps Long Grumman Drive," Missiles and Rockets 11 (December 10, 1962): 30-31; Hal Taylor, "Grumman Gets LEM Contract," Missiles and Rockets 11 (November 1962): 17; "Grumman Will Develop OAO Spacecraft," Aviation Week, October 17, 1960, pp. 28-30.

23. "Republic's Help to Long Island Is Depicted," New York Times, September 14, 1958, p. 58; "The Top 100 Nassau/Suffolk Companies," Long Island Daily Commercial Review, November 3, 1965, p. 1; "LEM Subcontracting Advanced," Aviation Week, February 4, 1963, p. 37; Grumman Annual Report for 1962, p. 7.

24. "The Tides Change," Newsday, September 10, 1965, p. 6; "The New Look of Industry," Newsday, September 10, 1965, p. 52; Alfred Wood, The Impact of Military Spending upon Manufacturing in the New York SMSA (Master's thesis, Columbia University, 1964); Franklin Letter 3 (February 1962): 1.

25. J. E. Ullman, "Conversion Prospects in the Defense Electronics Industry," in Hofstra University Yearbook of Business (Hempstead, N.Y.: N.P., 1965), pp. 60-75; "To Smooth out Peaks and Valleys, Aircraft Companies Turn to Diversification," Steel 145 (September 1959): 50-51; C. V. Murphey, "Plane Makers under Stress, Business Strategies for the 1960s," Fortune 61 (June 1960): 110-13, 134; "Will Guided Missiles Blast Aircraft Industry Plans?" Iron Age 179 (May 1957): 51-55.

26. W. L. Leonard and C. E. Storier, "Industry Looks at Long Island," in Hofstra College Bureau of Business and Commercial Research (Hempstead, N.Y.: N.P., 1956), p. 3; "Survey Finds Sperry Employees Moving to Nassau/Suffolk," New York Times, September 26, 1962, p. 117; Aspects and Analyses of the Social, Economic, and Housing Characteristics of Nassau County, New York

(Mineola, N.Y.: Nassau County Planning Commission, 1963), p. 18; New York Business Facts Book, 1965 Supplement (Albany: New York State Department of Commerce, 1965), p. 12; "A Peacetime Economy and Jobs on the Island," Long Island Daily Commercial Review, January 26, 1965, p. 10; "Defense Layoffs Reported to Hurt Long Island Plants," New York Times, October 2, 1957, p. 37; "Governor to Act in Long Island Job Crisis," New York Times, October 13, 1955, p. 26. See also New York Times: October 9, 1956, p. 37; October 10, 1957, p. 30; October 12, 1957, p. 21; February 10, 1962, p. 48; October 15, 1965, p. 47. Finally, see Smits, Nassau, pp. 39-46, 273-78.

4

The Failed Experiment: Military Aviation and Urban Development in San Antonio, 1910–40

David R. Johnson

Superficially, San Antonio was a city destined to have a long and profitable relationship with the military. The city's strategic location, first during the Texas War for Independence and then during the Mexican War, made it a natural focus for military activities. Afterward, roving bands of Indians along the Texas frontier ensured the continued need for the army's presence, and San Antonio became an important supply depot for frontier garrisons. Later in the century the city's climate and terrain combined with the army's need for good training camps to create Fort Sam Houston in 1876. Finally, the Spanish–American War once again demonstrated the efficacy of San Antonio's location for military training. Throughout its early development as a U.S. city, then, San Antonio had continuous ties to the military.

Yet these were not the sort of ties that fostered rapid urban growth. Except during emergencies such as the Spanish–American War, the army garrison was too small and the nation's commitment to things military too limited to create significant opportunities for sustained city building. San Antonio's business community recognized this. Already locked in a battle with Dallas and Houston for dominance of the state and region, local businessmen turned to the railroads, a traditional weapon among urban rivals, to secure a prosperous future. During the 1870s and 1880s San Antonians built four major rail routes into their hinterland and established the city as a service center for ranchers and farmers in southern and central Texas. This activity, not the army, made possible the city's first major development boom. By 1910 San Antonio had achieved its goal: it was the largest city in Texas.[1]

Dallas and Houston had not been idle, however, and the onset of the twentieth century gave both cities new opportunities to advance. The discovery of oil in east Texas in 1901, followed by a successful battle to become a port, created enormous economic opportunities for Houston. Dallas was busily constructing its own rail network, which, when combined with oil discoveries in west Texas in the 1920s, would make that city an equally serious challenger to San Antonio's primacy. San Antonio's business community could not rest upon its laurels; a service-oriented economy had limited potential for dynamic growth once the state's agricultural system began to mature. Local businessmen needed to continue to innovate if they expected to retain their dominance over their urban rivals.[2]

Recognizing a problem and solving it are two different things. San Antonio's business leaders had diverse opinions about how to achieve further growth. Established businessmen who had made their fortunes from the railroad boom would naturally favor proposals that reinforced San Antonio's role as a service center. Other entrepreneurs, especially those still searching for ways to achieve personal success, might seek other means to promote prosperity. As events unfolded, this latter group would in fact lead the initial efforts to stimulate urban development. Their control of economic policy initiatives in the years from 1910 to 1920 not only determined San Antonio's future as a major Texas city but also led to a fundamental change in the role of the military in local affairs. Ironically, these men did not succeed in preserving their city's primacy over its rivals, but their attempt to do so made the military a crucial, rather than a peripheral, presence in the economy.

The men who helped create this new role for the military shared certain characteristics. First, they were—either figuratively or literally—outsiders. Luther B. Clegg, Charles S. Fowler, and William B. Tuttle all arrived in San Antonio during its first major boom period. None was a native Texan. Clegg, who came in 1894, established the San Antonio Printing Company, an organization that quickly dominated local publishing. Fowler and Tuttle both arrived in 1906, and each had business interests that could thrive on rapid urban growth. Fowler would become a highly successful realtor, while Tuttle would guide the fortunes of San Antonio's privately owned traction and utility companies. None of these men belonged to the original socioeconomic elite, which had made possible the city's initial expansion. But they were all successful, ambitious men whose careers had, by 1910, become intimately intertwined with San Antonio's continued prosperity. And as newcomers unconnected to that original elite they would be more likely to seek innovative solutions to the difficulties of promoting further urbanization.[3]

Although few in number, these men occupied pivotal positions in the business community. Prior to 1910 that community had lacked any centralized means to coordinate economic policy. Numerous trade associations cluttered the landscape, but cooperation among them was practically nonexistent. San Antonio's spectacular growth and bright future convinced the Young Men's Business Club to propose a consolidation of effort. In response, the various business organizations established the San Antonio Chamber of Commerce in 1912. But some groups and individuals emerged with more influence in the new chamber than others. Specifically, the Young Men's Business Club, whose members did not belong to the original economic elite, controlled the chamber's structure, procedures, and policies. The chamber was organized along corporate lines. Individual businesses bought stock in the chamber, and their influence therefore depended upon the size of their investments. This dependence was especially true of elections for key officers such as the directors and president, in which the stock a member held could be voted according to his own preferences. And the more stock he owned, the more votes he had. Finally, the directors and president, who controlled policy, met secretly, while the general membership attended only the annual meeting.[4]

Because of this structure, Clegg and Tuttle were especially prominent. Tuttle, for example, was the largest stockholder in the chamber. Both men served continuously as directors through the critical first decade of the chamber's existence; both also served as president (Tuttle in 1913; Clegg in 1914 and 1915). In addition, Tuttle became the first chairman of the Industrial Committee. Finally, each man was either chairman or vice-chairman of the Military Affairs Committee from its inception in 1916 through the late 1930s. In sum, these two men occupied powerful positions in a chamber whose structure permitted a small group to control economic policy while claiming to represent (and make decisions for) the entire business community.[5]

Morris Sheppard, an outsider of a different sort, was a native Texan, a lawyer by training, and the heir to his father's congressional seat. When the elder Sheppard died in 1902, his son launched his own political career with a successful bid to complete his father's unexpired term in the Fifty-seventh Congress. After five terms in the House, Sheppard moved to the Senate when Joseph Bailey resigned his seat in 1913. An ardent prohibitionist, Sheppard would first achieve national prominence as the author of the Eighteenth Amendment. In the meantime, however, he was an extremely active legislator who rarely lost an opportunity to promote his state's interests. Throughout his career Sheppard would play a very important role in numerous urban development projects in Texas.[6]

As a group these men shared another crucial characteristic. Except for Fowler, they seem to have had a special regard for the military. The source of this affection is not clear, and it was expressed in different ways. Clegg, for instance, became a lifelong member of the chamber's Military Affairs Committee. In addition to that role, Tuttle had an even longer association with the military. At the age of 18, while an undergraduate at the University of Virginia, he joined a reserve unit, the First Virginia Cavalry, in 1892. During World War I he served the engineers. Like Clegg, Sheppard had no direct military experience. Upon his election to the Senate, however, he quickly sought a place on the Military Affairs Committee. He was an early advocate of Wilson's preparedness program and apparently helped write the National Defense acts of 1916 and 1920. This special interest in military matters on the part of these men was hardly typical of Americans at the time. It would, however, provide a common ground for cooperation among them as other events evolved.[7]

Aviation acted as the catalyst that transformed the military's role in San Antonio's development. Local civilian and military interest in aviation evolved independently, albeit simultaneously, until the two explicitly coalesced in 1915. From the army's perspective, San Antonio offered certain natural advantages for testing aircraft and flyers. The local climate and terrain were the strongest arguments in favor of flight tests near the city. San Antonio had more calendar days of optimal flight conditions than practically any other site in the nation. Furthermore, in the early twentieth century the relative lack of urbanization and the level terrain meant the army had available to it a large area suitable for air operations. Finally, the existence of Fort Sam Houston reduced the need for large sums to build an experimental airfield. Support facilities were already available. Even so, the army did not exactly leap at the opportunity to explore the aircraft's military potential.

The army had first used airships, in the form of balloons, for reconnaissance during the Civil War. Aside from establishing such airships as part of its Signals branch, however, the army subsequently chose to ignore their potential for the next 40 years. In the meantime various inventors such as Samuel P. Langley and the Wright brothers in the United States, as well as numerous Europeans, made major contributions to the development of aviation. Their cumulative successes led, between 1903 and 1910, to an explosion of public interest in the spectacular feats of early aviators. A few army officers, notably Lieutenant Frank Lahm, shared this general enthusiasm. Lahm became an internationally known balloonist in 1906, and he and other officers such as Benjamin Foulois became ardent advocates of an army air service. Brigadier General James Allen, chief Signal officer, impressed by these developments, created an aeronautical division within the Signal Corps in 1907. Then the Wrights, after innumerable rebuffs, finally convinced a reluctant Board of Ordnance and Fortifications to issue a contract for a single airplane. Although the contract was a milestone in military aviation, the army was still a long way from developing an air force. By 1909 Foulois was the only remaining officer in the aeronautical branch that was testing the Wrights' plane. General Allen transferred Foulois to Fort Sam Houston with orders to learn how to fly. Foulois did so in March 1910, but the future of military aviation looked rather bleak.[8]

While the army gingerly explored aviation, local civilian interest was more enthusiastic. The reasons for this attitude must remain conjectural owing to a paucity of extant evidence. However, it is clear that before World War I local advocates regarded aviation as an industry of considerable potential for urban growth. It is also clear that Clegg, Tuttle, and Sheppard were among the leading supporters of this industry. Tuttle, for example, apparently arranged the first "airshow" in San Antonio by inviting Louis Paulhon, a French aviator, to town for demonstration flights in February 1910—before Foulois had even assembled his plane from its packing crates. That same month a newspaper was already touting San Antonio as the "aeronautical center" of the United States. In April unidentified sponsors arranged a four-day aviation meet to coincide with Spring Fiesta, one of the most important social and economic events of each year. The meet's sponsors thus linked their enthusiasm for aviation with an event that they, and San Antonians generally, regarded as the quintessential expression of their city's uniqueness. Sheppard, at this point still a congressman, tried to help these local enthusiasts by proposing a bill to establish an experimental commercial airmail route between Washington and San Antonio. Although it failed to pass, this attempt marked the beginning of Sheppard's lifelong commitment to aviation.[9]

Continuing interest in aviation's potential, expressed in other public shows such as the international aviation meet in February 1911, promised to produce concrete economic benefits by early 1914. In March two St. Louis businessmen offered to build an aircraft factory in San Antonio. Tuttle chaired a chamber committee charged with conducting negotiations on the idea, and San Antonio seemed on the verge of becoming a leading center of a promising new industry.[10]

In the meantime the army slowly increased its commitment to aviation. Brigadier General George P. Scriven, Allen's successor as chief Signal officer, persuaded the secretary of war to approve an aviation center at San Antonio in May 1913. The reasons for choosing San Antonio illustrate the interaction between general military policy and personal preferences. In the summer of 1912 the army had surveyed the nation to select sites suitable for pilot training, given the technological limitations of the aircraft then available. The surveyors drew a line across the country at the 37° parallel. Army policy thereafter dictated that locations south of that line had precedence for flight training. Scriven probably selected San Antonio as one of those sites because he, like most regular army officers, had developed an affection for the city that hosted one of the army's most important posts. The new air base, Dodd Field, was in fact constructed at Fort Sam Houston in 1915.[11]

By 1915 a small group of civilian and military aviation enthusiasts had made sufficient progress to band together to promote their mutual interests. In June, Clegg (who was president of the chamber of commerce), Tuttle, and several other chamber members and directors met with a number of local businessmen and army officers to discuss forming an aviation club. General Funston told the assembly that the pilots of the air squadron soon to be installed at the fort would be available to give civilians flight training. Major Lyon discussed the commercial potential of aviation and spoke of the advantages an aero club would have in promoting San Antonio's "peculiar advantages" for aviation. Several businessmen responded that "it might be possible to develop a manufacturing industry here and make it [San Antonio] aeroplane headquarters." As a first step in achieving those goals, everyone at the meeting agreed to join a new organization, the Texas Aero Club.[12] This meeting subtly altered civil-military relations in San Antonio. Prior to 1915 the chamber of commerce had worked on an ad hoc basis with the army to secure improvements at the fort. This was the first time that the two had created a separate institutional basis for cooperation. Furthermore, this cooperative venture focused on future prospects rather than on immediate problems. Planning and developing an aviation program would require local businessmen to assume a more active role in a long-standing relationship in which they had previously been passive recipients of army largess.

Two other developments in 1915 encouraged a more entrepreneurial approach to the military. In May the National Security League, which had been organized to stimulate public concern over preparedness, asked the chamber to endorse its program. The chamber's directors readily did so and also agreed to organize a branch office on the grounds that it "was a matter of prudence and good business" to have an adequate national defense. Events in Europe were no doubt crucial in prompting this response. Nevertheless, the chamber had now linked itself with a national organization whose purpose, among other things, was to increase congressional appropriations for defense. This more aggressive attitude had immediate results when, in September, the chamber for the first time marshaled its political forces to increase the number of troops at the fort. Clegg directed a successful fight with Houston to acquire the 19th Infantry. These events, coupled with the founding of the Texas Aero Club, led the chamber to take yet one more step in formalizing its commitment to the military. In November the directors broached the idea of an annual banquet honoring army officers. Previously, the chamber had sponsored luncheons and banquets on an individual basis, usually for post or area commanders. Now the directors proposed to make this symbolic gesture of appreciation more systematic—a further indication that the military's role in San Antonio was assuming greater importance in their minds.[13]

In retrospect, 1915 was a turning point in San Antonio's relations with the military. Some businessmen had committed themselves to making the military a dynamic element in their continuing search for ways to promote urban growth. This did not mean that the entire business community agreed with that idea; nor did it mean the idea would succeed. At the time, however, San Antonio needed to find new ways to develop so as to perpetuate its current prosperity. Clegg, Tuttle, and others were hoping to stimulate local industrialization by encouraging the military to pursue aircraft development. Ideally, San Antonio would be in a position to offer the government land for bases to train a new, expanding branch of the service, while simultaneously offering industrialists who built aircraft plants contacts with officers whose needs would stimulate orders for their factories.

International events after 1915 accelerated military–civilian cooperation and created closer bonds between key businessmen and politicians. The Punitive Expedition against Mexico in March 1916 revealed deficiencies at Fort Sam Houston for large-scale operations. Senator Sheppard, visiting San Antonio during the expedition, learned about supply and space problems at the fort from Clegg. The two men seem to have worked with the base's commander in a plan to expand the fort's size and facilities significantly. Because this effort entailed a sustained lobbying campaign, and perhaps because of the obviously growing importance of the armed forces, the chamber forged another institutional link between itself and the military by creating a Military Affairs Committee.[14]

Local interest in aviation also received a boost from the Punitive Expedition. The army's experiment with aerial reconnaissance during the expedition had not been very successful. General Scriven argued that problems such as effective coordination between ground troops and aviation could only be resolved by an expanded aviation program. That argument, reinforced by the role aircraft were playing in Europe, prompted the secretary of war to approve a new base at San Antonio. Benjamin Foulois, now a major, selected a site for this airfield, which would be known as Kelly Field, approximately five miles southwest of downtown San Antonio. General Scriven approved the site in November 1916.[15]

The founding of Kelly Field marked the beginning of an explosion of military bases around San Antonio. With U.S. entry into World War I the army made San Antonio one of its principal locations for troop training. Fort Sam Houston and Kelly were considerably enlarged, but rapid national mobilization quickly exceeded the capacity of both bases. Accordingly, the army sought new bases. By 1918 Brooks Air Base, Camps Travis, John Wise, Stanley, Normolye, and Bullis, and an expanded Leon Springs Military Reservation practically surrounded San Antonio. In every case, either Tuttle or Clegg personally supervised site selection, and the chamber's Military Affairs Committee coordinated land acquisition and site preparation.[16]

An interesting pattern emerged from this flurry of activity. Bases that had the potential to promote urbanization and industrialization were located to the south of San Antonio. Those bases that did not have that capacity were sited to the north. (Fort Sam Houston, on the far east side, was an exception.) Postwar expectations may have dictated this pattern. Given past experience, the United States would not maintain a large army following the war. Local businessmen could not expect infantry and artillery camps (like Leon Springs and Bullis) to survive force reductions. Airfields and repair shops (Kelly, Brooks, and Normolye) were another matter, however, especially given the commitment Clegg, Tuttle, and their group had to aviation. Thus it would have been important for local boosters to take maximum care in selecting sites to offer the army for airfields.

And they did. By 1910 San Antonio's urbanization was shifting. Formerly, the city's subdivisions and suburbs had been developing to the north, but with the enormous population growth that occurred between 1900 and 1910 additional areas had to be opened for settlement. Much of the city's new residential and commercial growth shifted to the south in response to the demand for space.[17] From the army's perspective, air bases needed to be isolated from urban development as much as possible. Land that met that need was readily available on the east, south, and west sides of San Antonio. However, Kelly, Normolye, and Brooks all were sited along the southwest and southeast axes of growth, which had been clearly established well before the war. Although substantially removed from settled areas initially, all these bases could, and would, serve as magnets for further urban development.

Charles Fowler assumed a very direct role in promoting this type of development. Late in 1916 he accompanied Major Foulois to Washington to lobby Congress for money to buy the land for Kelly Field's original site. Sheppard successfully guided an appropriation bill through Congress for that purpose, and it may have been at this time that he and Fowler developed their lifelong friendship. Within a year Sheppard would be praising Fowler as one of San Antonio's most valued citizens. Fresh from this success, Fowler organized the South San Antonio Industrial Corporation in early 1917 and purchased substantial acreage adjacent to Kelly. Later in that year he helped Clegg and Tuttle secretly negotiate leases for a vast expansion of Kelly. Tuttle had in the meantime arranged a streetcar line extension linking Kelly with the downtown. Predictably enough, this new line terminated in South San Antonio's "business district." Fowler now had the means to promote rapid development adjacent to the airfield, and he proceeded to do so. In August, when Kelly was about to open, Fowler advertised residential, commercial, and industrial sites for sale in his private subdivision.[18]

The proliferation of bases benefited the entire city as well as individuals. Hundreds of small businesses opened their doors to serve the tens of thousands of soldiers pouring into the bases. Skilled and unskilled workmen flocked to San Antonio seeking construction jobs. Their housing needs provided numerous opportunities for local contractors and realtors to develop additional subdivisions around the city. Tourism flourished as parents traveled to town to visit their sons in the camps. Ranchers and farmers obtained lucrative contracts to supply the bases with meat and produce. And local businessmen made fortunes selling lumber, plumbing fixtures, sewer pipe, and innumerable other items to the army. In little more than two years federal appropriations for base construction and maintenance totaled almost $40 million; payrolls for troops and civilian workers exceeded $1 million a month.[19]

Problems, however, lurked beneath the surface prosperity. The war was the single best opportunity for local aviation boosters to secure the most critical element in their program: factories that would promote peacetime industrialization. Senator Sheppard, who believed "the future of aircraft is limitless,"[20] tried to help by authoring legislation for an Aircraft Board, which would encourage "industrial activities relating to aircraft."[21] He hoped that the board would find ways to promote commercial uses for aviation following the war. But neither Clegg, Tuttle, Fowler, nor their friends took up the challenge. San Antonio acquired flight training facilities and a motor repair shop, but civilian entrepreneurs in the infant aircraft industry chose not to locate in the city.

The reasons for the failure to attract aircraft factories remain conjectural. Part of the explanation may lie in a dissipation of the campaign to attract them. Sheppard, for example, became increasingly engrossed in his long-standing crusade for national prohibition. Tuttle joined the Army Reserve for the duration of the war. Fowler may have become immersed in the promotion of South San Antonio.

Clegg apparently spent most of his time dealing with the exhaustive details associated with developing the various bases. In sum, the men most crucial to the promotion of aviation may have lost direction or control over their own program for industrialization at just the crucial moment when it might have succeeded.

National developments also militated against success. The federal government's attempt to stimulate aircraft production had been a dismal failure. Businessmen who had extensive backgrounds in the automobile industry and in engineering dominated the nation's aircraft program after 1916. As members of the Aircraft Production Board, for instance, they supervised the distribution of contracts to their own, or their friends', benefit. Since San Antonio had not become a major automobile center before the war, it was hardly in a position to compete with Dayton and Detroit, two cities with strong ties to that industry. But even those cities did not fare well in the race to build airplanes. Technical and production problems reduced domestic manufacturing to an embarrassing trickle. In spite of its supporters' best efforts, the airplane did not emerge from the war capable of sustaining a major new industry. [22]

Whatever the reasons for the failure to attract factories, San Antonio entered the postwar era ill-equipped to promote urban growth. Rapid demobilization undermined the temporary prosperity that the bases had produced. Initially, the chamber of commerce tried to staunch the trend toward retrenchment by endorsing a separate Aviation Service in the army and by supporting universal military service. These ideas proved to be feeble protests against a more general, national sentiment for disarmament. By 1920 all the city's bases were either closed or operating at greatly reduced levels. Only the army's commitment to San Antonio as an aviation center and the affection regular army officers had for the city saved Kelly and Brooks from extinction. Even so, their status was tenuous indeed. Brooks survived by becoming a balloon training center. Kelly was reduced to training flight mechanics. [23]

The experiment with aviation, now a decade old in 1920, had produced three new bases (Normolye was also retained), but it had not fulfilled its sponsors' expectations. Businessmen with commitments to other ideas for growth now assumed direction of economic policies. While friendly to the military, they reverted to a passive role in the partnership. Nothing demonstrated the new situation more decisively than the attack they launched on San Antonio's lobbyist in 1916. But in 1920, when congressional cutbacks had heightened competition among cities for military contracts and base appropriations, the lobbyist was criticized for being unnecessary. His critics insisted that since the war had ended, his work was finished. Clegg tried to defend him, but he had lost the battle by early 1921. Even the Military Affairs Committee suffered a loss in status. It disappeared from the chamber's budget and was apparently relegated to a permanent committee of the organization's industrial division. The consequences of these maneuvers could be seen at Kelly and Brooks. Kelly Field lost its flight training role to Carlstrom Air Force Base in Florida in 1920, and Brooks was not designated a permanent base until 1922. [24]

   In their reduced circumstances the various bases would not have played a major role in an otherwise healthy local economy. San Antonio, though, was in trouble. During the 1920s the city lost some key industries, such as railroad car construction plants, and failed to find appropriate replacements. It was a pathetic commentary on the state of the economy that pecan shelling became the single largest industry by 1929. Wholesaling, especially in food products, remained the most important economic activity, but San Antonio's wholesalers displayed an extraordinary obtuseness concerning their own welfare. They failed to seize opportunities for dramatic growth, which beckoned to them from the burgeoning truck-farming business in the Rio Grande Valley. [25] Without suitable alternatives, federal expenditures for the military, even at the level of a few million dollars per year, loomed disproportionately large compared with local sources of income. Instead of helping San Antonio's economy soar, aviation now provided some of the wing splints that kept a wobbly economy aloft.

   At mid-decade local businessmen suddenly confronted the possibility that they might lose this vital crutch. Urbanization had continued adjacent to Kelly and Brooks since the war, and by 1926 their commanders had become concerned that the bases would soon be unable to conduct their operations safely. Major Ralph Royce accordingly drafted a report to his superiors in Washington recommending that Brooks, and possibly Kelly, be closed. The Air Service had no intention of abandoning San Antonio; in fact, Kelly's commander strongly urged the chamber of commerce to find an alternative field farther removed from the city. But other developments threatened the commitment to stay. Responding to the furor over the Billy Mitchell affair in 1926, President Calvin Coolidge had appointed a commission to investigate the problems of military air power. The following year the commission's report suggested a five-year expansion program. Congress partially implemented the suggestions in July and, among other things, set up a new Air Corps Training Center (ACTC). Although the army established the center's temporary headquarters at Kelly, the problems the local bases now faced with urban development made them less able to meet the service's needs. Army officials wanted a new location for training, and while they favored San Antonio, the battle other cities were prepared to wage for the new ACTC meant that Congress might not agree. [26]

Perhaps lulled by repeated army assurances, local businessmen did not take the prospect of losing the new training center seriously. The first signs of trouble arose in August 1927 when General Frank Lahm told Tuttle and the chamber's Military Affairs Committee that San Antonio must be prepared to offer a free site to the government for the new base. Lahm pointed out that other cities, Dallas among them, were already offering free land. Congressman Frank James, chairman of the House Military Affairs Committee, made the point more bluntly. He informed Tuttle that unless San Antonio would match its competitors' offers before Congress met in January, the city would lose not only the new base but Kelly and Brooks as well. In spite of this warning, the chamber simply assured James that a plan had already been worked out to provide a site. The congressman left town assuming the matter was settled; in fact, nothing had been done.[27]

Tuttle, as chairman of the Military Affairs Committee, did begin to assemble information on possible sites for the new base. By the end of September he had nine tracts ready for General Lahm's consideration. Yet Tuttle and Clegg apparently considered San Antonio's position so secure that both left town for lengthy vacations.[28] Nor did anyone take seriously the idea of donating land to the government. In December Tuttle and a delegation of businessmen in Washington tried to lobby Congress to appropriate money to buy land. They suffered a severe rebuff. Army officers told the delegation that "if it were not for the fact that [they] consider this city as one of the most desirable locations, it would not be considered in the matter . . . of this Field." Reporting to the chamber, the chastened delegation concluded that "the conditions of this day and time are such that the keenest competition prevails for the location of Governmental activities; . . . we cannot hope to secure such activities . . . unless we are public-spirited enough to meet the competition of other places." A sudden surge of public spirit might not suffice, however.[29] The delegation made its report on December 13; James had repeated his warning that a free site must be ready on January 1, 1928, or San Antonio would lose the race with its competitors.

Faced with what had now become a first-class emergency, the chamber attempted to redress its previous complacency with a burst of energy. With the chamber's blessing, Tuttle and Clegg organized the San Antonio Airport Corporation to solicit public contributions for land purchases. General Lahm had finally settled on a site northeast of the city that would cost an estimated $500,000. Unsure whether the public would be that generous, the corporation asked city officials to help. City Attorney Joseph Ryan stunned the chamber directors with an announcement that San Antonio's charter prohibited the use of public funds for such purposes. Furious, the Airport

Corporation sought aid from a more pliable source. A local judge opined that the city could indeed issue interest-bearing warrants for municipal purposes. That proved decisive. On December 19, when the public subscription drive had raised only $100,000, the city commissioners approved an ordinance for $0.5 million in warrants backed by uncollected delinquent taxes. Although the legality of the proceedings remained murky, the Airport Corporation had what it needed. Local banks agreed to lend it the money to buy land for a new base. Once the corporation had title to all the necessary parcels, the city would buy the land from it (whereupon the corporation repaid its debt and dissolved). Finally, the city would donate the site to the government. Congressman James, notified that a site that satisfied General Lahm was available, guided legislation through Congress establishing a permanent ACTC at San Antonio.[30]

San Antonio had salvaged its military industry, but the new base, Randolph Air Field, would not contribute to urban growth for some time. General Lahm had chosen a site well removed from San Antonio's prevailing direction of development. Furthermore, he resolutely opposed any attempt to encourage urbanization near the base. Ambitious developers tried to circumvent his opposition, plotting "Airport City" directly adjacent to Randolph in an imitation of South San Antonio. However, since the city's growth was away from, rather than toward, Randolph, this attempt fizzled.[31] Local contractors earned satisfying dividends from projects at Randolph during 1930 and 1931, but real estate developers had to await better times. As with the other bases since World War I, Randolph's payroll (about $4 million per year) became its major contribution to the local economy.[32]

Hailed at the time as a great step forward, Randolph in fact represented a barely successful defense of the status quo. San Antonio managed to retain its significant investment in military aviation, but it was an investment that paid disappointing dividends. The commercial aviation industry had bypassed the city in the 1920s, perhaps in part because the chamber indicated no interest in it, and government orders for planes went to plants located elsewhere. Training servicemen rather than building the machines they used had become San Antonio's specialty by the 1930s. As long as Congress took a dim view of defense appropriations, the bases would help sustain, but not promote, the local economy. Unable to develop satisfactory means to generate growth, San Antonio lost its primacy in the state and region. both Dallas and Houston easily surpassed it in population and economic development during the 1920s. The 1930 census confirmed the result: San Antonio ranked a poor third behind its more successful rivals.

The depression made a bad situation worse. San Antonio had become a relatively poor city by 1929; afterward it was desperately poor. The bases' food and maintenance requirements helped local businessmen somewhat, but that aid was minimal because the bases were themselves in bad shape. Niggardly funding had kept them all operating at minimum levels during the 1920s, and the depression only accentuated Congress's reluctance to spend money for the military. An inspection tour by members of the House Military Affairs Committee in 1935 revealed that all the installations were in serious disrepair and that their garrisons were below peacetime allocations. The army's inspector general put the matter even more bleakly two years later. He concluded that Kelly, in particular, could no longer fulfill its mission. Its buildings, mostly World War I vintage "temporary" structures, were collapsing, and its aircraft were the most outdated in the entire air corps.[33]

San Antonio's bases had become a poor crutch indeed for the local economy, but dramatic changes lurked on the horizon. In 1934 the city acquired a new, devoted champion in Congress when Maury Maverick won a House seat. Maverick had decided and outspoken views on defense matters. He was a harsh critic of the navy as the nation's first line of defense (a view held by such prominent politicians as President Franklin Delano Roosevelt). Capital ships, Maverick believed, had no place in a modern world that would soon be dominated by aircraft. Predictably, Maverick held passionately to the idea that air forces were the key to victory in future warfare. Also predictably, he urged the Congress to appropriate significant increases for the maintenance and expansion of air bases such as those in San Antonio.[34]

Maverick proved to be a persuasive man among his congressional peers. During his first term he obtained a seat on the House Military Affairs Committee and immediately wrangled large increases in appropriations for his district from the House. Local bases began receiving enough funding to remedy past defects and to bring garrisons to their authorized peacetime strengths. In his second term Maverick won a seat on the aviation subcommittee. While continuing to secure improved funding for local bases, Maverick expanded his activities by advocating more pilot training programs and the creation of an air force academy (to be located in San Antonio). Unfortunately for San Antonio, Maverick lost his bid for a third term. He returned home to wage a successful campaign for mayor, but his more ambitious projects in Congress collapsed with his departure. He had, however, made a significant contribution by restoring and enhancing the military's role in the local economy.[35]

In the meantime Sheppard had also been busy and had acquired considerable power to impose his views on the Senate. In 1933 he

became chairman of the Military Affairs Committee. Shortly thereafter, he began his own campaign to enhance the importance of the
air force. He continually introduced legislation designed to improve
the air force's efficiency and size. In the mid-1930s he had more
success persuading his colleagues to increase appropriations than
to change their attitudes toward general defense issues. Sheppard
worked assiduously to resurrect San Antonio's military industry and
shared the credit for that venture with Maverick.[36]

The news from Munich finally brought about the major shift in
defense policy that Sheppard and Maverick had been advocating. Prior
to 1938 President Roosevelt had slighted the air force in preference
to the navy as the critical component of defense. Munich changed his
mind. In September 1938 he summoned his key advisers to the White
House and announced that he wanted a major buildup of the air force.
He requested congressional authority for that policy in his January
message, and Sheppard introduced the legislation that became the
basis for Roosevelt's expansion program. Congress authorized
4,500 new pilots and 6,000 new planes in this initial step. Subsequent
events in Europe caused the numbers of men and planes to increase
rapidly.[37]

This shift to a larger air force had immediate and permanent
consequences for San Antonio. Randolph, as headquarters for the Air
Corps Training Command, quickly became one of the nation's key
bases. Kelly entered a period of extraordinary, nearly pell-mell
growth. Millions of dollars in contracts poured into the city as all
the bases acquired new or expanded roles in training, supply, and
maintenance functions.

As a result of these efforts the bases began to generate urban
growth once again. The bases' expansion created the need for hundreds and soon thousands of civilian workers. Fort Sam Houston led
the way. By 1936 it employed 7,601 civil service workers. The
change was most dramatic at Kelly, however. In 1938 Kelly had 873
civilians on its payroll. At the end of 1941 there were 8,962, and by
the end of 1942 there were 20,862. All those people, most from outside San Antonio, needed housing, food, clothing, and other amenities, which, thanks to generous federal pay scales, they had the
money to buy. Like the nation at large, San Antonio benefited enormously from the military buildup prior to and during World War II.[38]

Industrialization would not be a part of the renewed urbanization.
Unlike the situation prior to World War I, the San Antonio Chamber
of Commerce did not enter the period of rapid defense expansion
with a strategy for economic development. Instead, the inclinations
of the members who had dominated economic policy since the early
1920s—when they had rejected the initiatives of Tuttle and Clegg—
prevailed. The dominant group's ideas about development have not

yet been fully documented, but extreme caution seems to have been
a crucial characteristic. As new possibilities for rejuvenating the
local economy emerged in the late 1930s, the chamber's directors
resolutely refused to exploit them. A litmus test of this caution
occurred in early 1939 when an official of the National Aircraft
Corporation, in a move reminiscent of earlier days, offered to build
a factory in San Antonio. Considering the fact that Roosevelt's air
force expansion program was moving through Congress at precisely
this time, and that San Antonio's bases would obviously play a large
role in that program, the city had a great deal to offer such manufacturers. The directors accepted the proposal for the factory, but
they rejected a request for a free land site. Not surprisingly, the
factory was not built.[39]

That refusal to help a potentially important new industry indicates that the directors lacked an appropriately aggressive entrepreneurial spirit. Other events quickly confirmed that deficiency.
Between 1940 and 1942 military planners launched a successful campaign to disperse aircraft production. Federal monies became available for plant expansions, and several cities like Columbus, Omaha,
Louisville, and Dallas acquired aircraft factories at practically no
cost to themselves.[40] Mayor Maverick asked the chamber to help
him investigate the possibilities for obtaining such plants for San
Antonio. Accompanied by the chamber's general manager, Henry
Van Auken, Maverick visited Wichita, Kansas, to talk with aircraft
manufacturers. Upon their return, Van Auken reported that "in his
judgment it would be extremely difficult to move any of these factories
. . . to San Antonio, largely on account of this being a great military
reservation and in the Army's 'theater of operation.'" Apparently
the city's greatest asset for attracting industry had now become a
great liability. Van Auken's mangled logic ended the chamber's
interest in the subject, and San Antonio continued its nonindustrial
economic development.[41]

San Antonio thus began and ended 30 years of development as
a service center. Local boosters who had attempted to use the bases
as a lever for industrialization did not succeed. In effect, theirs was
a failed strategy. They had gambled on aviation and lost, not through
a lack of vision (at least in the period before World War I) but from
a lack of political and economic resources with which to realize
their ambitions. After 1939 a peculiar blindness to new opportunities
simply confirmed the failure of the original strategy. By way of
compensation, their efforts produced a legacy of much closer ties
to the military. Where once it had been a peripheral part of the city's
economy, the military had, by the late 1930s, become one of its
largest businesses. Various institutional and symbolic links, such
as the chamber's Military Affairs Committee, had been created to

establish the basis for closer cooperation. The active help of politicians like Sheppard, combined with the experience of dealing with
Congress and the army's bureaucracy from 1910 to 1940, habituated
local businessmen to the idea that the military could be a major
source of economic development. Even though San Antonio had failed
to industrialize, the bases could be viewed as appropriate substitutes
(especially after 1942). Finally, by the end of the period, thousands
of local residents had become dependent upon the bases for jobs.
That dependence influenced not only San Antonio's physical growth
by dictating the direction and location of new subdivisions, but it
also affected the well-being of all the businesses that served those
workers' needs. By the outset of World War II San Antonio had become a thoroughly military city.

NOTES

1. Caroline M. Remy, "A Study of the Transition of San Antonio
from a Frontier to an Urban Community, 1875-1900" (Master's
thesis, Trinity University, 1960); John Booth and David R. Johnson,
"Power and Progress in San Antonio's Politics, 1836-1970," in
Politics of San Antonio: Community, Progress, and Power, ed. John
Booth and David R. Johnson (Lincoln: University of Nebraska Press,
1983), pp. 1-32.

2. Seth S. McKay and Odie B. Faulk, Texas after Spindletop,
1901-1965 (Austin, Tex.: Steck-Vaughn, 1965), pp. 3-13; David G.
McComb, Houston: A History, rev. ed. (Austin: University of Texas
Press, 1981), pp. 66-68, 76-77.

3. Charles G. Norton, ed., Men of Affairs of San Antonio
(San Antonio, Tex.: San Antonio Newspaper Artists Association,
c. 1912), pp. 12, 46; San Antonio Express, September 10, 1954.

4. Charles Smith, "San Antonio Chamber of Commerce: A
History of Its Organization for Community Development and Service,
1910-1960" (Master's thesis, Trinity University, 1965).

5. San Antonio Chamber of Commerce, Minutes of the Board
of Directors (hereafter cited as Minutes of the Board of Directors),
1 (February 14, 1912); ibid., 2 (January 15, February 27, October 28,
1913); ibid., 4 (January 13, 1914). See also Smith, "Chamber of
Commerce," pp. 29, 44.

6. New York Times, April 10, 1941.

7. Minutes of the Board of Directors, 7 (May 9, 1916); ibid.,
8 (March 13, 1917); ibid., 8 (September 6, 1918); San Antonio
Express, September 10, 1954; U.S., Congress, Senate and House,
Congressional Record, 63rd Cong., 2d sess., 1914, 51, pt. : 16,
418; Reserve Officer 11 (February 1934): 3.

8. Carroll V. Glines, Jr., The Compact History of the United States Air Force, rev. ed. (New York: Hawthorn Books, 1973), pp. 42, 45-59; Lloyd Morris and Kendall Smith, Ceiling Unlimited: The Story of American Aviation from Kitty Hawk to Supersonics (New York: Macmillan, 1953), pp. 41-52, 66-67; Barney M. Gils, "Early Military Aviation Activities in Texas," Southwestern Historical Quarterly 54 (October 1950): 144-45.

9. Unidentified newspaper clipping of a column by William Reddell, in the Glassford Collection, Library of the Daughters of the Republic of Texas; San Antonio Light, February 21, 22, 1910; San Antonio Express, April 20, 1910; U.S., Congress, House, Congressional Record, 61st Cong., 2d sess., 1910, 45, H. Rept. 26833, p. 8144.

10. Minutes of the Board of Directors, 4 (March 14, 1914); Frances W. Isbell, "Military Aeronautics in San Antonio, 1910-1918" (Master's thesis, Trinity University, 1962), p. 18.

11. Isbell, "Military Aeronautics," pp. 42-44, 48-49; Gilbert S. Guinn, "A Different Frontier: Aviation, the Army Air Forces, and the Evolution of the Sunshine Belt," Aerospace Historian 29 (March 1982): 36; Clegg to J. H. Harte, April 2, 1918, Minutes of the Board of Directors, 8 (April 2, 1918) notes the affection of regular army officers for San Antonio.

12. Minutes of the Board of Directors, 6 (June 10, December 14, 1915). See also San Antonio Light, November 14, 1916.

13. Minutes of the Board of Directors, 6 (May 12, 25, September 15, November 23, 1915).

14. Richard C. Batz, "The Development of Fort Sam Houston and Its Importance to San Antonio" (Master's thesis, Trinity University, 1972), p. 77; Minutes of the Board of Directors, 7 (May 9, 1916).

15. New York Times, October 21, 1916; San Antonio Light, November 6, 13, 21, 1916.

16. Isbell, "Military Aeronautics," pp. 77-78, 134-36; Minutes of the Board of Directors, 8 (December 28, 1918).

17. San Antonio Light, February 20, 27, 1910.

18. Minutes of the Board of Directors, 7 (December 5, 1916); ibid., 8 (June 17, 19, 1917); U.S., Congress, Senate, Congressional Record, 64th Cong., 2d sess., 1916, 54, pt.   : 634; San Antonio Express, November 26, 1917; Jules A. Appler's General Directory and Households of Greater San Antonio (San Antonio, Tex.: Jules A. Appler, 1917); San Antonio Light, August 10, 12, 1917.

19. San Antonio Light, August 7, 10, 12, 19, 1917; Kelly Field Eagle, October 17, December 19, 1918; William C. Chase, "A Study of the Influence of Water on the Growth of San Antonio" (Master's thesis, Trinity University, 1957), p. 42.

20. San Antonio Express, November 26, 1917.

21. U.S., Congress, Senate, Congressional Record, 65th Cong., 1st sess., 1917, 55, p. 7: 6996-98; United States Statutes at Large (Washington, D.C.: U.S. Government Printing Office, 1919), 40, pp. 296-97.

22. Morris and Smith, Ceiling Unlimited, pp. 188-96.

23. Minutes of the Board of Directors, 8 (February 18, March 11, 1919); ibid., 11 (February 28, 1922); Kelly Field Eagle, November 21, 1918; ibid., May 22, 1919; "History of Kelly Field, Texas," 2 vols. (typescript; Kelly Air Force Base History Office, 1945), 1: 9-11.

24. Minutes of the Board of Directors, 7 (November 14, 1916); ibid., 10 (April 1, 1920; May 25, 1921); San Antonio Express, June 28, 1922.

25. Harold W. Schapir, "The Workers of San Antonio, Texas, 1900-1940" (Ph.D. diss., University of Texas, 1952), pp. 24-27, 38-41; Chase, "Influence of Water on the Growth of San Antonio," p. 44; Minutes of the Board of Directors, 11 (February 7, 1924).

26. Minutes of the Board of Directors, 12 (February 18, 1926); Fred M. Herndon to William B. Tuttle, June 18, 1926, William B. Tuttle Papers, Air Training Command History Office, Randolph Field (hereafter cited as Tuttle Papers); Office of the Historical Editor, "History of Randolph Field, Texas" (typescript; Air Training Command History Office, 1944), pp. 2-3, 7-8; Bruce E. Burgoyne, "Acquisition of Randolph Field" (Master's thesis, Trinity University, 1957), pp. 36-37.

27. Minutes of the Board of Directors, 13 (August 19, September 1, 1927).

28. Tuttle to Porter Whaley (General Manager, Chamber of Commerce), September 21, 1927, Tuttle Papers.

29. Tuttle to R. B. Brown, December 6, 1927, Tuttle Papers; Minutes of the Board of Directors, 13 (December 13, 1927).

30. Minutes of the Board of Directors, 13 (December 13, 14, 16, 22, 1927); San Antonio Light, December 14, 19, 1927; Burgoyne, "Acquisition of Randolph Field," chap. 3.

31. Lahm to Tuttle, September 19, 1928, Tuttle Papers; San Antonio Light, April 3, 1928; San Antonio Express, December 9, 1928; Service News, June 1, 1930.

32. Historical Editor, "History of Randolph Field," pp. 23-26, 68, and app. A; Burgoyne, "Acquisition of Randolph Field," p. 118.

33. San Antonio Light, October 31, 1935; Report of the Inspector General's Office, August 12, 1937, in "History of Kelly Field," 2: 257-59.

34. Richard B. Henderson, Maury Maverick: A Political Biography (Austin: University of Texas Press, 1979), pp. 61-62; U.S., Congress, House, Congressional Record, 74th Cong., 1st sess.,

1935, 79, pt. 6: 6328; ibid., 75th Cong., 3d sess., 1938, 83, pt. 9 (app.): 680-81.

35. U.S., Congress, Congressional Record, 74th Cong., 2d sess., 1936, 80, pt. 8: 8245; ibid., 75th Cong., 1st sess., 1937, 81, pt. 4: 4057, Senate, pt. 6: 6360-62; ibid., 75th Cong., 3d sess., 1938, 83, pt. 5: 5662-63, pt. 9 (app.): 2375, 2609; San Antonio Express, January 11, 1935; San Antonio News, July 14, 1936; Leader-News (Uvalde, Texas), October 23, 1936; Henderson, Maury Maverick, pp. 179-81.

36. New York Times, April 10, 1941; U.S., Congress, Congressional Record, 74th Cong., 2d sess., 1936, 80, pt. 2: 1698; ibid., 75th Cong., 3d sess., 1938, 83, pt. 5: 5189, 5377, 5883.

37. Glines, Compact History, pp. 146-47, 149-51; Guinn, "A Different Frontier," pp. 40, 42; U.S., Congress, Congressional Record, 76th Cong., 1st sess., 1938, 84, pt. 2: 2218-19; United States Statutes at Large, vol. 53, pt. 2, chap. 35, pp. 555-60.

38. Batz, "Development of Fort Sam Houston," pp. 81, 83; "History of the San Antonio Air Service Command from Inception to February 1943," 2 vols. (typescript; Kelly Air Force Base History Office, 1943), 1: iii-vi.

39. Minutes of the Board of Directors, 19 (February 23, 1939).

40. Guinn, "A Different Frontier," pp. 43-44.

41. Minutes of the Board of Directors, 19 (February 11, 25, 1941).

5

Norfolk and the Navy: The Evolution of City–Federal Relations, 1917–46

Christopher Silver

The rise of Norfolk, Virginia, to the stature of a New South metropolis owed immeasurably to its long-standing association with the U.S. Navy. Since the late eighteenth century, the strategic importance of Hampton Roads had been alluring to proponents of an enlarged navy. Yet as late as 1900, the sleepy port city of nearly 47,000 inhabitants gave few indications that it would mushroom into a military metropolis of more than 0.25 million and the home of the nation's largest naval installation by the late 1940s. Two world wars, in combination with an aggressive promotional effort by local leaders, help to explain Norfolk's emergence as a burgeoning military stronghold. In turn, the exigencies of war provided an impetus to those intent on placing Norfolk on a par with the region's leading urban centers.[1]

Turn-of-the-century Norfolk brimmed with the entrepreneurial spirit that inspired urban boosters throughout the South. Verbal imagery of Norfolk's urban destiny abounded in local promotional pieces which evoked unflagging optimism that the city could overcome nearly a century of inertia through aggressive promotion of its links to the sea. Resurrecting a local manufacturing base carried some appeal, but the focus of urban promotion centered on solidifying the city's maritime advantages. As the nexus of a flourishing commercial network in the Southeast, Norfolk assumed that its future rested with rails and cargo ships. Success is securing the terminus for the Norfolk and Southern rail line, which extended to Charlotte, North Carolina, and the Virginian line, which supplied a direct link to western coal fields, reconfirmed this assumption over the next ten years. To this Norfolk added enlarged direct foreign and coastal shipping service. Only through continuance of repair work at the Norfolk Navy

Yard, located across the harbor in neighboring Portsmouth, did the city exhibit any connection with the military.[2]

To further its ambitions as a South Atlantic trade center, Norfolk successfully challenged its inland rival Richmond as the site for the 1907 Jamestown Exposition. According to local boosters, the exposition was "an advertising opportunity unsurpassed in history" that could do for Norfolk what similar pageants had done for its urban rivals. The requirement that Norfolk raise $1 million to finance the celebration indicated how far it was willing to go to advertise the city to the nation. Although the exposition was a financial disaster, it produced one invaluable result: the decision by President Theodore Roosevelt to assemble the fleet for an around-the-world cruise at Hampton Roads in 1907 impressed upon local entrepreneurs the potential of establishing a naval base in Norfolk. Farsighted local boosters saw the military as a catalyst for accelerated economic development. Norfolk now went after the U.S. Navy to further its urban ambitions as tenaciously as it had sought new trade connections.[3]

Through a combination of natural advantages, strategic considerations, aggressive local promotion, and key political connections in Washington, Norfolk realized its objective within a decade. There appears to have been little impetus from the military expansionists to capitalize on Norfolk's natural and strategic advantages until local boosters planted the seed in the aftermath of the 1907 exposition. Yet once the idea of constructing a base had been floated, navy planners worked diligently to supply the appropriate strategic rationale for the enterprise. By 1921 outgoing Secretary of the Navy Josephus Daniels proclaimed the Norfolk installation "the greatest supply base on either coast. It is the great rendezvous of the fleet, and its importance in time of war is probably greater than any one yard." According to a 1923 navy plan for development of a system of permanent naval bases, Norfolk's facilities were the only ones in the nation that approached its concept of a naval base. This concept required "activities necessary to prepare, repair, and maintain the fleet ready for war, and to operate from during war," all in a contiguous area. Yet it was not until former Virginia Governor and U.S. Senator Claude Swanson became secretary of the navy under Franklin Roosevelt that Norfolk was assured that its marriage with the military would be permanent. It was no mere coincidence that under two Southern-born naval secretaries Norfolk secured, enlarged, and consolidated the city's hold over the Atlantic Fleet. The vigilance of Norfolk's boosters, as much as strategic consideration, had a bearing on the final outcome.[4]

To understand the influence of the military buildup on the process of growth and change in twentieth century Norfolk, one must examine indirect as well as direct influences. On the one hand, local boosters viewed a permanent naval presence after World War I as a necessary catalyst for continued expansion of the city's commercial base. According to Barton Myers, a former mayor and chamber of commerce president, Norfolk was in the midst of a business boom in 1920 that was destined to transform it into "a very large city." Although Myers asserted emphatically that this was "not a war expansion" but rather "a commercial expansion," he regarded permanent naval presence as an essential factor in making the city's waterfront attractive to new industrial concerns. The alleged boom failed to sustain itself beyond 1920, however. Indeed, the postwar recession that engulfed Norfolk was hastened in large part by a sudden and extended decline in naval activity and fostered ill feelings between the military and civilians that lingered until the rearmament of the late 1930s. Nevertheless, key urban boosters, headed by the chamber of commerce, recognized that even a reduced naval presence was better than nothing and maintained their vigorous backing of naval interests. [5]

As a vital component of urban promotional efforts, naval expansion also hastened change in local perceptions of public initiative in city development. The adoption of a city-manager government in 1918, an unprecedented willingness to bear the costs of extensive public improvements during the 1920s, annexation of the territory encompassed by the naval base, and experimentation with city planning all evidenced the city's faith in the future growth of military connections. Norfolk's experiences as a defense center during World War I demonstrated the inadequacies of local institutions and their capacity to respond to rapid urban growth. At the same time, the navy demanded improved city services as a prerequisite to future investments in Norfolk. This expectation became especially apparent as the military geared up for World War II and looked to the city to respond obediently and generously to its every need, even when it went against the local grain. The problem of housing war workers and military personnel pitted the navy against local real estate interests. In this instance, strong and direct pressure from the military forced Norfolk to abandon its laissez-faire posture toward a housing problem that had plagued the city since the turn of the century.

The combined effect of World War II and the acceptance of the navy as the city's dominant economic institution altered permanently Norfolk's belief in its ability to care for its own need. Unlike many Southern cities that shunned federal assistance for urban renewal in order to maintain local autonomy, postwar Norfolk performed an about-face and went after all it could get. The assumption of local political control by "progressive" business interests intent upon using every means to further the city's development explains, in part, the change in attitude toward federal assistance in the post-World War II era. Yet three decades of reliance on the military for urban sustenance also had convinced city boosters of the advantages of being a ward of the federal government and of the limits of their entrepreneurial talents in nonmilitary endeavors. As the following assessment will demonstrate, the confluence of city and sword in Norfolk between the world wars witnessed the gradual but steady emergence of city-federal interdependency in forging the modern metropolis.[6]

Although Norfolk had served the navy since the early nineteenth century through shipbuilding and repair work at its federal navy yard, the idea of accommodating a major base of naval operations must be traced to the aftermath of the 1907 exposition. Predictably, the idea grew out of a real estate scheme. Even before the exposition halls closed, a local developer, Theodore J. Wool, proposed to sell the 340-acre Jamestown Exposition site to the government to establish a navy base in Norfolk. He succeeded in getting Congress to consider a bill for purchase of the site during its 1908 session. President Roosevelt favored the bill but supplied no active support to the proposal. Furthermore, the $1 million asking price was well beyond what the government was willing to pay for land it had no immediate plans to use. Senator Eugene Hale of Maine, chairman of the Senate Naval Affairs Committee, indicated that a new coaling ship was more essential than a parcel of land. In the meantime, Wool formed the Fidelity Land and Investment Corporation, purchased the property for $235,000, and resumed his lobbying campaign in Washington. By enlisting support from the Norfolk Chamber of Commerce, Wool managed to get the bill reintroduced in 1909 but, as in the previous session, engendered little enthusiasm. The outbreak of war in Europe in 1914 and, more important, the appointment of North Carolinian Josephus Daniels as secretary of the navy under President Woodrow Wilson gave Wool renewed optimism in his speculative scheme.[7]

Selling Norfolk to the navy broadened into a city promotional campaign by 1915. The city's chamber of commerce formed a Naval Affairs Committee to pressure Washington for improvements at the navy yard and, with the assistance of Wool, used its political leverage to press for acquisition of the exposition grounds. In a November 1913 meeting with a Norfolk delegation in Washington, Daniels "expressed his cordial interest in the development of the Navy yard" at Norfolk. Less than two weeks later, Daniels was given a dinner in his honor at Norfolk to demonstrate the city's appreciation for its naval connections. Again in 1915 Daniels assured a contingent from the chamber that Norfolk "was the only place for the location of the dry dock" being proposed for the Atlantic region but gave no support to the idea of establishing a full-fledged base on the exposition site. Late in 1916

the secretary and members of the House Naval Affairs Committee
were persuaded to visit Norfolk to tour the navy yard but also to
examine the exposition site firsthand. While still impressed with the
need for expanded dry dock facilities at the navy yard, Daniels told
Norfolk's delegation, headed by Senators Thomas S. Martin and
Claude Swanson and Wool, that purchase of the waterfront site, at a
price that had risen to $1.5 million, was out of the question. "Gentle-
men," Daniels stated during the interview, "we do not need such a
base."[8]

Yet through vigorous behind-the-scenes lobbying by Swanson,
aimed particularly at the navy's strategists but gradually filtering
up to Daniels, interest in establishing a base in Norfolk was nurtured.
Since 1911, according to historian Henry Ferrell, Jr., Virginia's
junior senator had "centered his attention upon the naval affairs committee" as a way to curry political advantage from the Tidewater
area. Swanson essentially ran the committee, as South Carolina
Senator Benjamin Tillman's health failed during the war years. The
first dividends were reaped when the Roosevelt board report of
October 1915 mentioned the strategic importance of Norfolk. A
follow-up study of naval needs in 1916, conducted by Captain Josiah S.
McKean, reiterated the strategic arguments favoring acquisition of
the exposition site. The Norfolk base could serve as the primary
submarine base for the Atlantic, as a refueling and supply point for
the fleet, and as a training facility for new recruits. Its superb
harbor, deep channel, and mid-Atlantic location all reinforced Norfolk's strategic importance. Thus when Daniels insisted late in 1916
that there was no need for a Norfolk naval base (even after his requested study of the Norfolk site produced an unequivocal mandate
for development), it is likely that he was merely pressing Wool for
more favorable terms.[9]

This ploy was evidenced in Daniels's insistence that the land
for the base be leased rather than purchased. Nevertheless, Swanson
managed to push a bill for purchase through Congress (at a price substantially less than Wool's offer). With the imminence of U.S. involvement in World War I, President Wilson signed the bill in June 1917,
and construction of the Norfolk Naval Operating Base began immediately. Norfolk almost instantly became "the one great Battleship
Base" on the Atlantic coast.[10]

Between June 1917 and November 1918 the navy poured $7 mil-
lion into the base, mostly to fill the shallow shorelines to extend the
acreage of the base and to construct piers and aviation facilities.
Owing to severe time constraints, the navy opted for temporary
facilities with permanent buildings to be erected later. Those who
would later press for abandonment of Norfolk facilities used the cost
of replacing gerry-built World War I structures with permanent

buildings as their principal argument against further naval investments in the Tidewater city. Nevertheless, the substantial capital
investment by the navy in Norfolk between 1917 and 1921 ultimately
made abandonment impractical. When appropriations for improvements at the naval yard are included, the total federal expenditure
for naval expansion in Norfolk came to approximately $37 million by
1921. Thus Norfolk's success in luring the navy to its shores is owed
to locational advantages recognized by strategists and underscored
by local boosters and their congressional allies. Although a logical
site for naval expansion, the vigor of Norfolk's boosters supplied the
impetus for the city to capitalize on its maritime prowess.[11]

A sharp curtailment followed the boom in war-related naval
construction in Norfolk and lasted throughout the 1920s. The loss of
support from the navy secretary (once the base had been established,
Daniels, until leaving office in 1921, acted as if he had always favored
its creation) put Norfolk on the defensive. At the same time, the
Benjamin Tillman, Thomas S. Martin, and Swanson triumvirate in
the Senate, which vigorously espoused naval development in Southern
ports, fell apart after the deaths of Tillman and Martin. The first
sign of diminished Southern influence in naval affairs surfaced when
Swanson pressed for government purchase of the East Camp training
grounds in Norfolk, a site the navy had leased during the war. The
request fell on deaf ears in Republican-ruled Washington. In fact,
the Rodman Navy Yard Board report of 1923 recommended abandonment of the Hampton Roads Training Station in favor of expansion at
the Newport, Great Lakes, and San Diego facilities. The Rodman
report cited, in particular, the poor condition of Norfolk's temporary
buildings and the onerous costs entailed in modernizing them.[12]

Norfolk's business community responded quickly to this threat.
Two meetings between Navy Secretary Edwin Denby and members of
the Norfolk Chamber of Commerce's Naval Affairs Committee in
September 1923 elicited assurances that even if the training station
were removed, the Hampton Roads Naval Operating Base would
remain "the one great Battleship Base" on the Atlantic coast. Despite
Denby's contention that there would be "considerably more activity"
in Norfolk owing to anticipated expansion of the naval air station,
local boosters took nothing for granted. At home they moved to
demonstrate the city's fealty to the navy by wining and dining the
officers and men of the Atlantic Fleet in early November. At the
same time they stepped up their appeals to congressional supporters
to block the proposed transfer of the training station.[13]

Throughout the 1920s the chamber of commerce continued its
role as the liaison between the military and the city. The chamber
could be counted upon to funnel resolutions to Washington in favor of
pay increases for local officers or to the Navy Department to protest

the transfer of officials who had demonstrated a loyalty to the city. In April 1928 the chamber hosted a banquet in honor of two departing admirals, both of whom had served on the Naval Affairs Committee. It commemorated, in particular, retiring Fifth Naval District Commandant Admiral R. E. Coontz, who had helped to persuade the Navy Department to expand and make permanent the training facilities at the Norfolk base during a period of national naval retrenchment. Overall, there were four admirals, one commander, three captains, and one lieutenant who kept the chamber abreast of naval affairs in Norfolk during the interwar years.[14]

Besides local navy officers and the indomitable Swanson, Norfolk also had a strong supporter in James Byrnes, Tillman's successor from South Carolina. During the hearings on the 1923 appropriations bill, Byrnes questioned the veracity of the Rodman report's recommendations, noting that in a previous assessment of naval facilities it had been determined that Newport and Great Lakes be abandoned in favor of concentrations of training at Norfolk. He contended that Norfolk was being used to appease budget trimmers who had failed in their assault on other facilities and that the proposed removal of the Hampton Roads Training Station flew in the face of strategic considerations. Through the same sort of political maneuvering that enabled Illinois and Rhode Island to retain their naval installations, Norfolk also held on to its training station. In fact, the navy appropriations bill for 1929 included a request for $5 million to replace the temporary structures at Norfolk with permanent barracks and classrooms. It was not until Norfolk stalwart Swanson assumed the position of navy secretary, however, that the long-anticipated "permanent" improvements were realized in full.[15]

The Virginia delegation continued to work assiduously and in concert throughout the 1930s to defend Norfolk's interests. Even the most inconsequential attacks on Norfolk's naval affairs had to be challenged. In the 1932 naval appropriations bill, for example, all four training stations (Hampton Roads, San Diego, Newport, and Great Lakes) had their budgets trimmed, although Norfolk's facility was cut by only $4,000. The other three received far more drastic cuts, and as a result the Newport facility was to be closed. When Rhode Island's Senator Felix Hebert proposed that a few thousand dollars be taken from the other three training stations to maintain Newport for some future use, Virginia's Carter Glass, standing in on the naval affairs debates for the absent Swanson, vehemently objected to giving up anything from Hampton Roads to Newport. Hebert maintained that future defense needs warranted maintenance of the Rhode Island facility, especially since there was, in this view, "no harbor on the Atlantic seaboard which compares with that at Newport." Glass countered unequivocally: "The Senator needs to readjust his mind. The one at Norfolk is vastly superior to that at Newport."[16]

Moreover, the Virginia delegation continued to push for permanent improvements at the base to solidify Norfolk's naval connection. During the 1931 session, Norfolk congressman Menalcus Lankford introduced bills to acquire additional land for the Norfolk Naval Air Station, to complete barracks construction and a mess hall for the enlisted men, and to increase the anchorage grounds for navy ships. At the same time, they secured additional work for the navy yard. Modernization of two battleships, the Idaho and Mississippi, brought $24 million in work to the navy yard during the 1930s. According to historian Thomas Wertenbaker, Norfolk's marriage to the navy, however tenuous, "accounted for the comparative lightness of the impact of the depression on her life."[17]

The navy appropriations bill of January 1938 confirmed the permanency of Norfolk's role in national defense. Of the $1 billion requested for naval expansion, Congress earmarked $12 million for improvements at the Norfolk base. The plan called for repairs and improvements to the submarine base, dredging alongside the piers, construction of permanent officers' quarters and barracks, and enlargement of the Norfolk Naval Air Station. By 1940 the program of improvements included purchase of nearly 2,000 acres of additional land to enlarge the base, along with $4 million to convert the previously abandoned St. Helena Reservation to a repair yard for small vessels. Yet as Martin Schlegal observes, "Even these sums paled into insignificance beside the millions allocated to the Navy Yard for construction of warships." On July 29, 1940, and approximately 33 years after his uncle Theodore first drew attention to the strategic potential of Norfolk harbor, Franklin Roosevelt came to inspect the sprawling naval facilities. The trip signified more than obeisance to family tradition. The commander in chief's choice of Norfolk for an inspection of U.S. defenses confirmed that the city had become, as Wertenbaker put it, "the center of the modern navy." To local leaders the visit implied something more: no longer was the navy one among many factors in the city's quest for greatness. Having been frustrated in its efforts since the early 1900s to turn the city into a commercial-industrial giant, Norfolk acknowledged its role as a massive military encampment after 1940. In the process, moreover, the city became the ward of the federal government.[18]

The failure of Norfolk to build an industrial base is apparent in comparisons of its work force prior to World War I and following World War II. In 1914 approximately 14,000 were employed in local manufacturing, while work at the U.S. navy yard supplied only 3,000 jobs. By late 1945 the proportional strengths of employment in navy-related and civilian industrial sectors reversed themselves. Approximately the same number of Norfolk residents worked in manufacturing as had in 1914, but more than 21,000 were employed in military-related jobs, accounting for 25 percent of the city's civilian work force. Overall, in 1945 more than 43 percent of the total income payments in Norfolk came from naval activities.[19]

Beyond merely recasting the city's economic base, changes in city-federal relations after 1940 also exerted a substantial effect on the evolving character of public policy in Norfolk. Yet it is possible to trace the origins of these changes to the city's previous experiences as a military outpost. As early as the 1920s, the naval presence in Norfolk influenced the manner in which local government defined its responsibilities. Conditions during World War I underscored the city's inability to accommodate rapid urban growth. For one thing, Norfolk found itself unable to supply enough water to meet the demand of the navy base and, consequently, was forced to purchase additional supplies from neighboring Portsmouth. Navy Commandant F. R. Harris warned that the federal government "would cease construction and pull out" if additional water did not flow. The city council immediately appropriated funds for additional lines, and in 1920 Norfolk residents voted overwhelmingly for a bond issue to construct an enlarged system. Pressure from local boosters played a key role in making the costly improvements in the city's water supply system that the navy demanded. As early as 1917 it had been pointed out that an inadequate water supply would discourage industrial expansion. In 1920 boosters came more to the point. The Naval Affairs Committee of the chamber admonished city council that "negligence in supplying adequate water to the Norfolk Operating Base . . . could lead to withdrawal" of the navy.[20]

Expansion of the city's water system was but one facet of the public improvements package enacted in the early 1920s. Between 1918 and 1924, the city accumulated an indebtedness of more than $30 million to underwrite long-overdue public improvements throughout Norfolk but especially near the base. Extensive street paving, the addition of miles of new sewers, and construction of a new market and several schools indicated an unprecedented willingness on the part of the city to bear the costs of modernization and confidence that the wartime boom would translate into enduring prosperity. Annexation of 30 miles of new territory in 1923 officially attached the military to the municipal body. The enlarged city included the entire area encompassed by the Naval Operating Base, the East Camp (which local entrepreneurs sought to sell to the navy throughout the interwar years), and the Army Supply Base. The annexed area received an additional $2 million for improvements, affording further evidence that the city would pay to cement ties to the military.[21]

The demands generated by a more activist local government also precipitated a movement for administrative reform in Norfolk. Soon after Washington announced its plans to establish the fleet base at Norfolk in June 1917, city voters overwhelmingly approved a charter change to institute a city manager, five-member city council form of government. Norfolk's move to put city administration on a more businesslike footing stemmed from a local reform campaign initiated in 1915. Local boosters believed that a modernized government would enhance the city's chances of luring new business. In this sense, government reform emerged from urban development initiatives that proved successful in luring the navy to Norfolk. Moreover, it was Norfolk's chamber of commerce that guided the charter reform movement while tenaciously pursuing naval investments through establishment of a fleet base. Although the city manager became the city's official mouthpiece on naval affairs after 1918, he acted in concert with Norfolk's leading business interests.[22]

At the same time, the inauguration of the new governmental structure ensured proponents of urban growth a stronger voice in the city's affairs. As noted in the Norfolk Virginian-Pilot in the mid-1920s: "The first six years of the life of the present form of city government saw more changes in municipal affairs than had, perhaps, taken place in any quarter of a century prior to that time." Most important, it marked city government's "participation in public affairs on a scale unprecedented in municipal life."[23]

Naval-induced expansion of the city also compelled local leaders to take a more serious posture toward planning. As in the case of public improvements, the original impetus for stronger planning control on urban development flowed directly from local boosterism. In 1917 civil and business interests formed a Beautifying Commission to function as the city's unofficial planning body. The majority of the 25 members favored what they referred to as a visionary type of planning as distinguished from the purely pragmatic concerns of patching up the city's capital structure. The visionary types who regarded their approach as "real city planning" maintained that a carefully planned Norfolk could become "the most beautiful city between Detroit and Savannah." Yet when the revised charter of 1918 relegated planning responsibilities to the city's director of public works, in consultation with two citizen advisers, it ensured that the visionary approach would remain subservient to the more limited goal of charting public improvement. The "city beautiful" impulses that sought to refashion a drab little city into a spectacular metropolis failed to hold sway in local policy decisions.[24]

Throughout the 1920s and 1930s, the planning commission concentrated on guiding city expansion, enacting regulations to protect property affected by annexation and changing land uses, and providing guidance to downtown development so that economic expansion would "be as little restricted as possible." In 1923 the city hired the Technical Advisory Corporation to draw up a master plan for a system of street and highway development, playgrounds and parks, and zoning, all of which were deemed "necessary for the proper future growth of Norfolk City." Yet after paying $30,000 for the plan, city council decided that the cost of having it printed for public scrutiny was wasteful. Consequently, the plan was never acted upon. As in numerous cities during the 1920s, Norfolk's planning process failed to produce a "working" blueprint for community improvement but instead amounted to an innocuous exercise in outlining a new city form. The limits of local planning would not be acknowledged until much later, however. According to a member of Norfolk's planning commission in the mid-1950s, "It was not until the end of World War II that the citizens of Norfolk realized the need for an overall planning program to assist and integrate the physical, social, and economic factors of the community."[25] Most important, it was the wartime experience, and the demands of a burgeoning martial metropolis, that spurred a conscientious urban planning effort after 1945.

The refusal of city council to release the master plan in the mid-1920s coincided with a sudden cessation of publicly backed improvement initiatives. The apparent halt in naval expansion, coupled with a sharp downturn in economic growth, engendered a move toward retrenchment in public expenditures. Although Norfolk remained an active port throughout the decade, owing to increases in import and export business, the expectations of a boom remained unfulfilled. Even though the city added 30,000 new residents when it annexed the periphery in 1923, the official population growth for the decade amounted to only 14,000. The 1930s witnessed a continuation of sluggish population growth. Not until after 1940 did Norfolk experience the long-awaited takeoff that pushed its population above the 200,000 mark.[26]

The poignant sign of urban stagnation in the interwar years was the depressed state of the local real estate market. Owing in large measure to the inability of the navy to sustain the wartime level of demand for housing, real estate values in Norfolk and adjacent areas plunged during the 1920s. The conversion of 1,000 government-owned homes to private ownership in the early 1920s compounded the vacancy problem. By 1929 housing values sank to approximately 50 percent of their peak in 1920. Conditions became still worse in 1931 following transfer of a major part of the Atlantic Fleet to the West Coast, an exodus that led to the vacating of approximately 800 units by navy officers. Not only were few new structures built during the 1920s, but those that had been constructed prior to World War I were poorly maintained. Consequently, housing blight, a problem that had been highlighted by the rapid mobilization of Norfolk during World War I, became even more acute in the interwar years. Lacking any local programs to foster upgrading, the only alternative was to tear down those structures that became uninhabitable. In fact, between 1932 and 1936 demolitions greatly exceeded new housing construction in Norfolk. The bulk of new houses built were for middle-class occupants. Virtually no new units for renters were constructed.[27]

Efforts to alleviate the city's housing crisis, and at the same time address growing unemployment, reinforced ties between the navy and the city during the depression years. As early as October 1930 the navy agreed to begin construction of new barracks at the base to assist in alleviating rising unemployment. In September 1933 an attorney representing local landowners forwarded a proposal to Navy Secretary Swanson for construction of a major highway connecting the center city and the navy installations. The project's intent went beyond merely improving accessibility to and from the navy base, however. It would provide a much needed source of employment and, through careful zoning, increase the supply of prime commercial and industrial land. The proposal called for the designation of two "free port zones" along its path, which could serve as a powerful allurement to new businesses. The landowners were willing to donate the right-of-way for the highway to secure the free port designation. It was evident that those who had speculated in land near the base saw the project as a way to recoup losses sustained during the depressed 1920s. Although local navy officials lent support to the proposal, Swanson refused to endorse it, maintaining that efforts such as these "should be a local matter." The attempt to link militarism with commercial expansion remained an unfulfilled dream of local entrepreneurs.[28]

This was not the first time that the city had called upon the federal government, through its naval connections, to address what most cities regarded as a local problem. During World War I, Norfolk's business leaders, under the auspices of the chamber of commerce and the Board of Trade, solicited federal assistance to undertake a $9 million housing effort in Norfolk and Portsmouth. Not until early in October 1918, just one month prior to the armistice, did construction begin on government housing projects aimed at supplying approximately 4,000 new units. The planned neighborhood of Glenwood—a carefully designed blend of detached, semidetached, and row houses along with a town square, a boulevard, and ample open spaces—was to be built adjacent to the navy base. Almost immediately after ground was broken on the first units, the war ended and Norfolk's only United States Housing Corporation project was scrapped. Had it been built, it would have added further to the interwar housing glut.[29]

When concern over housing resurfaced during the military buildup in the late 1930s, it was the navy that urged an aggressive housing and slum clearance initiative in the face of stiff local opposition. Nearly two decades of depressed housing conditions made local leaders hesitant to support any sudden spurt of government-built housing. Admiral Manley Simons, commandant of the Norfolk Navy Yard, maintained that existing housing resources could not accommodate his enlarged work force. By early 1939 employment at the navy yard was up to 6,500 (a threefold increase over the level of employment in the 1920s), and by the end of the year it had grown to over 11,000. Discouraged by local inertia, Simons took the housing matter into his own hands. Using navy funds, he planned and built a neighborhood development adjacent to the yard the following year.[30]

It was the commandant of the Naval Operating Base in Norfolk, Admiral J. K. Taussig, who voiced the loudest criticism of the growing housing problem and the city's refusal to participate in the federal public housing program as a way to alleviate it. Throughout 1939 Taussig made numerous public statements urging Norfolk to establish a local housing authority. When city council followed the advice of local real estate interests and voted against such a move in June 1940, Taussig stepped up his public indictment and accused Norfolk of attempting to sabotage the defense effort. While stung by the admiral's implied charge of treason, the argument that public housing was a defense measure enabled the council to reverse itself just one month later and vote unanimously to create the Norfolk Housing Authority. Navy support had supplied the critical backing that those in Norfolk who desired improvement in housing conditions through slum clearance and public housing construction had lacked previously.[31]

Taussig went one step further. While lending support for Norfolk's application to Washington for public housing funds, Taussig secured, within a few weeks, additional assistance from the navy's Bureau of Yards and Docks for construction of 50 homes for enlisted men inside the base. By mid-October 1940, even before the Norfolk Housing Authority broke ground for the Merrimack public housing project, Taussig's housing was ready for occupancy.[32]

The need to confront Norfolk's depressed housing conditions owed to more than the anticipated wartime emergency. The 1940 census revealed serious deficiencies in local housing that had plagued the city since World War I but that had gone unaddressed during the interwar years. The military buildup after 1938 exacerbated the crisis. It produced a dramatic decline in housing vacancy, which by 1940 amounted to only 3 percent of the combined sales and rental stock. Surprisingly, the census takers rated only 6.1 percent of the city's housing units as overcrowded. As to its physical state, however,

the census revealed that much of Norfolk's housing failed to meet
even minimal quality standards. Almost 20 percent needed major
repairs; 34 percent lacked a private bath; and over 40 percent had
been built prior to World War I. Additionally, owners occupied a
mere 28 percent of the city's housing. Progressive business leaders
who favored public action to address the housing crisis recognized
the value of obliterating all signs that Norfolk was a backward port
city. Since the early 1920s, however, they had been stymied by a
resurgence of conservative impulses in city council. The pressures
of the naval buildup and an impending war supplied the leverage necessary to overcome the city's intransigence and to allow experimentation in publicly backed housing efforts. [33]

It should be noted, however, that the experience of the depression era, along with increased dependency on federal military spending, had begun to make Norfolk less dogmatic in its self-reliance
prior to 1940. In the 1930s the city looked for the first time to the
federal government for assistance beyond that engendered by wartime
exigencies. Construction of a bridge over the Lafayette River supplied
an essential link between the navy base, the Marine Hospital, and the
Norfolk Navy Yard and came about through federal funds secured
after vigorous lobbying by the city manager with federal officials. A
$2 million federal office building and a new municipal airport repre-
sented additional fruits of Norfolk's quest for outside assistance.
Clearly in the case of Norfolk, New Deal programs "had lasting
effects which were to be vitally important in shaping the city's development during the next two decades" by making the federal government "an ever-increasing part in the development of cities themselves." [34]

Yet even as Norfolk acknowledged its dependency upon the
federal government to address a range of local needs, city voters
in 1940 elected as mayor one of the standard-bearers of old-line
politics. The election of Joseph D. Wood, who would serve as mayor
throughout the war years, epitomized the city's continued commitment to the assumption that cities could, and should, shape their own
destiny. Wood opposed the New Deal and the expanded prerogatives
of the central government. Instead, he favored a local and essentially
private approach to resolving urban problems, especially in the
housing field. Yet when it came to public improvements, Wood evidenced a willingness to substitute federal funds for scarce city funds
on a limited basis. For one thing, he actively supported a plan to
employ federal funds in the construction of a combination of bridge
and tunnel between Norfolk and Portsmouth and reluctantly endorsed
federal support for a new city auditorium.

Moreover, the war experience awakened Wood to the importance of a more vigorous local planning agency. The mayor supported

a resolution to reorganize the "old Planning Commission which does not function" and to equip it with a professional staff, but he balked at a move, supported by Norfolk's progressive business interests, to raise planning to a functional level in city government. Wood's partial conversion to the planning persuasion did not constitute a shift to liberalism per se but merely to recognition that postwar Norfolk would no longer be able to rely on its traditional ad hoc methods of framing public policy. Wood left office in 1944 still firmly wedded to the view that "a super Santa Claus in Washington" was nothing short of "Un-American."[35]

Nevertheless, it was during Wood's tenure that the Norfolk Housing Authority moved decisively to meet the navy's demand for additional housing and that the city nurtured its links to federal assistance that would dominate the postwar era. By October 1940 the housing authority had under way its housing program, which resulted in the construction of more than 3,000 units by 1945. Through the combined initiative of Admiral Taussig and successor Manley Simons, the Norfolk Housing Authority, and the backers of a greater Norfolk, a planning effort had been set in motion that "would work permanent changes in the face and outlook of the city." (See Table 1.) As John Bauman noted in his study of Philadelphia during World War II, the experiences of the war solidified those forces seeking to restructure the center city to combat the problems of slums and provide space for expansion of the central business district. In Norfolk a similar coalition emerged victorious in the 1946 city council election and would preside over city policy direction for the next three decades. It was early in the 1960s that the city boasted proudly that after 1946 there was never a single negative vote in council when proposals for the federal urban renewal and related public improvements initiatives came up for consideration. A political consensus had emerged to guide Norfolk into an era of increased city-federal interdependency.[36]

To supply direction to public policy initiatives the city's new leadership sought two key objectives: to strengthen Norfolk's planning function and to explore the potential of consolidating the Tidewater communities, most of which had federal connections through the military pipeline, into a single metropolis with Norfolk as its core. Creation of a new city planning commission in 1946 under the sponsorship of Norfolk's progressive political leaders aimed at supplying guidance to urban development that had been absent during the war years. The planning commission was enlarged from three to five members and given a broader mandate to counter growing criticism over its ineffectiveness. Change was not wholesale, however. Whit P. Tunstall, one of the original three members of the commission in 1919, continued in his role as chairman. Nevertheless, the reorganized

TABLE 1

Housing Developments during World War II:
Norfolk, Portsmouth, and Norfolk County

	White	Black
Public		
Number of projects	12	5
Number of units occupied	9,882	2,219
Apartments	2,323	666
Houses	4,399	750
Temporary units	3,154	803
Constructed		
1941 or before	360	0
1942	2,561	179
1943 or later	7,065	2,170
Private		
Number of projects	24	4
Number of units programmed	3,369	483
Constructed		
1941 or before	1,371	188
1942	270	0
1943 or later	1,728	295

Source: Charles F. Marsh, ed., The Hampton Roads
Communities in World War II (Chapel Hill: University of
North Carolina Press, 1951), p. 129.

planning commission formulated a revised agenda that incorporated
a broadened set of urban concerns, including a civic and cultural
center; a major highway plan; a housing strategy; recreation, park,
and school improvements; a plan for transportation and local transit;
and a scheme for capital expenditures. Yet the most pressing problem was the lack of space for industrial expansion. Since 1940, the
planners noted, the federal government had acquired 1,334 acres of
land for enlargement of the navy base, of which 599 acres had been

zoned for heavy industry. To develop a more diversified economic base, annexation of the periphery was critical. In March 1948 the planning commission hired a consulting firm to conduct a land-use survey as the basis for future annexation, noting that even the most cursory examination of land availability in Norfolk "showed little space for industrial development because of Navy acquisitions." Evidently, accommodating the navy made planning for urban expansion a significant concern in postwar Norfolk.[37]

Norfolk's new leadership also seriously explored the idea of consolidating the Hampton Roads communities into a single urban entity. The Lower Peninsula Planning Commission (LPPC), formed in 1944, grew out of the wartime necessity for coordinated planning among Tidewater localities, but it was envisioned by Norfolk as an instrument to consolidate its hold over the region. There was reason for Norfolk to be concerned about the rivalry engendered by the various Tidewater communities who were pursuing development independently. Portsmouth maintained its independence largely on the strength of the Norfolk Navy Yard but kept relatively close ties with its neighbor Norfolk. On the other hand, Newport News and Hampton posed a far greater challenge to Norfolk's continued dominance. Although Norfolk usually backed proposals for naval construction and repair work at the Newport News Shipbuilding and Drydock Company, it gave first preference to the Norfolk Navy Yard when it came to choosing between local vendors. Evidence of Newport News's threat to Norfolk was its sharp increase in shipping during the war, which reduced Norfolk's share from 72.5 percent in 1939 to 64.9 percent in 1946. As a company town dominated by Colis Huntington's shipbuilding concern and the Chesapeake and Ohio Railroad, Newport News complemented but did not seriously rival Norfolk prior to 1940. In fact, between 1900 and 1930 Newport News increasingly fell further behind Norfolk in population growth. World War II brought a boom to Newport News as significant as that in Norfolk, however. During the war, the Newport News Shipbuilding and Drydock Company turned out 49 new navy vessels and made repairs on or refitted an additional 1,497 crafts. At its peak in 1943, the shipbuilding concern employed over 30,000 workers.[38]

The prosperity of the war years and the continued military presence after the war nurtured Newport News's quest for metropolitan status independent of Norfolk. When the Lower Peninsula Planning Commission released its proposal for consolidating Tidewater communities in 1950, Norfolk was left out of the scheme. The plan called for merging Warwick, Newport News, Hampton, Elizabeth City County, and Phoebus into a single city. Although the plan failed to receive the necessary approval of the localities involved, mergers did occur during the 1950s. In 1958 Newport News and Warwick consolidated into a greater Newport News. Hampton, Elizabeth City, and Phoebus formed themselves into a greater Hampton. As a result Norfolk found itself surrounded by rival military cities intent on and capable of maintaining their independence from Norfolk. Hemmed in by its rivals, Norfolk looked to urban redevelopment as a way to promote growth and sustain the level of prosperity engendered by the war.[39]

Having secured not only a political consensus favoring active solicitation of federal funds to underwrite the costs of urban improvements but also assurances that the war boom in military facilities would form a permanent economic foundation, Norfolk sought to complete the process of modernization initiated after World War I. The navy's decision to retain Norfolk as the base of the Atlantic Fleet ensured, as a postwar economic analysis suggested, "a comparatively high level [of Navy activity] as compared with the pre-war period." Yet, as the report went on to note, military expansion in the Norfolk area failed to generate economic spin-offs as it had elsewhere.

> There is evidence that only a limited relationship has developed so far to create new enterprises and employment in the non-military industrial economy. It is true that large quantities of supplies have been purchased locally, particularly for the feeding and maintenance of personnel, and that heavy volumes of local retail goods and services have been purchased both officially by the military institutions and individually by military and civilian workers and their families. However, the military in the area does not constitute a major primary "industry" that has generated behind it a wide variety of secondary and tertiary industries comparable to what is found in most large metropolitan regions.[40]

Yet at the same time, naval presence exacted a high price in terms of city resources. As in the post-World War I era, Norfolk found itself after 1945 trying to catch up with neglected urban improvements. Between 1946 and 1956, for example, Norfolk expended $107 million to upgrade its infrastructure. Creation of a port authority was seen as a way to foster economic activity along the city's underused waterfront. Nevertheless, as City Manager Charles A. Harrell observed in testimony on federal housing legislation in 1951, the navy consigned one fifth of Norfolk's land area to a nontaxable status while contributing significantly to increased demands for housing, schools, new streets, and sewers and demanding fire, police, health, and recreational services. "All of us recognize the importance of

the military in our community life. . . . In the over-all, it is a
distinct advantage to the community to be host of such an organization," Harrell noted. Because of its naval connections, however,
Norfolk could survive and prosper only through increased federal
assistance in coping with various local public responsibilities. To
be a keeper of the nation's defense, Norfolk required the full backing
deserved by a ward of the federal government. As Harrell's testi-
mony acknowledged, unlike most Southern cities in the early postwar
period, Norfolk willingly accepted its dependency on a higher authority in return for assistance in forging a modern metropolis. Through
the confluence of war and a quest for urban greatness, Norfolk molded
itself into a model of the evolving federal city of the New South.[41]

Ironically, Norfolk's dreams of greatness led to ever-increasing
dependency. In order to best its urban rivals and to throw off or at
least loosen the control of outside cities like New York, Norfolk had
to accept a colonial connection to the federal government itself.
Within the rapidly urbanizing Tidewater region, Norfolk was forced
to accept equality with, rather than superiority over, its urban rivals,
all of whom also drew sustenance from the military wellspring. Still,
Norfolk's dependency on the navy was not unilateral. The city helped
to shape the distribution of federal resources, lent strength to the
drive for rearmament, and would lend unflagging support to the continuing necessity to maintain a high level of military spending. In
return, Norfolk secured a recession-proof, if not a dynamic, economic base capable of sustaining the desired growth of the city. The
dependence was mutual. The federal government secured an unequivocal proponent of militarism. Norfolk filled a deep void in its quest
for metropolitan greatness through its expansive naval pipeline. In
one sense the failure of local boosters to succeed in their full range
of objectives necessitated reliance on its military connections. On
the other hand, the emergence of Norfolk as a prototype of the martial metropolis underscores how closely wedded the needs of defense
and the politics of urban growth became in twentieth century America.

NOTES

1. Norfolk Navy Yard, Guide and Brief Historical Sketch
(Norfolk, Va.: Norfolk Navy Yard, 1928); Clare Beverley Whitehead,
History of the Norfolk Navy Yard (Norfolk, Va.: Methodist, 1942);
Charles F. Marsh, ed., The Hampton Roads Communities in World
War II (Chapel Hill: University of North Carolina Press, 1951). For
a persuasive discussion of the relationship between military develop-
ment and urban rivalry, see Roger W. Lotchin, "The City and the
Sword: San Francisco and the Rise of the Metropolitan-Military

Complex, 1919-1941," Journal of American History 65 (March 1979): 996-1020. Also see Jonathan J. Wolfe, "Virginia in World War II" (Ph.D. diss., University of Virginia, 1971).

2. Thomas Jefferson Wertenbaker, Norfolk: Historic Southern Port, 2d ed. (Durham, N.C.: Duke University Press, 1962), pp. 278-85; The Story of Norfolk: City of Great Opportunities (Norfolk, Va.: Norfolk Board of Trade, 1908); Whitehead, Norfolk Navy Yard.

3. Carl Abbott, Kenneth Galchus, Norman Pollack, and Raymond Rosenfeld, The Evolution of an Urban Neighborhood: Colonial Place, Norfolk, Virginia (Charlottesville: University of Virginia Institute of Government, 1975), p. 3; Theodore A. Curtin, "A Marriage of Convenience: Norfolk and the Navy, 1917-1967" (Master's thesis, Old Dominion University, 1969), pp. 10-11; Wertenbaker, Norfolk, pp. 296-98; U.S. Naval Station, Norfolk, Postscripts Jamestown Exposition, 1907 (Norfolk, Va.: Naval Station Library, 1957); Carl Abbott, "Norfolk in the New Century: The Jamestown Expository and Urban Boosterism," Virginia Magazine of History and Biography 85 (January 1977): 86-96.

4. U.S., House of Representatives, Naval Affairs Committee, Sundry Legislation affecting the Naval Establishment, 1921 (Washington, D.C.: Government Printing Office, 1924).

5. Naval Affairs Committee, Hearings, 1921 Naval Appropriations Bill (Washington, D.C.: Government Printing Office, 1921), pp. 1065-66.

6. For an assessment of evolving city-federal relations beginning with the 1930s, see Mark I. Gelfand, A Nation of Cities: The Federal Government and Urban America, 1933-1965 (New York: Oxford University Press, 1975); Philip J. Funigiello, The Challenge to Urban Liberalism: Federal-City Relations during World War II (Knoxville: University of Tennessee Press, 1978).

7. W. H. T. Squires, "Norfolk in Bygone Days," Norfolk Ledger-Dispatch, November 11, 1937; Curtin, "A Marriage of Convenience," p. 13. The Norfolk Chamber of Commerce set out early in Daniels's tenure to curry his favor. A dinner in honor of Daniels and the new navy yard commandant on November 20, 1913, sought to demonstrate local appreciation of its ties to the navy; see Executive Committee Minutes, Norfolk Chamber of Commerce, October 29, November 11, 1913, Library, Norfolk Chamber of Commerce.

8. Curtin, "A Marriage of Convenience," pp. 19, 32; W. H. T. Squires, "The Navy and Norfolk," Known Norfolk, Virginia 6 (August 1944): 61; Henry C. Ferrell, Jr., "Regional Rivalries, Congress, and MIC: The Norfolk and Charleston Navy Yards, 1913-20," in War, Business, and American Society: Historical Perspectives on the Military-Industrial Complex, ed. Benjamin Franklin Cooling (Port Washington, N.Y.: Kennikat, 1977), p. 95; Executive Committee

Minutes, Norfolk Chamber of Commerce, November 11, 1911; ibid.,
February 7, 1914; ibid., September 14, 17, 1915.

9. Board for the Development of Navy Plans to the Navy Department, June 27, 1916, Josephus Daniels Papers, Library of Congress; Robert G. Albion, Makers of Naval Policy, 1798-1947 (Annapolis, Md.: U.S. Naval Institute, 1980), p. 149; Ferrell, "Regional Rivalries," p. 67; idem, "Claude A. Swanson of Virginia" (Ph.D. diss., University of Virginia, 1964), pp. 265-67.

10. Curtin, "A Marriage of Convenience," p. 34: The Fidelity Land Corporation received only $367,194 for its land. The total area taken was 474 acres, which included not only the old exposition grounds but the Pine Beach area. The latter tract had been the focus of unsuccessful resort development ventures since the 1870s, the last of these being a resort for blacks in the decade following the exposition. See U.S., Department of the Navy, Report of the Board Covering Valuation of Site for Naval Operating Base, Hampton Roads, Virginia (Washington, D.C.: Government Printing Office, 1918), pp. 5-30.

11. U.S., House of Representatives, Naval Affairs Committee, Hearings, Estimates Submitted by the Secretary of the Navy, 1919 (Washington, D.C.: Government Printing Office, 1919), p. 472; idem, Hearings, Naval Appropriations Bill, 1922 (Washington, D.C.: Government Printing Office, 1921), p. 315.

12. Naval Affairs Committee, Hearings, Estimates Submitted by the Secretary of the Navy, 1920 (Washington, D.C.: Government Printing Office, 1920), pp. 1045-73; idem, Hearings, Naval Appropriations Bill, 1925 (Washington, D.C.: Government Printing Office, 1924), pp. 207, 272-79. Apart from a copy of the navy yard plan of 1916, there is no evidence in the Daniels papers that he considered the Norfolk base essential until 1917. The first and only reference to it in his diary came on the heels of congressional consideration of the appropriation for purchase in May 1917; see E. David Cronon, ed., The Secret Diaries of Josephus Daniels, 1913-1921 (Lincoln: University of Nebraska Press, 1963), pp. 145, 162-63.

13. Executive Committee Minutes, Norfolk Chamber of Commerce, February 7, October 23, November 30, December 6, 1923; ibid., January 4, February 19, 1924.

14. Ibid., March 23, April 6, June 1, 1928.

15. U.S., House of Representatives, Naval Affairs Committee, Hearings, Naval Appropriations Bill, 1925, pp. 242, 250-57; idem, Hearings, Naval Appropriations Bill, 1929 (Washington, D.C.: Government Printing Office, 1928), p. 268. Throughout the late 1920s, Norfolk continued to cultivate strong ties with local navy officials through the energetic lobbying of the chamber of commerce. When the navy began to shift its fleet to the Pacific, Norfolk considered a

formal protest but abandoned it because "Chinese/Japanese disturbances" made it "inadvisable at this time." See Executive Committee Minutes, Norfolk Chamber of Commerce, April 6, May 7, June 1, 1928. According to W. H. T. Squires, the Norfolk Association of Commerce, the Norfolk Advertising Board, and other civic groups under the leadership of Thomas P. Thompson, later Norfolk's city manager, fought successfully to retain the Norfolk base in the late 1920s. See Squires, "The Navy and Norfolk," p. 61.

16. U.S., Congress, House, Congressional Record, 72d Cong., sess., 1931/32, pt. : 13139–40.

17. Ibid., H.Rept. 438; ibid., H.Rept. 439; ibid., H.Rept. 2925; Norfolk Virginian-Pilot, January 1, 1931; Wertenbaker, Norfolk, p. 329.

18. Norfolk Virginian-Pilot, January 1, 1939; ibid., July 30, 1940; Marvin W. Schlegal, Conscripted City: Norfolk in World War II (Norfolk, Va.: War History Commission, 1951), pp. 40–41; Memorandum, February 17, 1941, NA 8/NI-13, General Correspondence, U.S. Secretary of the Navy, National Archives.

19. Norfolk Industrial Commission, The Sunrise City by the Sea (Norfolk, Va.: Board of Commerce and Industry, 1914); James Bertram Haugh, Power and Influence in a Southern City (Washington, D.C.: University Press of America, 1980), pp. 17-18; Lorin Thompson, An Economic Summary and Analysis of Norfolk, Virginia (Charlottesville: Bureau of Population and Economic Research, University of Virginia, 1947), p. 4.

20. Norfolk Virginian-Pilot, March 21, October 11, 1917; ibid., March 6, 9, 1918; ibid., February 25, 1920; U.S., Naval Affairs Committee, Hearings, 1920, pp. 1015–44; Executive Committee Minutes, Norfolk Chamber of Commerce, February 2, 1920.

21. Norfolk Virginian-Pilot, January 1, 1925; Walter H. Taylor III, "Planning for the City of Norfolk—Past, Present, Future," October 1943, in Minutes of the City Planning Commission, Department of Planning and Community Development, Norfolk, Virginia.

22. Norfolk Virginian-Pilot, November 21, 1917; Executive Committee minutes, Norfolk Chamber of Commerce, June 1, August 21, 1915; Bureau of Municipal Research, Norfolk, Virginia: Report on a Survey of the City Government (Norfolk, Va.: H. B. Vessey, 1915).

23. Norfolk Virginian-Pilot, January 1, 1925.

24. Ibid., March 1, 7, 20, April 3, 23, October 2, 1917; Executive Committee Minutes, Norfolk Chamber of Commerce, August 11, 1924.

25. Technical Advisory Corporation, Master Plan for Norfolk, Virginia (unpublished maps, 1923); Taylor, "Planning for the City of

Norfolk"; Minutes, City Planning Commission, 1922-1924; "Your
Planning Commission," Norfolk 19 (August-September 1954): 7-9.

26. See Wertenbaker, Norfolk, pp. 318-27. Frustration with
the failure of the military to sustain economic growth compelled city
council, in a 1924 pamphlet, to warn against future reliance on the
military. It referred to the military as a "government pap which has
proved none too nourishing food in the past" and rebuked the city's
role as "a government maintained Navy resort." The impetus for
the pamphlet was the attempt by the navy to disband the training station along with the gradual transfer of the fleet to the Pacific; see
Norfolk City Council, The City of Norfolk (Norfolk, Va.: Keyser-
Doherty, 1924), p. 6. Norfolk's city population totaled 46,624 in
1900; 67,453 in 1910; 115,777 in 1920; 129,710 in 1930; 144,332 in
1940; and 213,513 in 1950; see Statistical Data about Norfolk, Virginia (Norfolk, Va.: Norfolk Chamber of Commerce, 1953), p. 1.

27. Memorandum, Highlights of Special Summary Survey of
Norfolk and Portsmouth, Virginia, July 9, 1937, Record Group 195,
Home Owners Loan Corporation City Survey File, 1935-1940, National Archives. See also U.S., Bureau of Labor Statistics, The
Impact of War on the Hampton Roads Area (Washington, D.C.: Government Printing Office, 1944), which includes data on World War I,
interwar, and World War II eras.

28. Secretary of the Navy to Manalcus Lankford, October 27,
1930, NB2/L8-3(11), Box 3123, Office of the Secretary of the Navy,
General Correspondence, National Archives; Minton W. Talbot to
Claude A. Swanson, September 21, 1933, ibid.; Swanson to Rear
Admiral A. St. Clair Smith, September 11, 1933, NB2/N2, ibid.

29. Arthur Kyle Davis, Norfolk City in War Time: A Community
History (Richmond, Va.: n.p., 1925), pp. 36, 38-40; U.S., Department of Labor, Report of the United States Housing Corporation,
Vol. 2 (Washington, D.C.: Government Printing Office, 1919),
pp. 285-91.

30. Curtin, "A Marriage of Convenience," p. 103.

31. Norfolk Virginian-Pilot, June 29, July 2, 3, 10, 24, 1940;
Schlegal, Conscripted City, pp. 9-16. Concern with spreading slum
conditions in Norfolk surfaced in 1937 as a consequence of investiga-
tions carried out by Norfolk's Citizens' Committee on Crime. Yet it
was slum clearance rather than construction of public housing that
represented the thrust of local recommendations for improvements.
Pressure from Taussig to pursue public housing construction temporarily diverted city leaders from slum clearance, although efforts
after the war concentrated on this approach to urban revitalization.
See Norfolk Housing Authority, This Is It (Norfolk, Va.: NHA, 1946),
pp. 3-6.

32. Norfolk Virginian-Pilot, August 8, 1940; U.S. Navy Department, Building the Navy's Bases in World War II, I (Washington, D.C.: Government Printing Office, 1947), p. 372. Simon took up the gauntlet in 1941 when he replaced Taussig as commandant of the Fifth Naval District and rebuked publicly local real estate interests for failing to meet the navy's critical defense needs in the housing area. See Schlegal, Conscripted City, p. 83; Norfolk Virginian-Pilot, November 7, 1941.

33. See Marsh, Hampton Roads Communities; Hampton Roads Regional Defense Council, Housing and Population Report, November 21, 1941, Housing Series #2 (Norfolk, Va.: HRRDC, 1941).

34. Wertenbaker, Norfolk, pp. 333–43.

35. Joseph Wood to Admiral Manley Simon, October 8, 1941; Wood to J. F. Taussig, February 13, 1942; Wood to Representative Winder R. Harris, March 17, 1942; Wood to Garlon W. Johnson, April 10, 1942; Wood to George S. Mooney, July 13, 1943; Wood to Dr. J. W. Reed, July 29, 1943; Wood to Albert James, January 12, 1944; Undated Memorandum by Wood; Resolution from W. S. Harney, Norfolk Association of Commerce, to Wood, January 26, 1944, favoring expansion of the City Planning Commission into a department of city government and solicitation of funds from the federal government to support planning—all in Joseph Downing Wood Papers, Miscellaneous Correspondence, Old Dominion University Library, Norfolk, Virginia. Also see Carl Abbott, The New Urban America (Chapel Hill: University of North Carolina Press, 1981), p. 113.

36. Curtin, "A Marriage of Convenience," p. 110; Norfolk Housing Authority, This Is It, pp. 7–9; John F. Bauman, "Visions of a Post-War City: A Perspective on Urban Planning in Philadelphia and the Nation, 1942-1945," Urbanism: Past and Present 6 (Winter-Spring 1981): 2. For a brief assessment of postwar urban renewal and public improvement ventures, see Norfolk City Manager, The Norfolk Story, Annual Report for 1949-1950 (Norfolk, Va.: 1951); Minutes, City Planning Commission, 1946, 1947, 1948, 1949; Norfolk Chamber of Commerce, Statistical Data about Norfolk, Virginia.

37. Norfolk City Planning Commission, Minutes, February 11, 1946; ibid., October 9, 1947; ibid., March 2, 1948; ibid., January 28, September 30, 1949. Norfolk annexed 11.2 square miles in 1954 and an additional 13.5 square miles in 1955. For a discussion of annexation as a pivotal issue in postwar Norfolk politics, see Abbott, The New Urban America, pp. 173–74.

38. See Parke Rouse, Jr., Endless Harbor: The Story of Newport News (Newport News, Va.: Historical Commission, 1969); Donald Ransome Taylor, Out of the Past—The Future: A History of Hampton, Virginia (Hampton, Va.: Prestige Press, 1960).

39. Rouse, Endless Harbor, p. 75; Taylor, Out of the Past, p. 42.

40. Hammer and Company Associates, Norfolk in the Hampton Roads Economy (Washington, D.C.: HCA, 1964), pp. 57-60.

41. Norfolk City Manager, The Norfolk Story, Annual Report for 1949/50 (Norfolk, Va.: February 15, 1951); U.S., Senate, Banking and Currency Committee, Hearings, Defense Housing Act (Washington, D.C.: Government Printing Office, 1951), pp. 333-340.

6

Airplanes to Aerospace: Defense Spending and Economic Growth in the Los Angeles Region, 1945–60

Martin J. Schiesl

Few urban centers in the United States have been more influenced by federal defense expenditures than the Los Angeles region. World War II mobilization boosted the output of local aircraft companies to major proportions and made the metropolis one of the nation's leading areas of military production. This development gave Los Angeles a decided advantage in the postwar decade when planes dominated the procurement program. As a result aircraft employment became highly dependent upon fluctuations of government policy toward national security. The increasing emphasis on missiles and electronics transformed the aircraft into the aerospace industry to the extent that by the late 1950s planes were no longer the largest segment of its military business. Los Angeles's emergence as the space-age center of the American West proved to be a powerful demonstration of the impact of defense spending on the economic character and prosperity of large metropolitan regions.

The outbreak of World War II triggered a massive migration into the western United States. Seeking better employment opportunities, millions of workers flocked to defense industries in the Southwest and along the Pacific coast. California experienced the biggest growth, adding 1 million persons during the war.[1] The majority of newcomers settled in the southern portion of the state. Between 1940 and 1945 Los Angeles's population rose from 1.5 million to 1.8 million in the city and from 2.7 million to 3.4 million in the county.[2]

The aircraft industry provided the largest number of defense jobs. In 1939 aircraft manufacturing was a relatively small-scale business in the metropolis, characterized largely by skilled tradesmen numbering about 20,000. The eruption of hostilities in Europe led to Los Angeles's receiving large orders for military planes.

Douglas, Hughes, and North American opened new plants, while Lockheed enormously enlarged its Burbank facilities.[3] After Pearl Harbor brought the United States into World War II, aircraft orders greatly increased. President Franklin Delano Roosevelt called for an output of 60,000 planes a year, a large proportion of them to be built in aircraft factories on the West Coast. Los Angeles's companies shared engineering data, exchanged information on tooling and equipment, and developed assembly-line techniques and mass production. By 1943 aircraft employment totaled 243,000, representing over half of the factory workers in Los Angeles County.[4]

This rapid expansion pushed aircraft manufacturing to staggering levels. Douglas concentrated on A-20 bombers for the air corps, SBD dive-bombers for the navy, and C-54 transports. By 1945 its plants at Long Beach, Santa Monica, and El Segundo had turned out more than 20,000 planes. Lockheed built P-38 fighters, B-17 Flying Fortresses (on consignment from Boeing), and C-69 Constellation transports. In its peak year, 1943, the company produced nearly $700 million worth of aircraft out of the $10 billion in contracts let in the Los Angeles area during the war. North American built B-25 bombers, P-51 fighters, and AT-6 combat trainers. By the time peace came, it had assembled 42,683 planes, about 14 percent of all U.S. aircraft.[5]

The aviation industry emerged from the war with vastly improved production techniques and more competent administrative organization. Adjusting to peacetime status was not easy, however. Large-scale cancellation of military contracts ended over 100,000 aircraft jobs in 1945 and 1946.[6] Lockheed saw its backlog of orders drop from $417 million to $153 million, and its employment from 57,000 to 16,000. North American laid off about two thirds of its workers. Jobs were also lost in the metals and machinery industries, which supplied parts and tools to the aircraft factories.[7] This sharp reduction of employment, however, did not indicate that aircraft production was yielding its war-created position as the leading enterprise in Los Angeles. "The industry . . . is still in a young and expansive phase," two close observers of aircraft operations pointed out in 1946.

> Survival chances for Los Angeles plants . . . are good, because most of the local plants are privately owned, whereas a majority of inland plants were government-built during the war. Furthermore, the southern California climate is an advantageous factor.[8]

Developments in 1947 and 1948 confirmed this optimism. North American, Hughes, and Lockheed continued to occupy a strong

position in what was left of the military market. North American saw
its backlog of orders jump from $160 million to $380 million, and
employment from 8,000 to 22,000. The development of jet planes
absorbed most of its productive capacity. North American came up
with the B-45 bomber, the P-82 Twin Mustang fighter, a new training
plane, and the FJ-1 Fury jet fighter for the navy. Lockheed's backlog
increased from $111 million to $181 million, with corresponding effects on earnings and employment. It built F-80 Shooting Stars, P2V
Neptune patrol bombers for the navy, and TF-80 jet trainers.[9]
Hughes's facility in Culver City harbored one of the nation's most
talented groups of engineers in the field of military electronics.
Headed by Simon Ramo and Dean Wooldridge, they developed fire
and navigational control systems, airborne radar, and airborne
computers.[10]

This construction of faster and more complex planes led to a
reappraisal of governmental policy toward aviation. In July 1947
President Harry S. Truman appointed an Air Policy Commission to
study various areas of U.S. air power and make proposals for establishing an integrated national aviation program.[11] Among the aircraft leaders appearing before the commission was North American
president J. H. Kindelberger. He urged the adoption of a long-range
preparedness program that would be "strong enough to meet and
contain any potential military threat to national security." The most
important phase of this defense policy, Kindelberger contended, was
the maintenance of a healthy aircraft industry capable of expansion
in an emergency situation.[12] Similar arguments were voiced by
military officials and other aircraft executives. The commission
proposed an air force of 70 groups and 22 special squadrons, with a
total of 12,400 modern planes. It also recommended an annual procurement program of 30 to 40 million pounds of airframe weight for
maintaining an adequate level of aircraft production.[13]

The Air Policy Commission's proposals never materialized,
however. In the fall of 1948 the Truman administration cut the budgets for the military services substantially. Air Force Secretary
Stuart A. Symington proceeded to cancel nearly $300 million in
defense contracts.[14] By 1949 thousands of aircraft workers in the
Los Angeles area were looking for new jobs. The downswing at Lockheed and North American was particularly disturbing; they had been
distinctive in keeping their production facilities closely connected to
military requirements. Both companies laid off nearly a quarter of
their workers in early 1949 and operated at that reduced level, sometimes lower, for the rest of the year.[15] This slump represented a
serious vulnerability in Los Angeles's postwar economic readjustment: the tenuous relationship between national defense and employment stability. Whether such a situation meant periodic labor

dislocation depended on policies and decisions beyond the reach of the aircraft industry. Lockheed president Robert A. Gross related his company's position, which was typical of other aircraft firms: "Until such time . . . as there is adopted a long range military program, we . . . must be alert to changing volume, up or down, and be constantly ready to adapt our company insofar as possible to these changing programs."[16]

Cold war tensions ended this anxiety over defense policy. In April 1950 the National Security Council delivered a top-secret document to President Truman numbered NSC-68. Predicting continual friction with the Soviet Union and its Communist allies, the report called for a massive rearmament program to counter the Soviet global design U.S. defense analysts thought existed. The outbreak of the Korean War in June 1950 seemed to validate the premises of NSC-68. Truman and his aides believed that the Soviet Union had masterminded the North Korean attack on the Republic of South Korea; it followed that failure to intervene in the conflict would encourage Soviet aggression in other areas of the world. The Korean War provided the Truman administration with an opportunity to launch a program of military expansion as part of the U.S. global strategy for the next decade.[17] Government expenditures on artillery, combat vehicles, planes, and other military hardware shot up from $3.9 billion in 1950 to over $17 billion by 1953.[18]

This new defense spending set off a major surge of migration into southern California. Los Angeles County experienced the largest growth of any U.S. county during the Korean War, adding about 400,000 persons. Many of the newcomers were lured by the region's congenial climate and varied landscape. Economic opportunities provided the main magnet, however. Attracted by relatively higher wages and salaries, large numbers of engineers, technicians, and production workers from other states flocked to Los Angeles's defense-related industries.[19] Employment in aircraft and parts manufacturing soared from 66,000 in 1950 to 167,000 in 1953, an increase of 153 percent. Wartime demands also created thousands of new jobs in the ordnance and electrical machinery and equipment sectors. Together the aircraft, electrical machinery, and ordnance industries accounted for over one third of all manufacturing workers in the Los Angeles region.[20]

Military planes continued to be the largest segment of the metropolis's defense business. Douglas Aircraft's output was especially impressive. The late 1940s had seen the company's total sales decline from $744 million to $120 million. Korea's battlefields reversed this slump drastically. Douglas's military sales jumped from $100 million in 1950 to over $400 million in 1952, and employment from 25,000 to 62,000. It built AD Skyraiders for the navy, Boeing-

designed B-47 jet bombers, and F4D Skynights. Large orders were
also placed for C-74 and C-124 transports.[21] War contracts in 1950
and 1951 doubled Lockheed's backlog of orders from $450 million to
$900 million. It concentrated on F-94 fighters, T-33 jet trainers,
and P2V patrol bombers. By 1952 Lockheed was delivering one out
of every six military planes. North American, too, reached remarkable production levels during the Korean conflict. The company saw
its backlog increase from $311 million to $1 billion, and its employment from 18,000 to 45,000. North American produced F-86 Sabre-
jets, F-82 Twin Mustang fighters, and T-28 jet trainers.[22]

Complementing the output of military planes was the increased
emphasis on nuclear weaponry. Shortly after the United States entered the Korean conflict, President Truman appointed former Chrys-
ler Corporation president K. T. Keller to head a new office of guided
missiles in the Defense Department and to put into production any
missile showing promise of quick delivery. The Jet Propulsion Laboratory (JPL) at Pasadena met this requirement easily. Operated by
the California Institute of Technology for the Army Ordnance Corps,
the JPL housed one of the nation's ablest groups of scientists and
engineers in the missile and rocket field. They had pioneered the
first all-electronic radioguidance system in the Corporal E test
vehicle. Keller recommended the missile as a tactical weapons
project in late 1950, and the Defense Department agreed. With a
team of JPL engineers accompanying it, the Corporal was trans-
ported to the army's White Sands Proving Ground in New Mexico.
By 1952, 30 rounds had been fired, and the first stage of development
was complete. JPL personnel continued supervising the Corporal
project to actual production at the Firestone Tire & Rubber Company
in Los Angeles.[23]

The aircraft companies played a greater role in the national
missile program. Unlike their competitors in eastern metropolitan
areas, they took experimental projects as well as high-profit production awards.[24] Douglas Aircraft, with its notable engineering
talent and excellent testing sites in southern California, received
contracts from Army Ordnance, the navy, the air force, and several
large electrical firms. Its plant at Santa Monica built a multitude of
missiles during the Korean War, including the Nike Zeus. North
American's facility at Downey, California, did significant work on
rocket motors and guidance and control systems. Hughes' personnel
designed and developed numerous missiles, including the Falcon air-
to-surface missile. The company also supplied much of the electronic
equipment for planes and missiles, with deliveries rising from $8.6
million in 1950 to nearly $200 million in 1953.[25]

Such concentration of military work in the aircraft sector
aroused concern among respected observers of Los Angeles's

industrial economy. "In the event of cuts in the defense expenditures,"
the Southern California Research Council, an organization of prominent educators and businessmen, warned in 1953, "reductions of
employment in the aircraft industry would be the most serious problem facing the Los Angeles area." The Research Council urged local
industries to prepare plans for expanding civilian production to offset the effects of a defense cutback.[26] Similar concerns were voiced
at a meeting of the Southern California Planning Institute in 1954.
Two public administration analysts, discussing the impact of military
spending on the metropolis, pointed out that aircraft production accounted for 27 percent of all local manufacturing employment. Each
new defense job in aircraft plants also created two additional jobs in
supporting industries. Drawing on this information, Frank Sherwood,
professor of political science at the University of Southern California,
estimated that a 10 percent reduction in military expenditures would
eliminate 187,000 jobs in the Los Angeles region. These figures, he
noted, indicated that defense spending was the most "unstable variable" in the planning program designed to maintain economic stability.[27] Unfortunately, it was the one over which Los Angeles's civic
and industrial leaders had little, if any, control. The Research
Council, in a special report on the "strengths and weaknesses" of the
metropolitan economy, bluntly related the situation: "A continuance
of the present high level of aircraft production will be determined
more by changes in the international situation and by governmental
decisions than by any local programs."[28]

Developments in Washington confirmed these expectations.
Seeking ways to reduce the heavy military budget he had inherited
from the Korean conflict, President Dwight D. Eisenhower instructed
the Joint Chiefs of Staff to make a complete study of the nation's
defense needs and to look at fiscal factors as well as military considerations. They recommended reducing U.S. forces overseas and
building up a mobile reserve at home to back up European allies.
They also advocated primary reliance on nuclear weapons as a deterrent against any Communist aggression. Both proposals were adopted
by the Eisenhower administration.[29] This "New Look" of the U.S.
military led to basic changes in the patterns of defense procurement.
Purchases of ordnance, vehicles, and production equipment fell
sharply in the mid-1950s. The result was a huge loss of defense
business for New York and the east central states, where such manufacturing had been heavily concentrated. During the same period,
aircraft, missile, and electronics contracts went to the newer industrial states in the Mountain and Pacific regions. California, with its
large aircraft firms and numerous electrical machinery companies,
received the biggest slice of the defense pie. It secured 16 percent

of all prime military contracts and more than two thirds of those awarded west of the Mississippi River.[30]

This massive outlay of government funds opened up another reservoir of defense employment. Seeking better economic and professional opportunities, thousands of scientists, engineers, and technicians migrated to southern California during the mid-1950s.[31] San Diego County, with its many defense plants and government military installations, received a large number of the new settlers. Most of the increase in employment occurred in the aircraft industry; aircraft and parts production accounted for 70 percent of the county's industrial work force. The bulk of military business, however, continued to be concentrated in Los Angeles County. Employment in the electrical equipment sector increased from 54,000 to 66,000, making it the county's second largest industry. The aircraft and parts sector became the largest single manufacturing activity in the region. Aircraft employment reached 213,000 in 1957, representing nearly one third of all factory workers.[32]

Missile contracts absorbed an increasing proportion of the skills and productive capacity of the aircraft industry. "The business that goes with strong defense is going to be big," Lockheed president Robert E. Gross observed in 1955. "It is going to be with us for many years to come. And we must readjust our company's sights to view and appreciate properly the role we play in national defense." Lockheed opened a new missile center at Van Nuys and developed Q-5 ballistic missiles for the army and X-7 supersonic ramjet vehicles.[33] Douglas fabricated the Thor Able booster rocket, the Nike Ajax air-to-surface missile, and the Honest John surface-to-surface missile for the army. Important work on propellant systems was done in 1955 and 1956 at North American's Rocketdyne Division at Canoga Park; its field propulsion laboratory in the Santa Susana Mountains was the largest high-thrust test center in the world. Rocketdyne built and tested liquid fuel engines for the Atlas and Thor intercontinental missiles and the army's Redstone missile.[34]

Equally significant were the missile programs of the JPL and the new Ramo-Wooldridge Corporation. In 1954 Army Ordnance awarded a contract to JPL to develop a flexible surface-to-surface missile having a solid-fuel rocket engine. Dubbed the Sergeant, the weapon project involved path-breaking studies in propulsion, systems design, airframe guidance, launching equipment, and other areas of rocket technology.[35] Ramo-Wooldridge occupied a more strategic position in the missile market. Worried that moody Howard Hughes might sell his aircraft company, Simon Ramo and Dean Wooldridge left the firm in 1953 and set up their own technological organization at Inglewood. Joining them were a large number of scientists and executives from Hughes Aircraft. The following year Ramo-Wooldridge received a contract to provide technical supervision and system engineering for the government's entire intercontinental ballistic missile (ICBM) program. Working closely with the air force's Western Development Division located in Inglewood, Ramo-Wooldridge in 1955 and 1956 supervised flight programs, monitored design work, and issued technical directives to industrial contractors. It also manufactured navigational and control equipment for planes and missiles.[36]

The feast-or-famine characteristic of defense business surfaced again, however. In January 1957 President Eisenhower submitted a budget to Congress for fiscal year 1958 that included $38 billion for military goods and services. Feeling that defense expenditures were already too extravagant, Congress chopped off $1 billion from the president's request.[37] As a result the Defense Department had to cancel a large number of contracts. Lockheed and Douglas suffered from the cutback in military planes. Lockheed laid off 13,600 people at its Burbank plant, while 7,000 persons working at Douglas's facilities at El Segundo and Long Beach lost their jobs.[38] The biggest defense casualty in the Los Angeles region was the Navaho missile project. North American's plant at Downey had won a contract in 1956 to do all of the design, fabrication, and testing for the weapon system. The Navaho cancellation was a major blow to the company, its employees, and the city. North American laid off 16,000 workers in the summer of 1957. Company president J. T. Atwood, reporting on the military market of Los Angeles's aircraft industry, regretted "the series of drastic actions" taken by procurement agencies to hold down defense spending and expected that "the downward trend in employment and sales" would continue indefinitely.[39]

Soviet breakthroughs in rocket science changed this situation rapidly. In August 1957 the Soviets fired the world's first ICBM. Two months later they propelled the first earth satellite, Sputnik, into outer space. These displays of Soviet technical expertise led to demands from congressmen, service officials, and prominent scientists for a sustained effort to catch up with and overcome the Soviets in the missile and rocket fields.[40] Defense expenditures on missiles and spacecraft shot up from $2 billion in 1957 to over $4 billion in 1959, constituting almost one quarter of all military procurement.[41]

Los Angeles's aircraft companies received the biggest piece of the aerospace cake. By this time few defense industries in southern California or in any other large urban center could match their technical know-how, superior testing facilities, and productive capacity. Together Douglas, Hughes, North American, and Lockheed garnered nearly one fifth of all prime military contracts in 1958 and 1959.[42] Large portions of this defense business were subcontracted to local electrical machinery firms, which specialized in the development and manufacture of missile guidance and control equipment. By 1960 the Los Angeles region accounted for one quarter of all the missile workers in the United States.[43]

This expansion of defense employment, however, was not nearly enough to offset the continuing decline in aircraft jobs. Those workers who had skills that were important in the production of military planes found their skills to be inadequate for the new space age. The result was another major jolt to aircraft employment. Wage and salary earners in aircraft and parts manufacturing fell from 213,000 in 1957 to 143,000 by 1960, a drop of 33 percent.[44] In the process, emphasis shifted from mass production and assembly-line techniques to fewer and more sophisticated projects involving a great amount of research and development. In 1958 and 1959 Lockheed received over $800 million in contracts to work on missiles, satellites, and spacecraft. Its plant at Van Nuys concentrated on X-7 ramjet vehicles, Kingfisher target missiles for the army, and Agena satellites. The air force used the Agena as the injection stage in its Discoverer program. Douglas's missile and space sales in 1959 exceeded $500 million and constituted over half of its military business. The company fabricated Thor surface-to-surface missiles, Nike Zeus and Skybolt air-to-surface missiles, and Thor and Delta space launch vehicles. North American developed the X-15 supersonic research plane, the Hound Dog air-to-surface missile, and rocket engines for satellites. It also made guidance and control hardware for Boeing's Minuteman Missile.[45]

JPL and Ramo-Wooldridge also entered the new space technology with considerable success. In January 1958 JPL, in collaboration with the Army Ballistic Missiles Agency, launched the Explorer, the first man-made satellite to orbit the earth. Several months later President Eisenhower signed an executive order that transferred JPL property and personnel from army jurisdiction to the new National Aeronautics and Space Administration. In 1959 JPL teamed again with the Army Ballistic Missiles Agency to launch the nation's first successful moon probe.[46] Less spectacular but even more important was the transformation of Ramo-Wooldridge from an air force think tank to a leading aerospace firm. Ramo-Wooldridge had become very frustrated with contract provisions that prohibited it from manufacturing any ICBM hardware. Making things worse was the fact that Thompson Products, an auto and aircraft parts outfit in Cleveland, Ohio, with hardware-selling ambitions of its own, was financing the company. Determined to acquire a larger share of the business generated by missile contracts, the two organizations merged in 1958 to make Thompson Ramo Wooldridge, a new corporation. In the next two years military sales of TRW rose from $340 million to $460 million. It established an independent subsidiary at Inglewood called the Space Technological Laboratories (STL) to continue performing the technical direction and systems engineering of the ICBM program. STL also designed, built, and tested airborne and ground equipment for various space projects.[47]

Such heavy concentration of defense business in the Los Angeles area aroused resentment from other regions of the nation. Especially critical of the distribution of military contracts was New York's congressional leadership; they complained about their state's falling share of the procurement program. "Today, with U.S. defense expenditures of $45 billion representing over half of the federal budget, defense contract awards and procurement policies have a profound impact on the economic well-being of almost every major industrial region in the country," Senator Jacob K. Javits told a meeting of a subcommittee of the Senate Armed Services Committee. "It is for this reason that every member of New York's congressional delegation is vitally concerned with the declining percentage of defense dollars spent in New York as compared with other states, particularly California."[48] With the assistance of Senator Kenneth B. Keating, Javits composed the Armed Services Competitive Procurement Act in May 1959. The measure required, among other provisions, that procuring agencies consider "the strategic and economic desirability of allocating purchases to different geographical areas of the nation." Keating assured the subcommittee that the bill was "not designed to benefit any one section of the country, but to benefit all sections by a more equitable distribution of contracts."[49]

California Senator Thomas H. Kuchel disagreed. He saw the measure as an ill-conceived scheme to divert military work away from the Golden State. "If a substantial percentage of contracts for aircraft, missiles, rockets, electronic equipment and other weapons goes to companies operating or based in California," Kuchel informed the Armed Services Subcommittee, "that is for good and justifiable reasons." He singled out excellent testing sites and the pool of technical and scientific manpower.[50] Similar arguments were advanced by the Los Angeles Chamber of Commerce. Convinced that the Javits-Keating bill was a "conspiracy" of Easterners to "raid" Southern California's aerospace complex, the chamber organized an industrial task force against the measure. Composed of defense industry executives and the leaders of several chambers of commerce, the task force prevailed upon economist Gerhard Rostvold of Pomona College, a close student of local military production, to write a report explaining California's disproportionate share of defense contracts. Focusing on Los Angeles's aerospace business, Rostvold highlighted the large number of competent scientists and technicians working in the missile and electronics fields. He also pointed out that the region's defense firms had willingly accepted research as well as lucrative production contracts. Armed with this information, the task force traveled to Washington and presented Rostvold's report to California's congressional delegation. They, in turn, persuaded the Armed Services Subcommittee to table the Javits-Keating procurement bill.[51]

Los Angeles was thus ensured of remaining the nation's largest center of military production. Federal defense expenditures in the metropolitan area in 1960 totaled more than $2 billion, constituting about 13 percent of all military contracts, although the region's population was only 3.8 percent of the national total.[52] The launching of the space race and the reliance on missiles had catapulted the metropolis from being a leading aircraft producer to being the most sophisticated scientific-technological complex in the United States. Los Angeles's rise to this new position was not an unmixed blessing, however. Sudden reductions in defense spending in 1945, 1949, and 1957 had put thousands of people out of work. This economic vulnerability persisted into the 1960s, often with far greater suffering. There was also the growing problem of structural unemployment. Aircraft workers seeking jobs outside the aerospace industry would find it difficult, if not impossible, to secure employment at skills and pay commensurate with their training and experience.[53] It remained to be seen whether Los Angeles's civic and industrial leaders could effectively resolve these unpleasant manifestations of the metropolis's defense-oriented economy.

NOTES

1. Gerald D. Nash, The American West in the Twentieth Century: A Short History of an Urban Oasis (Englewood Cliffs, N.J.: Prentice-Hall, 1973), pp. 196-98.
2. Los Angeles City Planning Commission, Accomplishments, 1945, p. 7.
3. William G. Cunningham, The Aircraft Industry: A Study in Industrial Location (Los Angeles: Lorrin L. Morrison, 1950), p. 89; John Caughey and LeRee Caughey, "Adjusting to War and to Peace," in Los Angeles: Biography of a City, ed. John Caughey and Laree Caughey (Berkeley: University of California Press, 1976), p. 359.
4. Donald W. Douglas, "60,000 Warplanes a Year!" Los Angeles Times Magazine, December 13, 1942, pp. 4-5; Caughey and Caughey, "Adjusting to War and to Peace," p. 359.
5. Rene J. Francillon, McDonnell Douglas Aircraft since 1920 (London: Putnam, 1979), pp. 27, 29; Lockheed Aircraft Corporation, Annual Report of the President, 1943, p. 1; North American Aviation, Annual Report, 1945, p. 4.

6. North American Aviation, Annual Report, 1945, pp. 5-6; Urbanomics Research Associates, Southern California Economic Trends: 1940-1970 (Claremont, Calif.: Urbanomics Research Associates, 1969), p. 82.

7. Lockheed Aircraft Corporation, Annual Report of the President, 1944, p. 1; idem, Annual Report of the President, 1946, p. 5; North American Aviation, Annual Report, 1946, p. 9.

8. Frank L. Kidner and Philip Neff, Los Angeles: The Economic Outlook (Los Angeles: Haynes Foundation, 1946), p. 20.

9. North American Aviation, Annual Report, 1947, pp. 3-5; idem, Annual Report, 1948, pp. 1, 5; Lockheed Aircraft Corporation, Annual Report of the President, 1948, pp. 5, 7.

10. Christopher Rand, Los Angeles, the Ultimate City (New York: Oxford University Press, 1967), pp. 75-76. After earning a doctorate in the sciences at the California Institute of Technology, Simon Ramo went east in 1940 and became director of the physics section at the General Electric Laboratories. Feeling that an electronics industry could be built on the West Coast, he left General Electric in 1946 and found a home for his vision at Hughes Aircraft. Joining him was Dean Wooldridge, a brilliant classmate of his at Cal Tech who had been supervising the physical-electronics department at Bell Telephone Laboratories. He and Ramo established an electronics research laboratory and recruited over 400 engineers with advanced degrees to staff it. See Robert Sheehan, "Thompson Ramo Wooldridge: Two Wings in Space," Fortune 67 (February 1963): 97-98; Rand, Los Angeles, pp. 74-75.

11. President's Air Policy Commission, Survival in the Air Age (Washington, D.C.: U.S. Government Printing Office, 1948), p. v.

12. North American Aviation, Annual Report, 1947, pp. 10-11.

13. President's Air Policy Commission, Survival in the Air Age, pp. 25, 46; also see John B. Rae, Climb to Greatness: The American Aircraft Industry, 1920-1960 (Cambridge, Mass.: MIT Press, 1968), pp. 193-94.

14. Rae, Climb to Greatness, p. 195.

15. Lockheed Aircraft Corporation, Annual Report of the President, 1949, p. 4; North American Aviation, Annual Report, 1949, p. 9.

16. Lockheed Aircraft Corporation, Annual Report of the President, 1948, p. 9.

17. Walter LaFeber, America, Russia, and the Cold War, 1945-1980, 4th ed. (New York: John Wiley, 1980), pp. 97-100, 104, 106-8.

18. George A. Steiner, "Research Report," in Committee for Economic Development, Southern California Associates, National

Defense and Southern California, 1961-1970 (Los Angeles: Southern California Associates, 1961), p. 92.

19. California State Chamber of Commerce, Research Department, "Economic Survey of California and Its Counties," in California Blue Book: 1954 (Sacramento, Calif.: 1954), pp. 709-10; Doris Ikle, Southern California's Economy in the Sixties (Santa Monica, Calif.: Rand Corporation, 1960), pp. 2-3.

20. California State Chamber of Commerce, "Economic Survey of California," pp. 711-13, 715.

21. Francillon, McDonnell Douglas Aircraft, pp. 32-33; Douglas Aircraft Company, Annual Report, 1951, p. 2; idem, Annual Report, 1953, pp. 13-14, 30.

22. Lockheed Aircraft Corporation, Annual Report of the President, 1950, p. 3; idem, Annual Report of the President, 1952, pp. 6-7.

23. Clayton R. Koppes, JPL and the American Space Program: A History of the Jet Propulsion Laboratory (New Haven, Conn.: Yale University Press, 1982), pp. 43-46, 51-55.

24. James L. Clayton, "Defense Spending: Key to California's Growth," Western Political Quarterly 15 (June 1962): 284.

25. Douglas Aircraft Company, Annual Report, 1951, p. 27; idem, Annual Report, 1953, p. 16; North American Aviation, Annual Report, 1951, p. 8; idem, Annual Report, 1952, pp. 6-7; Sheehan, "Thompson Ramo Wooldridge," p. 98.

26. Southern California Research Council, The Effect of a Reduction in Defense Expenditures upon the Los Angeles Area (Los Angeles: Southern California Research Council, 1953), pp. 9, 34.

27. Jenniellen Ferguson and Lyndon R. Musolf, "The Role of Government in the Future Economy of the Los Angeles Metropolitan Area," in Planning for the Economic Growth of Southern California, ed. Ernest A. Engelbert (Berkeley: University of California, University Extension, 1955), p. 97; Frank Sherwood, "Discussion," ib., p. 103.

28. Southern California Research Council, The Los Angeles Economy: Its Strengths and Weaknesses (Los Angeles: Southern California Research Council, 1954), p. 20.

29. Robert A. Divine, Eisenhower and the Cold War (New York: Oxford University Press, 1981), pp. 35-37. Successful testing of the hydrogen bomb by the United States and the Soviet Union in 1952 and 1953 showed that nuclear warheads could be made small enough to be carried by an intercontinental ballistic missile. See Rand, Los Angeles, p. 76.

30. Roger E. Bolton, Defense Purchases and Regional Growth (Washington, D.C.: Brookings Institution, 1966), pp. 117, 122-24; Merton J. Peck and Frederic M. Scherer, The Weapons Acquisition

Process: An Economic Analysis (Boston: Graduate School of Business Administration, Harvard University, 1962), pp. 110-12.

31. David L. Clark, Los Angeles, a City Apart: An Illustrated History (Woodland Hills, Calif.: Windsor, 1981), p. 156.

32. California State Chamber of Commerce, Research Department, "Economic Survey of California and Its Counties," in California Blue Book: 1958 (Sacramento, Calif.: 1958), pp. 940-42, 946, 1031, 1033; Steiner, "Research Report," pp. 81, 87; also see Clayton, "Defense Spending," pp. 288-89.

33. Lockheed Aircraft Corporation, Annual Report of the President, 1955, p. 16; idem, Annual Report of the President, 1957, p. 9. Much of Lockheed's missile research and production was, and still is, done at its facilities at Sunnyvale, California.

34. Douglas Aircraft Company, Annual Report, 1955, pp. 29-30; idem, Annual Report, 1956, pp. 26-27; North American Aviation, Annual Report, 1955, pp. 21-23; idem, Annual Report, 1956, pp. 10-11.

35. Koppes, JPL, pp. 63-64.

36. U.S., Congress, House, Committee on Government Operations, Organization and Management of Missile Programs, 86th Cong., 1st sess., 1959, H.Rept. 1121, pp. 83-85; Sheehan, "Thompson Ramo Wooldridge," pp. 99, 134, 139.

37. Herbert S. Parmet, Eisenhower and the American Crusades (New York: Macmillan, 1972), pp. 498-501.

38. Lockheed Aircraft Corporation, Annual Report of the President, 1957, p. 5; Douglas Aircraft Company, Annual Report, 1957, p. 28.

39. North American Aviation, Annual Report, 1957, pp. 3-4, 6-7.

40. LaFeber, America, Russia, and the Cold War, p. 199; Koppes, JPL, p. 84.

41. Steiner, "Research Report," p. 92.

42. U.S., Congress, Joint Economic Committee, Background Material on Economic Aspects of Military Procurement and Supply, 86th Congress, 2d sess., 1960, p. 26.

43. Robert K. Arnold et al., The California Economy: 1947-1980 (Menlo Park, Calif.: Stanford Research Institute, 1960), p. 251; U.S., Department of Labor, Bureau of Employment Security, Missiles and Aircraft: Recent Manpower Developments, Industry Manpower Surveys, no. 95 (Washington, D.C.: 1960), pp. 16-17.

44. Steiner, "Research Report," p. 87.

45. Lockheed Aircraft Corporation, Annual Report of the President, 1958, pp. 8-9; idem, Annual Report of the President, 1959, pp. 5, 10; Douglas Aircraft Company, Annual Report, 1959, pp. 4, 6-7, 9-10; North American Aviation, Annual Report, 1958, pp. 10, 23, 27; idem, Annual Report, 1959, pp. 14-15, 18, 20.

46. Koppes, JPL, pp. 88-93, 98-99.

47. U.S., Congress, House, Missile Programs, pp. 88-91; Sheehan, "Thompson Ramo Wooldridge," pp. 96-97, 139-40.

48. U.S., Congress, Senate, Military Procurement, Hearings before a Subcommittee of the Committee on Armed Services, 86th Cong., 1st sess., 1959, pp. 25-26.

49. Ibid., pp. 22-24, 103. Similar procurement legislation was also introduced in the House.

50. Ibid., pp. 127-28.

51. Seyom Brown, "Southern California's Precarious One-Crop Economy," Reporter, January 7, 1960, p. 28.

52. Walter Isard and James Ganschow, Awards of Prime Military Contracts by County, State and Metropolitan Area of the United States, Fiscal Year 1960 (Philadelphia: Wharton School, Department of Regional Science, University of Pennsylvania, 1960), pp. 8, 13.

53. Steiner, "Research Report," p. 131; Arnold et al., California Economy, p. 265. The 1960s witnessed a variety of proposals by government officials, economists, and professional planners to diversify California's aerospace industries and provide broader employment opportunities for defense workers. See, for example, Werner Z. Hirsch and Richard N. Baisden, eds., California's Future Economic Growth (Berkeley, Calif.: Diablo Press, 1965), chaps. 4, 5, 6, 8.

7

The City Loses the Sword: The Decline of Major Military Activity in the New York Metropolitan Region

Kenneth T. Jackson

New York has had a long and occasionally distinguished military history. The oldest of major U.S. cities, it was the scene of both Indian and Dutch massacres in the 1640s and of protracted conflict between the English and the Dutch throughout the entire seventeenth century.[1] In the decade preceding the Declaration of Independence, New Yorkers exhibited every one of the appropriate revolutionary responses, including riots against stamp tax collectors, a tea party in 1773 similar to that which occurred in Boston, and numerous rallies around the Liberty Pole. During the American Revolution, the British selected New York City as the pivot of their military operations because of its splendid harbor and its location at the mouth of a waterway that divided the colonies. The strategic plan, of course, called for General William Howe to occupy New York City, to extend a line north to control the Hudson, and to meet a Canadian expedition coming down toward Albany under General Guy Carleton.[2]

The military operations of both sides in the environs of New York City were of major significance. On June 29, 1776, Royal Navy warships first appeared off Sandy Hook, and by mid-August the British had concentrated 32,000 soldiers and 10,000 sailors, along with 400 transports and 30 ships-of-the-line, in New York harbor. It was the most massive demonstration of military power ever seen in the New World. On August 22 about 20,000 redcoats and heavily booted Hessians began landing at Gravesend Bay in what is now the borough of Brooklyn. In the course of the next week, George Washington's Continental army was defeated so soundly in the Battle of Long Island that it was said even the women camp followers of the British army took prisoners. General Washington was appropriately discouraged, and only a middle-of-the-night, Dunkirk-style evacuation—

151

possible only because Admiral Howe foolishly failed to send even a patrol boat into the East River—enabled the revolutionary army to escape certain destruction.[3]

The U.S. military debacle in Brooklyn was followed by a series of battles between September and November 1776 in Westchester County and on Manhattan Island that were almost equally disastrous for the new United States. The worst single day came on November 16 when Fort Washington (at present-day 183rd Street in Manhattan) and its 2,818 soldiers surrendered to the forces of King George III. Most of them ultimately died on the notorious British prison ships, which lay at permanent anchor in Wallabout Bay on the Brooklyn side of the East River.[4]

The only good result of the New York campaign for the Americans was that General Washington learned several valuable strategic lessons, the most important of which was that his poorly trained soldiers could not compete with the perfectly disciplined redcoats in any large, set-piece battle. His best option, like that of Ho Chi Minh two centuries later in Vietnam, was to strike hard at small enemy formations and to fade into the countryside before powerful reinforcements could appear. Henceforth, the Americans favored hit-and-run tactics and avoided major engagements (Saratoga and Yorktown were each the result of special circumstances). Meanwhile, the British remained firmly in control of New York City, and Evacuation Day, when the last Royal Navy vessels sailed through the Narrows, did not occur until November 25, 1783.[5]

Two decades after national independence was achieved, Gotham surged past Philadelphia to become the dominant city in the Western Hemisphere. In 1801 the federal government purchased the Brooklyn Navy Yard, which became a respected builder of ocean-going and innovative vessels. For example, the steamboat Fulton was constructed there in 1814/15 from the inventor's plans. During the War of 1812, the British chose not to attack the new nation's busiest seaport, and the small forts that surrounded the harbor were never tested.[6]

By the time of the Civil War, the defenses around the city had become even more elaborate. Forts Hamilton and La Fayette, the latter having three tiers of guns, guarded the eastern side of the Narrows, while Forts Tompkins and Richmond on Staten Island covered the other flank. To protect the inner harbor and upper bay, Forts Columbus and Castle William were supported by the works on Bedlow's and Ellis islands. Incredibly, the city furnished 116,382 men to the Union cause during the rebellion, even though New York was concentrated in lower Manhattan (well below present-day 42nd Street) and counted less than a million people. Its regiments stood at Gettysburg and marched with General William T. Sherman through

Georgia, while its factories almost alone outproduced the entire Confederacy. Gotham shipyards increased the size of the U.S. Navy, and they outfitted the Monitor, the famous ironclad that outdueled the Merrimac at Hampton Roads in 1862.[7]

The Monitor was but the first of a succession of famous warships to be built or outfitted along the New York docks. The ill-fated battleship Maine, the mysterious sinking of which touched off the Spanish-American War in 1898, slid down the ways at the Brooklyn Navy Yard in 1890. The battleship Arizona, which exploded during the Japanese attack at Pearl Harbor on December 7, 1941, and which continues as a memorial to the 1,200 sailors who are entombed in its hull, was built in Brooklyn in 1915, as was the battleship Missouri (built in 1944) on whose decks World War II was formally ended in Tokyo Bay on September 2, 1945.[8]

Like many U.S. cities, New York throbbed with military activity between 1940 and 1945, and its hotels and rooming houses were jammed with servicemen on leave or about to ship out. In the Red Hook section of Brooklyn, the 40,000 employees of the Todd Shipyard worked on round-the-clock shifts to keep their boast that they could take a vessel that had been badly damaged by a German torpedo and put it back into service in a matter of days. A mile farther north, at the Brooklyn Navy Yard, employment jumped from 17,000 to 71,000, and the neighborhood outside its Sands Street gate established itself as New York's "Barbary Coast." At Floyd Bennett Field, a few miles to the east, the runways of one of the navy's busiest air stations were rarely quiet.[9]

Perhaps the heart of New York's great effort in World War II was the Brooklyn Army Terminal. Just west of Sunset Park and north of Bay Ridge, the 97-acre site included two giant eight-story factory buildings with 961-foot-long atriums and four massive piers, each of which could handle several ships at a time. It was the army's main East Coast supply terminal and as such was the arrival and departure point for millions of tons by military hardware and for tens of thousands of servicemen described by President Franklin D. Roosevelt as: "Our sons, pride of our nation." Indeed, National Geographic recently reported that the Brooklyn Army Terminal processed every GI sailing for Europe during World War II.[10]

THE URBAN DISTRIBUTION OF DEFENSE SPENDING
AFTER VIETNAM

After the collapse of the Axis powers in 1945, New York City's 300-year role as a center of important military activity in the Western world slowly began to erode. The rapid demobilization of the armed forces after the end of hostilities understandably affected all regions of the United States and all sectors of the economy. But beginning with the Soviet detonation of a nuclear device in 1949 and continuing with the Korean War in the early 1950s and with renewed military activity in Europe as part of the North Atlantic Treaty Organization (NATO), the Department of Defense assumed a semipermanent status and size that made it, as its publicity officers were proud to boast, the largest "business" on earth. The benefits of its largesse were not equally distributed, however. Norfolk and San Diego became the world's largest naval installations, while air force bases breathed new economic life into dozens of declining agricultural communities. In Texas, San Antonio prospered from the 1980 paychecks of 40,500 active-duty military personnel stationed at Randolph, Brooks, Lackland, and Kelly Air Force bases and at Fort Sam Houston. Not far away, Houston similarly benefited when Fort Hood, the home of 38,000 soldiers of the First Cavalry and Second Armored divisions, became the most populous of all army posts. Similarly, Charleston, Los Angeles, Pensacola, Jacksonville, and San Francisco became familiar second homes to the nation's men and women in uniform. [11]

The shift actually began at least as early as 1919 when the Veterans Bureau built many hospitals in the Carolinas and elsewhere in the South and West even though the greatest demand for beds was in the North and East, the home of the majority of veterans. The Northern hospitals tended to be overcrowded, while the Southern ones remained underutilized. By June 1923 there were 25,588 beds available, but only 16,655 patients in them. Meanwhile, many men in need of hospitalization were unable to squeeze into the available facilities near their homes. [12]

Whenever and however the shift took place, its impact was particularly clear in the New York Metropolitan Region, which, in contrast to rivals in the Sunbelt, was extraordinarily unsuccessful in retaining its traditional military installations, let alone acquiring any new ones. Westhampton Air Force Base, Mitchell Field (once the headquarters of the First Air Force), Camp Upton, the Brooklyn Army Terminal, the Brooklyn Navy Yard, Floyd Bennett Field, and 21 of the 22 forts (including Fort Wadsworth, which had been in continuous service since 1663 and which ranked as the oldest military installation in the United States) all were closed by 1983. The most recent casualty, Todd Shipyards, shut down its New York City operations in June 1983, after 135 years of continuous activity. Practically the only survivor of the carnage has been Brooklyn's Fort Hamilton, but it operates at a relaxed level at best. [13]

The Pentagon has typically downplayed the disastrous economic consequences of installation closings by emphasizing possible alternative uses for each site and by making such facilities available at bargain basement prices. With some exceptions, however, the rosy projections rarely materialize. For example, in 1983, eight years after the Brooklyn Army Terminal was abandoned by the Department of Defense, the 6-million-square-foot industrial complex, replete with rail connections and deep-water piers, remained empty as real estate developers and the city's Economic Development Administration fought over which revitalization plan to follow. [14]

In order to give some numerical expression to the declining significance of New York in the nation's defense strategy, I have analyzed data in a revealing publication of the Community Services Administration in the Executive Office of the President. Entitled Geographic Distribution of Federal Funds, 1980, this document annually records the distribution of tax monies to the various governmental jurisdictions of the country. As Table 2 indicates, the New York City standard metropolitan area ranked ninth in the United States on an absolute basis in 1980, trailing Los Angeles, which has been the actual center of the U.S. military effort for decades, Washington, Norfolk/Newport News, St. Louis, Dallas/Fort Worth, San Diego, Hartford, and Seattle. San Francisco would also have exceeded the Gotham total if the various suburbs around San Jose and Sunnyvale had been added. On a per capita basis, the showing of the Hudson River metropolis was more dismal, as New York fell to the bottom among the great cities of the United States. [15]

A comparison of the distribution of defense expenditures by type of activity in the major military winners is especially revealing. As Table 2 indicates, Washington, San Diego, and Norfolk profit greatly from the presence of large numbers of servicemen on active duty, while Los Angeles, Newport News, St. Louis, Dallas, Hartford, and Sunnyvale are prominent primarily because of their military suppliers. In San Diego and San Antonio, retired military personnel are a dominant force. New York, in contrast, is the only city to receive its defense money primarily in the form of service contracts (recruit advertising, for example).

The figures in Table 2, admittedly less precise than they appear, are in general in agreement with analyses completed by other researchers. In the early 1970s, Governor Nelson Rockefeller raised the proposition that New York State's problems arose in part from an imbalance in its fiscal relations with the federal government. Washington responded with the first of its annual reports from the Community Services Administration (itself a creation of President Lyndon B. Johnson's antipoverty program). Breaking down various national expenditures to the county level, the report argued that New York in fact received more in federal outlays than it paid in taxes. The Empire State and the Empire City were told that they did not have a legitimate complaint.

TABLE 2

Distribution of DOD Expenditures in the Ten Metropolitan Areas Receiving the Most Funds in Fiscal Year 1980 (millions of dollars)

	Civilian Pay	Military Pay	Construction	RDTE	Services	Supplies	Reserve Pay	Retired Pay	Total
1. Los Angeles	292	129	—	1,383	749	3,941	45	213	6,752
2. Washington*	1,050	746	8	119	393	312	18	154	4,635
3. Norfolk/ Newport News	342	827	23	20	355	1,335	9	119	3,030
4. St. Louis	315	25	1	557	224	2,209	9	18	3,358
5. Dallas/ Fort Worth	63	19	6	206	185	2,758	38	94	3,369
6. San Diego	474	1,437	56	281	330	275	34	325	3,212
7. Hartford	10	—	—	93	106	2,571	1	1	2,782
8. Seattle*	32	21	1	398	174	1,096	12	55	2,498
9. New York	77	35	1	22	1,014	396	64	49	1,658
10. Sunnyvale	18	16	1	247	252	1,023	2	8	1,567

DOD = Department of Defense

RDTE = Research and development total expenditures

*In the Seattle and Washington metropolitan areas, I was unable to determine the exact distribution of expenditures in some suburban jurisdictions. The subtotals in those two cases will not add to the grand total.

Source: Geographic Distribution of Federal Funds, 1980, Executive Office of the President, Community Services Administration, Federal Information Exchange, 1980.

The matter did not rest there. With substantial assistance from Erik Johnsen of the Technical Assistance Center of the State University of New York at Plattsburgh, Senator Daniel Patrick Moynihan made a detailed study of the various Federal Outlays reports. He discovered that New York was credited with receiving almost half of the interest paid on the national debt and more than 40 percent of the foreign aid payments of the United States, when in both instances the money was simply being funneled through big Wall Street banks on its way around the country and across the world. Senator Moynihan corrected the numbers and in 1977 began to release his own annual report, New York and the Federal Fisc. Over the first five years of his analysis (1976-80), the 50 states, collectively, received $145 billion more in federal outlays, while New York State received $11.5 billion less than it sent to Washington.[16]

Senator Moynihan also called attention to the mix of outlays, demonstrating that New York received a high proportion of "soft" money (medicaid and food stamps) and a low proportion of "hard" money (water projects and defense contracts, for instance). In 1980, for example, he reported that New York State received 10.4 percent of Housing and Urban Development expenditures but only 5.3 percent of military-related items. Senator Moynihan argued that the difference was significant because hard money created infrastructure and future prosperity, while soft money simply enabled the poor to survive.[17]

A more recent analysis of the economic impact of federal programs, and one that focuses more narrowly on defense spending, was first issued in 1979 by Employment Research Associates, a private Lansing, Michigan, firm led by Marion and James Anderson. (See Table 3.) Dr. James Anderson's 1982 study, entitled "Bankrupting American Cities," considered the Pentagon's projected $214 billion budget for fiscal year 1983 and attempted to measure the real gains or losses that such spending would have on the nation's 266 standard metropolitan statistical areas (SMSAs). It concluded that Washington, where Pentagon officers are routinely reminded not to wear their uniforms so that the public will not be overwhelmed by the military presence, was the largest beneficiary of the war economy, getting back more than $2 for every tax dollar it contributes to the defense budget. Other big winners were San Diego, St. Louis, Newport News, and Dallas. On a per capita basis, Newport News, with a net gain of $27,600 per family, was the most successful area.[18]

Most of the nation's metropolitan regions, however, were net losers, according to Dr. Anderson's calculations. The biggest burden fell on the New York City area, which received only $3 billion in 1983 spending while paying out about $11.8 billion in taxes for defense and military contracts. According to the Employment Research study,

TABLE 3

The Pentagon Tax Burden and Expenditures by Metropolitan Area,
Fiscal Year 1983
(millions of dollars)

SMSA	Military Projected Expenditures	Pentagon Tax Burden	Net Gain or Loss	Net Gain or Loss per Family
Winners				
Washington	9.8	4.2	+5.6	+6,200
San Diego	4.9	1.6	+3.3	+6,600
St. Louis	5.8	2.5	+3.2	+4,600
Newport News	3.2	0.3	+2.9	+27,600
Dallas	5.7	2.9	+2.8	+36,000
Losers				
New York	3.0	11.8	−8.7	−3,100
Chicago	1.8	8.9	−7.0	−3,400
Detroit	2.3	5.2	−2.9	−2,200
Houston	0.6	2.9	−2.4	−3,200
Cleveland	0.5	2.3	−1.8	−3,100

SMSA = standard metropolitan statistical area
Source: James Anderson, "Bankrupting American Cities,"
Employment Research Associates, Lansing, Michigan, 1982.

"The federal government acts as a giant siphon funneling tax money
out of 176 metropolitan areas into those which have large military
bases or very high military contracts."[19]

CONCLUSION

The purpose of this chapter has been to demonstrate that U.S.
historians have not adequately considered the domestic impact of
defense expenditures. War is usually treated as a departure from
"normal" activity, and its impact is only slightly understood in
spatial terms. Yet the growth of the military-industrial complex in
the United States has meant that the Pentagon has a profound and
continuing impact on urban economics. More particularly, I have

traced the decline of the New York Metropolitan Region in terms of its relative importance within the U.S. military establishment. The evidence for such a result is overwhelming and not the subject of dispute. The reasons for the shift are less clear but for convenience may be divided into technological and political factors.

The increasing sophistication, speed, and range of modern weaponry have completely altered pre-twentieth century notions of time and space. New York City no longer requires thick-walled forts to protect its harbor or local military detachments to put down periodic rioting. Similarly, the dry climate and wide-open spaces of the West and South have become important to air operations and armored warfare at the same time that the cost of real estate has meant that the federal government has tended to utilize its extensive landholdings west of the Mississippi River for defense activities.

Technology, however, has been less important than politics in determining the spatial distribution of defense largess. For at least a generation, Southern congressmen have been following the lead of Representative R. Mendell Rivers of South Carolina, who secured 12 major military installations for his Charleston district, transforming an economic backwater into a thriving twentieth century metropolis. The Texas contingent is an important case in point. Although it is no longer the one-party, all-white, all-Democratic, unabashedly conservative delegation of the past, its members have been meeting regularly to discuss "pork barrel" strategy for a third of a century. Senator John Tower is chairman of the Senate Armed Services Committee and the leading supporter of President Ronald Reagan's plan for a vast buildup of military might, despite cutbacks in social programs and the pressure of rising budget deficits. Democrats and Republicans in Texas know that the home state of the Alamo boasts a proud military tradition and, more important, a powerful industry dependent upon it. When federal funds are available, the entire Texas delegation ignores their broad ideological disagreements and closes ranks behind any program that benefits any part of the state. Whether this solidarity is born of regional defensiveness or whether it merely reflects unusual political skills, it is no coincidence that Houston, which is no closer to the moon than any other part of the country, is the home of the National Aeronautics and Space Administration or that Texas trails only California in the contracts it receives from the Department of Defense. Unfortunately, a slavish devotion to the tenets of more and more military preparedness is often rewarded with lucrative procurement contracts for a representative's district.

Although the congressional representatives and senators for the New York area have been as capable as those of Texas or any other state, several factors have worked against their success in securing a "fair share" of defense monies for their region. A dearth of standing committee chairmanships—especially since Representative James Delaney of Queens, the chairman of the House Rules Committee, lost his reelection bid in 1978—has hurt the New York delegation. Moreover, reflecting a constituency less interested in military hardware than in immigration quotas and more interested in Ireland, Israel, and Italy than in the army, navy, and the air force, New York area representatives carry the image of being against increases in the Pentagon budget. Jacob Javits, a highly respected and intelligent leader in the Senate until his 1980 defeat, is a case in point. Senator Javits took an important role in shaping U.S. foreign policy in the 1960s and 1970s, but he was singularly ineffective and largely uninterested in helping his state gain a more equitable share of the nation's defense activities. Similarly, Congressman Joseph P. Addabbo, a Democrat from Queens, is currently a senior member of the Armed Services Committee. But Addabbo is a relative dove on a committee of hawks, and this fact sadly influences decision making at the highest levels. [20]

In conclusion, the real explanation for the uneven distribution of defense expenditures is not national security, which is arguably damaged by the obscene level of our outlays for ever more deadly weapons, but politics. To some degree, the New York Metropolitan Region has been shortchanged by the Pentagon because of jealousies within the delegation. But the most important factor has been, and will continue to be, the perception, correct I believe, among New Yorkers that the military budget is already bloated and should be reduced rather than expanded.

NOTES

1. New York City was founded in 1624 by the Dutch, who called the settlement Fort Amsterdam and later New Amsterdam. When the English captured the city in 1664, they renamed it in honor of the Duke of York, brother of King Charles II of England. Because the earlier settlements at St. Augustine (1565), Jamestown (1607), and Plymouth (1620) either disappeared or declined into insignificance and because Boston (1630), Philadelphia (1682), and Charleston (1670) were founded at a later date, New York stands as the oldest important community in what is now the United States.

2. Willard M. Wallace, Appeal to Arms: A Military History of the American Revolution (New York: 1951), is the best survey of the campaign around New York City.

3. A Loyalist woman who lived near the evacuation site sent a black slave to warn the British of the American escape, but the first

officer encountered was a Hessian who did not understand the message and put him under arrest.

4. As many as 11,500 Americans may have perished on the prison ships, far more than died in any of the campaigns. There is, however, no adequate account of the horror. The best work available includes: Larry G. Bowman, Captive Americans: Prisoners during the American Revolution (Athens, Ohio: 1976), pp. 2-20; Danske Dandridge, American Prisoners of the Revolution (Baltimore, Md.: 1967), pp. 202-6; and Charles H. Metzger, The Prisoner in the American Revolution (Chicago: 1971).

5. The last shot of the American Revolution was fired by an English ship as it passed out of New York harbor into the Atlantic Ocean.

6. The best volume on the growth of New York as a world leader in maritime commerce is Robert G. Albion, The Rise of New York Port, 1815-1860 (New York: 1939), pp. 3-87; see also Myron H. Luke, The Port of New York, 1800-1810 (New York: 1953).

7. J. Miller, Miller's New York as It Is (New York: 1866), pp. 92-93; and Robert Macoy, History and How to See New York (New York: 1876), p. 25.

8. The Brooklyn Navy Yard first rose to importance during the War of 1812, when it outfitted and armed more than 100 ships. During World War II, the yard constructed five large attack aircraft carriers, three battleships, and eight big landing ships; it also repaired 5,000 vessels and converted 250 others to military use.

9. There is no scholarly history of the New York area during World War II. A useful general study is Gerald T. White, Billions for Defense: Government Finance by the Defense Plant Corporation during World War II (Tuscaloosa, Ala.: 1980).

10. Alice J. Hall, "Brooklyn: The Other Side of the Bridge," National Geographic 163 (May 1983): 587.

11. On the importance of military expenditures to the economy of San Antonio, see New York Times, December 28, 1981.

12. Willard E. Waller, The Veteran Comes Back (New York: 1944), p. 236; Stanley Frost, "What's a Few Sick Veterans between Friends," Outlook, September 19, 1923, pp. 106-9.

13. Appropriately, Todd Shipyards, which had fitted the Monitor with its armaments in 1862, closed because it was underbid for a major renovation contract by a South Carolina firm. On the closing of Fort Totten in Queens, see New York Times, October 17, 1982.

14. The various controversies over the navy yard and army terminal are covered in the following issues of the New York Times: January 1, 1965; January 10, 1965; January 29, 1978; May 21, 1978; April 26, 1979; September 20, 1980; October 12, 1980; December 4, 1980; October 4, 1981; January 30, 1983; and June 6, 1983.

15. Community Services Administration, Executive Office of the President, Geographic Distribution of Federal Funds, 1980 (Washington, D.C.: 1981), v. 44. See also "Distribution of DOD Contracts by State, City, and Contractor," American Statistic Index File 3544-22, Congressional Information Service (Washington, D.C.: 1981); "The Second War between the States," Business Week, May 17, 1976, pp. 92-96; "Federal Spending: The North's Loss Is the Sunbelt's Gain," National Journal 8 (June 1976):   ; and "A Trillion for Arms—Just to Catch Up," U.S. News and World Report, July 21, 1980, pp. 69-70.

16. Letter from Senator Daniel Patrick Moynihan to his constituents, September 4, 1981.

17. New York State and the Federal FISC, V (Washington, D.C.: 1981).

18. Employment Research Associates, "Bankrupting American Cities" (Lansing, Mich.: 1982); see also Washington Post, September 28, 1982.

19. Ibid. The most recent analysis in book form is Robert Jay Dilger, The Sunbelt/Snowbelt Controversy: The War over Federal Funds (New York: 1983).

20. On the efforts of other states to win defense contracts, see New York Times, October 10, 1982; ibid., March 4, 1983; and ibid., April 29, 1983; see also James C. Cobb, The Selling of the South: The Southern Crusade for Industrial Development, 1936-1980 (Chapel Hill, N.C.: 1982).

8

Planning for the Home Front in Seattle and Portland, 1940–45

Carl Abbott

THE PROBLEM OF WARTIME PLANNING

Mobilization of the American home front at the start of World War II raised high hopes among city planners. After the disorderly improvisation of the "first New Deal," the second half of the 1930s had brought support for urban planning goals with the Greenbelt towns of the Resettlement Administration, the Tennessee Valley Authority, the public housing program authorized by Congress in 1947, and the increasing prominence of the National Resources Planning Board (NRPB). Expanding the commitment of earlier relief agencies, the WPA had channeled more than $16 million into local planning work from 1936 to 1939.[1] The expansion of military bases and defense industries in 1940 and 1941 created pressing needs for new housing and public facilities in dozens of cities and seemed to ensure a major role for local city planning agencies and for the state and regional planning boards coordinated through the NRPB. Walter Blucher, executive secretary of the American Society of Planning Officials, summed up the optimism a few months after U.S. entry into the war: "No year in the last twenty has seen such interest in city planning as developed in 1941. . . . Defense activities created problems which could be solved only through the planning process."[2]

The author would like to acknowledge the suggestions of Nohad Toulan and the assistance of a Portland State University faculty research grant.

Leaders of the planning profession could be forgiven their enthusiasm, for U.S. city planning as a local government function needed help at the start of the 1940s. Following the lead of New York in 1916, most large cities had created independent planning commissions and adopted comprehensive zoning ordinances. By 1941, 91 percent of the cities with more than 100,000 residents had planning commissions or zoning agencies, and 88 percent regulated land uses through zoning. The figures for cities of 25,000 to 100,000 were 68 percent with planning agencies and 67 percent with zoning.[3]

The good showing on paper masked the precarious status of local planning. Most commissions were boards of volunteer businessmen, realtors, architects, and lawyers. Only 46 cities had spent $5,000 or more on planning in 1929, and only 39 spent that much in 1936, out of 1,200 communities with planning or zoning boards. Full-time staff were available to assist the commissions in only 10 percent of the smaller cities and 64 percent of the larger at the time of Pearl Harbor. In many cases, planning commissions had to borrow space and staff. The American City Planning Institute (forerunner of the American Institute of Certified Planners) had fewer than 200 professional members at the start of the war.[4] As advisory bodies, planning commissions and their staffs were accustomed to seeing their proposals ignored and decisions overturned by mayors and city councils. In 1940 Robert Walker described how little progress had been made "toward more closely integrating the planning agency with local government." Amateur standing and narrow focus on zoning relegated planning agencies to "the periphery of the urban administrative structure."[5]

As Blucher anticipated, the war required hundreds of decisions about streets, sewers, water mains, schools, and housing in every defense boom city. It also triggered local, state, and national efforts to plan for postwar readjustment and the anticipated economic crisis. Looking at the period as a whole, Mel Scott has described "a national renaissance of city planning" that included dozens of examples of transportation planning, housing programs, and economic studies as "local governments from coast to coast more and more fervently embrace . . . postwar planning." A special Committee on the War Effort echoed Walter Blucher in its report to the American City Planning Institute in 1942. The committee argued that the profession should try to persuade cities and federal agencies to introduce "more and better planning methods and procedures for the war effort" in order to prepare a firmer position for planners in the postwar era.[6]

Paradoxically, the very quantity and pressures of wartime planning hindered rather than helped in the establishment of city planning as a central function of local government. The similar experiences of Portland and Seattle, two of the nation's major war production centers, cast doubt on any optimistic assessment of the war as a promoter of city planning. The present analysis focuses on the most prominent new planning initiatives required by the mobilization—housing and economic planning—with attention to political context and support as well as to specific goals and accomplishments. Despite a continuity in basic local planning concerns for transportation and zoning, established planners and planning agencies took a major role in shaping local responses to the defense buildup only in 1940/41. During the later stages of rapid population and employment growth (1941–43) and during a second period of postwar planning (1943–45), the civic leadership in both cities turned to ad hoc organizations and short-range solutions to solve immediate problems. The choices that molded the future of Portland and Seattle were made by hastily assembled committees, corporate executives, nervous politicians, and federal bureaucrats, while local planning agencies ended the war with no more influence than they had at its start.

SEATTLE AND PORTLAND IN THE 1940s

Seattle and Portland ranked high on every list of cities that were transformed by the war effort. The Bureau of the Census published special reports on their growth. Members of the House Committee on Naval Affairs held Portland and Seattle hearings on the problems of the home front and troubleshooters from the President's Committee for Congested Production Areas pitched in to help harried local officials at the height of the war. "Seattle, 1942, is definitely a boom town," wrote Business Week six months into the war. "The crowds are there, and the air is vibrant." Only a few months later, Fortune reported that the summer boom town had turned sick by autumn, "full of many more people than could be efficiently absorbed into its war industries." The same columnist found that Portland "neither likes nor knows how to accommodate its Virginia City atmosphere."[7]

Since the emergence of Seattle in the 1880s, the two cities had shared the metropolitan functions of the Pacific Northwest. They were major export markets for wood products, wheat, and other farm commodities. Portland was the import and finance center for Oregon and the Inland Empire of the Columbia-Snake River system. Seattle played the same role for Puget Sound and Alaska and competed for the business of eastern Washington.[8] Manufacturing held a secondary position in both economies in 1940, accounting for 19 percent of Portland's jobs and 20 percent in Seattle.[9] According to a classification based on 1940 employment data, Seattle at the start of the war was a wholesaling center and Portland a diversified wholesale/retail/manufacturing city. [10]

The defense buildup turned both cities into manufacturing centers, with most of the new business channeled through a handful of corporate giants. Two huge Kaiser Corporation shipyards in Portland built hundreds of Liberty ships, Victory ships, and T-2 tankers, while a third Kaiser yard across the Columbia River in Vancouver, Washington, added dozens of escort carriers and landing craft. Kaiser and smaller Portland-area shipyards launched more than a thousand ocean-going ships. Boeing factories in Seattle, Everett, and suburban Renton turned out thousands of B-17s and B-29s during the same years. The Todd-Pacific shipyard built destroyers and a score of other shipbuilders in the Seattle-Everett area added cargo ships, patrol boats, and minesweepers. Dozens of foundries, machine shops, and sheet metal plants subcontracted for Boeing and the shipyards and filled other defense orders. [11] War contracts totaled $2.34 billion for the Seattle area between 1940 and 1945 and $1.74 billion for Portland. The manufacturing expansion had the same relative impact on the two cities. Seattle's 35 percent margin in value of contracts was proportional to its 32 percent edge in population. [12]

Thousands of new jobs meant tens of thousands of new residents demanding housing, schools, water service, and seats on the bus. During the 1930s, the city of Seattle had added only 2,000 residents, and the city of Portland only 3,000 (Table 4). By the middle of 1944, Seattle counted an additional 46,000 citizens, and Portland an extra 54,000. Metropolitan Seattle grew by 18 percent during the same four years, and metropolitan Portland by 25 percent. And 25 percent of Seattle's residents and 30 percent of Portland's were newcomers since the last census. On the far side of Puget Sound from Seattle, Kitsap County with the Puget Sound Navy Shipyard grew from 44,000 to 97,000. Clark County, Washington (Vancouver), facing Portland's back door across the wide Columbia River, also doubled from 50,000 to 99,000.

Seattle faced its wartime boom with an unventuresome civic leadership that was interested in stabilizing downtown business and putting an end to 40 years as a wide-open city. Through most of the depression decade, Seattle had been a battleground for organized labor. Dave Beck's Teamsters had led other conservative unions in an ongoing fight with the Washington Commonwealth Federation and the Longshore union of Harry Bridges. The business community had watched from the sidelines as city and state gained a reputation for radical politics and bizarre candidates. In 1938, however, Arthur Langlie won the mayoral election as a businesslike reformer against candidates backed by the Teamsters and the Commonwealth Federation. His victory and landslide reelection in 1940 marked "a new era

TABLE 4

Seattle and Portland Area Population, 1930-50

	1930	1940	November 1943	May/June 1944	1950
Seattle	366,000	368,000	—	414,000	468,000
King and Snohomish counties	542,000	594,000	686,000	700,000	844,000
Kitsap County	31,000	44,000	92,000	97,000	76,000
Portland	302,000	305,000	—	359,000	373,000
Multnomah, Clackamas, and Washington counties	415,000	451,000	555,000	562,000	620,000
Clark County	40,000	50,000	95,000	99,000	85,000

Sources: U.S., Bureau of the Census, Characteristics of the Population, Labor Force, Families, and Housing: Puget Sound Congested Production Area, Series CA-3 no. 8, June 1944; idem, Wartime Changes in Population and Family Characteristics, Portland-Vancouver Congested Production Area, Series CA-2 no. 6 and CA-3 no. 6, May 1944; idem, County and City Data Book (Washington, D.C.: Government Printing Office, 1947).

of conservatism and stability" in which the city government deferred to cost-conscious property owners and businessmen. Langlie's elevation as governor in 1941 opened the mayor's office to Democrat Earl Millikin for one year in 1941/42, but Millikin in turn lost decisively to William F. Devin, an attorney stamped from the same mold as Langlie.[13] Devin advocated tight law enforcement and civil defense and asked the voters to choose between "Devin for Mayor or Beck for Boss."[14] Serving from 1942 to 1952, Devin "received non-partisan support from civic organizations which were interested in a passive, custodian-type of government that was honest and efficient. Devin . . . capitalized on the image of the 'clean-cut young man' devoted to promoting civic virtue."[15]

Portland's Earl Riley filled much the same role as mayor from 1940 to 1948. The 1940 election offered Portland a choice between upper-class and middle-class conservatism. After eight years as finance commissioner, Riley made the race with the backing of the Oregonian, the Oregon Journal, the state Republican leadership, and the city's utilities, bankers, and downtown property owners. His opponent attacked Riley as a friend of both the "over-world" and the underworld, complained about police corruption, and promised lower property taxes for the decent homeowner. Riley's victory gave the city a capable administrator who disliked intervention in the private economy, opposed public housing, and showed little interest in land-use planning. Under Portland's commission form of government, city planning was the responsibility of Public Works Commissioner William Bowes, a political ally of Riley who thought of planning as a branch of civil engineering and who modeled himself after Robert Moses.[16]

The crowds of newcomers constituted the overriding wartime problem for both Riley and Devin, their administrators, and their city planners. In the short term, few ships would slide down the ways and few bombers roll off the assembly lines until war workers and their families were adequately housed. Each city's longer-range concern was to find ways to absorb new residents within its postwar economy. In both cases the explosive growth of the metropolis threatened to upset a carefully won political equilibrium as housing agencies and economic planners tried to fit the migrants into functioning urban systems.

MOBILIZATION FOR DEFENSE

World War II arrived in the Pacific Northwest in the spring of 1940. Within little more than a year, the defense buildup had become a home-front crisis. From the summer of 1941 through the summer of 1943, the growth of Portland and Seattle as manufacturing and military centers outpaced the ability of local officials to provide public services and the capacity of the private market to supply housing. Despite attempts at careful planning during the first year of the boom, the mobilization crisis caught the cities with planning agencies that were still inadequate in staff, program, and political support. The response was to bypass established planning organizations in favor of institutional improvisation in the hope of quick solutions to specific problems.

The key to the boom in Seattle was the mounting pile of orders for Boeing bombers from the U.S. Army Air Corps and the Royal Air Force (RAF). The Boeing work force rose from 6,000 in January 1940 to 8,800 in January 1941 and to 22,000 by Christmas. Construction started on the huge Renton plant in September 1941.[17] Civilian employment at the Puget Sound Naval Shipyard soared from 3,000 in 1939 to 10,000 at the start of 1941 and to 17,010 by the beginning of 1942. Extra ferries purchased from San Francisco after the opening of the Bay Bridge carried 5,000 daily commuters from Seattle to Bremerton.[18]

After absorbing the local labor surplus in 1940, the boom began to attract migrants in the summer of 1941. While private home construction reached a new high in August, only 1 house or apartment in 200 was available for new Seattlites.[19] Sociologist Calvin Schmid described the last half of 1941 and the first months of 1942 as a year of crisis housing, with families jammed into single rooms and unmarried workers living in tourist courts, trailer camps, tents, offices, and chicken coops.[20]

Portland felt the same explosive growth. Its first shipyard contract went to the Commercial Iron Company early in 1940. The Albina Shipyard and Willamette Iron and Steel began to build small warships the next year. The U.S. Maritime Commission also approved development of the new Oregon Shipbuilding Company, to be operated by a consortium of Todd Shipbuilding Corporation and Henry Kaiser's construction empire. The lower Columbia was the site for aluminum reduction plants to use electric power from the new Bonneville Dam. Alcoa opened a factory at Vancouver in 1940. Additional plants opened the next year at Troutdale, 15 miles east of Portland, and Longview-Washington, 40 miles to the west.[21]

Oregon Shipbuilding launched its first freighters in September 1941. In the first months after Pearl Harbor, Kaiser put two more shipyards into operation and began to scour the backcountry for workers. The company emptied out the small towns along the lines of the Union Pacific and Northern Pacific, took out help-wanted ads through the Northwest and Great Plains, and ran in trainloads of workers from Chicago and New York.[22] The arrival of young families nearly doubled the number of children under ten, placing new demands on parks and schools. By the end of 1942, every third face in line for the double bill at the Paramount or Broadway Theater belonged to a newcomer.[23]

In every boom city of World War II, rapid growth combined with national shortages to create a crisis for local governments. Portland's specific problems matched the lists detailed by urban expert Louis Wirth and City Manager L. P. Cookingham of Kansas

City.[24] Newcomers jammed rented rooms and fought for apartments
in a city whose vacancy rate fell to 2 percent in the spring of 1941
and 0.5 percent by early 1942.[25] Rubber and gasoline rationing put
severe demands on public transit systems as every boom town competed for new buses. Military service and high wages in private
industry took scores of trained police and fire fighters. To the serious concern of Riley, Millikin, and Devin, city officials also had to
learn their way around new federal bureaucracies as they worked for
allocations of defense housing and building supplies, subsidies for
utilities, and deferments for vital personnel.[26]

Portland encountered its wartime problems with a mixed record
in planning from the New Deal years. In the middle 1930s, under the
direction of City Commissioner Ormond Bean, the Planning Commission had taken an active part in traffic improvements, park system
expansion, downtown waterfront redevelopment, and rezoning. Social
reformers in the Portland Planning and Housing Association had taken
satisfaction in a revised housing code that the Housing Code Commission enacted in 1934. Despite a recommendation from the Planning
Commission and the Housing Code Commission for establishment of
a housing authority, however, the city council ducked the issue by
submitting it to an advisory referendum. In November 1938 Portlanders voted 32,000 to 18,000 to reject a public housing program.
After Bean resigned his city council seat in 1939 to take an appointment as Oregon public utilities commissioner and was replaced by
William Bowes, the Planning Commission focused more narrowly on
zoning. Reed College professor Charles McKinley resigned as president of the Planning Commission in July 1940 with a criticism of its
probusiness bent in zoning cases. A six-month absence by planning
director Harry Freeman compounded the problems.[27]

Despite its problems, the Portland City Planning Commission
tried to guide Portland's reaction to the unanticipated boom during
the spring and summer of 1941. Most of the commission's attention
centered on North Portland, a peninsula flanked by industrial areas
along the Willamette and the Columbia. With a strong commitment
to professional practice, the commission and its small staff took
seven months to agree on a plan for traffic improvements. It also
tried carefully to balance the demands of a growing city with the
accepted principles of land-use planning in recommending a site for
Portland's first public housing project of 400 permanent apartments.
Although the location for Columbia Villa met general approval from
federal and city officials, the elaborate process for comparing the
competing sites seemed excess baggage to a pragmatist like Bowes.[28]

The initiative in housing policy shifted in December when the
city council created the Housing Authority of Portland. Since April
a Greater Portland Defense Housing Committee had been working to

coordinate real estate offerings and to build support for public housing. In the aftermath of Pearl Harbor, the council picked a realtor, banker, apartment owner, and trade union leader from the Defense Housing Committee to serve on the new Housing Authority board. The agency was justified as a war emergency measure and gained legitimacy in conservative Portland from its origins in an ad hoc committee. It obtained necessary expertise by borrowing half of the time of Planning Commission director Harry Freeman.[29]

In replacing the Planning Commission as the focus for public housing policy, the Housing Authority had to decide the total number of public housing units needed and to pick the sites. It was several months before the Housing Authority learned to think in the scale required by the emergency. Initial debate on the first question threatened to split the board between differing views of housing requirements. Protracted deliberations in February and March traced and retraced the same ground as board members tried to decide whether to request 3,100 temporary units or 2,500 temporary and 600 permanent. As exasperated officials of the National Housing Administration tried to suggest, arguments over a few hundred apartments were inconsequential by the end of May, when the Housing Authority asked for an allocation of an additional 10,000 units.[30] Similarly, the Housing Authority spent much of its energy during the spring on a plan for placing temporary housing on vacant lots within established neighborhoods that provided only 700 homes during the course of the war. By June, in contrast, the Housing Authority and Planning Commission rubber-stamped a location decision for a 2,000-unit project. At the end of November the board members were willing to accept a package of sites for another 2,000 units on the word of the Federal Public Housing Authority.[31]

The crisis for Portland housing came in July 1942. The 4,900 apartments under construction at midsummer appeared painfully inadequate to the United States Maritime Commission and to shipyard executives whose workers were leaving town because they could not find decent accommodations. Representatives of the Kaiser yards, which had the highest labor demand, were especially insistent that the Housing Authority was acting too slowly. Housing already under construction was delayed by its low priority in claims on lumber, plumbing, and wiring. At the same time, city officials worried over population projections, which indicated an immediate need for 32,000 housing units beyond those already authorized (the July estimate of maximum employment proved to be 60,000 over the actual figure).[32] The Housing Authority convened an emergency meeting of contractors, shipyard executives, and civic leaders on July 2. The same afternoon, the city council endorsed an ad hoc Citizens Committee organized by E. B. McNaughton of the First National Bank, retailer

Aaron Frank, and Edgar Kaiser to deal with the problems of appropriations and priority ratings. The committee dispatched a team to Washington to hound the bureaucrats and to mobilize Oregon's delegation on Congress.[33]

The key decision for Portland's defense housing came without the direct knowledge of the city council or the Planning Commission. Meeting behind closed doors at the beginning of August, Edgar Kaiser contracted with the Maritime Commission to build a massive housing project of 6,000 units (soon raised to 10,000). The Maritime Commission approved the actual site on a square mile of Columbia River floodplain just north of the Portland city limits on August 18.[34] Housing Authority members were as surprised as other Portlanders when Kaiser's bulldozers broke ground three days later. As nearly 5,000 workers set the foundations and raised the frames for 700 identical buildings on the muddy flats of Kaiserville, the Housing Authority members grumbled about the lack of consultation and complained that the project was convenient only to the Kaiser yards. In fact, they had no alternative but to accept management of the instant community, whose first tenants moved into "Vanport" on December 12, 1942.[35]

The obvious characteristic of the two crucial years for Portland housing policy was improvisation. Portland's political leadership bypassed formal planning institutions by establishing new advisory committees and creating new agencies. Indeed, the city effectively deactivated the Planning Commission at the height of the housing crisis. At the beginning of September 1942, Harry Freeman left his job with the Planning Commission to become full-time executive for the Housing Authority. A month later, William Bowes closed the Planning Commission offices and transferred the remaining staff to his Public Works Department. The Planning Commission held no meetings from September to December and convened only occasionally in 1943 to rubber-stamp decisions made by the city council.[36]

The same improvisation shifted the locus of influence on planning policy. The Greater Portland Defense Housing Committee of 1941 had a civic committee's customary mix of businessmen and community spokesmen, but the smaller Housing Authority clearly represented the city's housing industry. The makeup of the Housing Authority and the deemphasis of the Planning Commission reduced the influence of the city's liberal planning lobby but opened opportunities for input from new elements in the community, of whom Edgar Kaiser was the most conspicuous. If the creation of Vanport was not sufficient evidence of Kaiser's influence, Mayor Riley also ceded him the primary responsibility for choosing replacement members of the Housing Authority.[37]

The implementation of emergency housing in Seattle also required ad hoc committees. The Housing Authority of Seattle had been
established in March 1939 to build federally assisted low-rent housing
under the Housing Act of 1937. Its first project in 1940 under the
guidance of Executive Director Jesse Epstein was Yesler Terrace,
690 low-cost apartments on the southwest edge of downtown Seattle.
However, clearance of the Yesler site brought the Housing Authority
as many enemies as friends. In the fall of 1940 the Real Estate Board
and the Municipal League questioned the need for the 200-unit Sand
Point Homes, a project designed for married enlisted personnel at
the Seattle Naval Air Station. City council hesitated to approve Sand
Point Homes without the assurance that the apartments would not
later be converted into permanent public housing.[38] At the same
time, the Seattle _Times_ complained that liberal "housers" were ex-
ploiting the defense buildup for their own purposes. Through the
first half of 1941 the newspaper repeatedly questioned the Housing
Authority's definition of a housing crisis, cited the real estate boom
and bust of World War I, and argued that the private market was
capable of meeting Seattle's housing needs.[39]

The successful record of the Housing Authority of Seattle
reflected the strong leadership of Epstein and the willingness of Earl
Millikin and other elected officials to commit themselves to emergency housing. The Seattle Planning Commission benefited from no
such support. Established in 1925 and reorganized in 1932, it functioned in 1940 as a zoning appeals board with the help of a part-time
executive secretary borrowed from the Engineering Department. In
the 1930s the city council had several times overruled the Planning
Commission without a required public hearing. The commission in
turn operated without a master plan and refused to give opinions on
"controversial" issues like the Lake Washington Bridge.[40]

Early in the war years, three mayors in succession raised the
issue of a stronger Planning Commission but failed to follow through
in the press of politics and the mobilization emergency. In March
1940 Arthur Langlie aired plans to restructure the Planning Commission for better long-range planning. As the chairman of the commission told the newly inaugurated Earl Millikin a year later, "Langlie
had in mind a new ordinance which would give more responsibility to
the Commission and perhaps provide funds, but he never got around
to do it."[41]

Earl Millikin stirred new expectations in March 1941 by announcing _his_ intention to revitalize the commission. Three months
later he appointed six new commissioners and told city council that
he was interested "in the creation of a Planning Commission for the
City of Seattle with powers to proceed with the making of plans for

the growth of this city, for the providing of better housing and sanitary conditions, and for the absorbing of the shock of cessation of defense industries at the close of the present emergency period." Significantly, he reassured council that the Planning Commission should not be given enough power to "bring criticism and embarrassment to your honorable body." To make sure, the council ignored his suggestion that the Planning Commission be enlarged to allow the recruiting of "more varied talent."[42]

The third round belonged to William Devin, who told the city council in June 1942 that "when this war is over, Seattle has the opportunity of becoming one of the nation's largest cities. . . . We must be prepared to expand intelligently and not haphazardly. It would be well for us through the Planning Commission to prepare a master plan for the Seattle of the future and to construct each improvement in accordance with that plan, to lay out on paper our future parks, playfields and schools, our civic centers and boulevards, our industrial and commercial areas." At the same time, however, he appointed an ad hoc War Production Transport Commission to deal with traffic and street congestion, excluding the Planning Commission from one of the two areas in which professional planning had specialized for the last two decades. Without further support from the mayor's office or council, the Planning Commission's agenda was limited to three or four zoning petitions per month.[43]

There was greater interest in formal planning outside the city limits of Seattle than inside. In 1940 the King County Planning Commission noted the need for long-range planning to avoid the detrimental impacts of "temporary, emergency solutions" during the expected boom. The King County planners also worked with the Washington State Planning Council (WSPC) and the NRPB to organize the Puget Sound Regional Planning Commission (PSRPC) in December to deal with wartime problems in a 12-county region. The monthly meetings of the PSRPC brought together more than a score of city, county, and port district officials in 1941 and 1942. Its agenda included a regional highway plan, coordination of new public facilities, and encouragement of the formation of local planning agencies. Most of the day-to-day work of Executive Secretary Joshua Vogel involved collection of basic planning data and technical assistance to smaller cities and counties on hospital needs, school district consolidation, housing sites, and traffic surveys.[44]

In the fall of 1942 the NRPB and the WSPC decided that the Puget Sound Commission was ready to sponsor a comprehensive regional study. Puget Sound Region: War and Post-War Development appeared in May 1943. The work was conceived and supervised by professionals within the federal planning network—Joshua Vogel, Pat Hetherton of the WSPC, and Roy Bessey of the Pacific Northwest

Regional Planning Commission in Portland. The chapters were contributed by planners tied into the NRPB network and by university
professors. The result was a data inventory rather than a planning
document. Its analysis of natural resource development and growth
through the 1930s gave an economic profile of the region at the start
of the war, but its final paragraph was a request that local governments translate the data into action. As Roy Bessey admitted to the
NRPB's Charles Eliot, "Since the Puget Sound Regional Planning
Commission feels that it has only advisory status, the recommendations may not be as concrete as might have been hoped for."[45]

POSTVICTORY EMPLOYMENT

The three-year boom in Seattle and Portland slowed in the
second half of 1943, giving city officials some breathing space in
their scramble to provide services and turning the attention of civic
leaders to peacetime reconversion. Beyond the immediate worries
about traffic jams and trailer camps, both cities feared a postwar
recession. In the Seattle area the index of economic activity for the
Puget Sound counties held a plateau from mid-1943 through the
early months of 1944 but dropped in the spring. A more limited index
of Portland department store sales had jumped by 90 percent from
1940 to 1943 but grew only 9 percent from 1943 to 1945, while bank
clearings and building permits fell from 1943 highs.[46]
The indexes reflected the stabilization of metropolitan populations. Both Portland and Seattle had neared their wartime highs by
November 1943. The Portland area added only 7,000 more residents,
and the Seattle area only 14,000 more by the beginning of the next
summer (Table 4). Employment in Seattle area manufacturing topped
out in November 1943. Portland's private shipbuilders and Bremerton's federal shipyard reached their largest payrolls early in 1944.[47]
By the start of 1944, politicians proclaimed victory over the
disruption of mobilization. Announcing his candidacy for a second
term on December 13, 1943, William Devin asserted that Seattle
in the previous 18 months had "met every challenge and responsibility given to her by reason of the war. . . . She has housed and trans-
ported her thousands of new citizens and maintained efficient functioning of all public services in the face of regulations, shortages,
and countless handicaps." The next spring, Earl Riley could claim
to have "solved the problem of expanded service . . . housing,
policing, transportation, fire protection, recreation, and the scores
of other emergencies that have come with the war and with the tens
of thousands of new homes and workers."[48] A follow-up report by
the Subcommittee on Congested Areas of the House Naval Affairs

Committee agreed that the two cities were well prepared for the intensification of the Pacific war. A year after the subcommittee's hearings in October 1943, its staff found "greatly improved" housing conditions in the Puget Sound area and a housing surplus in Portland-Vancouver.[49]

Civic leaders realized that the problems of postwar readjustment were just as serious as the short-term crisis of mobilization. Polls conducted by Kaiser executives in Portland and the Seattle Chamber of Commerce showed that more than 75 percent of each city's war industry workers hoped to remain after the war.[50] Massive layoffs at the shipyards and defense plants and the return of military personnel would be only partly offset by the revival of the civilian economy and the return of women workers to their homes. Nathaniel Engle, head of the University of Washington Bureau of Business Research, calculated that King County would need 117,500 more jobs after the war than it had in 1939. Estimates of potential unemployment for metropolitan Portland hovered around 70,000; a calculation using Engle's method gives a requirement of 78,000 jobs over the prewar total.[51] Business Week summarized the concern: "How to absorb these people into the Portland economy, or—better still, from a narrow point of view—how to thank them and send them home, is the No. 1 problem in the No. 1 problem city of the area with the most debatable postwar future."[52]

Portland's politicians turned to an ad hoc organization rather than to established planning agencies for a reconversion strategy. In February 1943 William Bowes appointed a Portland Area Postwar Development Committee "to study and recommend action on the problems of postwar planning for employment and healthy urban growth in the Portland metropolitan area during the remaining term of the war and during the critical immediate postwar years." The 47 members represented the city government, banks, utilities, local retailers, manufacturers, labor unions, the real estate and construction business, newspapers, and civic and religious groups. The chair was David Simpson, current president of the chamber of commerce and past president of the National Association of Real Estate Boards. Advisers came from the Pacific Northwest Regional Planning Commission, the Northwest Electric Company, and the Bonneville Power Administration. The committee's larger mandate included planning for improved transportation connections, industrial expansion, and suburban development. More immediately, it focused attention on the development of a public works program.[53]

Since William Bowes had oversight of both the new committee and the Planning Commission, he periodically reassured the commission that it would be included in the deliberations of the Postwar Development Committee. However, he assigned it no specific tasks.

Given that three of the Planning Commission's members served on
the Postwar Development Committee, Bowes may have felt that
formal communication was redundant, but the fact remains that
Portland's political leaders judged their established planning organization inadequate for the job of economic planning and public works
programming. Even when the Planning Commission gained a new
technical director in September 1943, it had to share his time with
the Postwar Development Committee, for which he was director and
secretary. [54]

Indeed, members of the Portland Area Postwar Development
Committee themselves had relatively limited influence on the final
form of the city's postwar plans. The committee spent its first seven
months setting up subcommittees and holding desultory meetings.
By August, Edgar Kaiser could no longer contain his impatience and
made his own arrangements to bring New York City's Robert Moses
to Portland. Even William Bowes, who cultivated the image of the
no-nonsense pragmatist, was taken aback by the speed with which
Kaiser dispatched the question. "Mr. Kaiser called the postwar planning group and others into the Arlington Club and laid the whole program before them," Bowes reported. "It was just one, two, three
with him! I was amazed at the energy and push of that man." Under
Kaiser's prodding, the Postwar Development Committee agreed to
front for an invitation that had already been accepted. The $100,000
cost of the consultation was shared by the city of Portland, Multnomah
County, the port of Portland, the Docks Commission, and the Portland School District. "Don't be surprised if Mr. Moses comes with
a staff of about forty people," Bowes warned the Planning Commission. "What they will do is give us a shot in the arm. He is bringing
his port engineer . . . and six attorneys. These are the people who
know all the larger ones in Washington. They know where money is
available." [55]

The plan for Portland improvement that Moses presented on
November 9 matched his reputation as a "boulevard builder and city
planner." More than a dozen engineers and planners had spent two
months assembling their report from a suite in the Multnomah Hotel.
Moses himself spent six days in Portland to supervise the progress
and to add to his reputation by ostentatiously refusing public appearances. [56] As intended by Kaiser, the resulting document was a
massive public works program designed to "stimulate business and
help bridge the gap between the end of the war and the full resumption
of private business." [57] Moses and his associates proposed that
Portland-area governments undertake a $60 million construction pro-
gram to employ up to 20,000 workers during the first two postwar
years. The list included $20 million for a freeway loop around the
central business core; $20 million for improvements to sewers,

schools, public buildings, and the airport; $12 million for upgrading existing parks and streets; and $8 million for highway construction outside the city. The program placed greatest stress on the design of an efficient citywide system of arterial highways and on the enhancement of Portland's physical appearance by landscaping the Willamette waterfront, modernizing the railroad depot, and building a civic center.

Portland's elite endorsed the Moses report with enthusiasm. Bowes summarized its findings in a radio address on November 15, describing the drama of the Moses visit and arguing that his suggestions gave Portland an opportunity to build the wartime boom into permanent prosperity. Both the Oregonian and the Oregon Journal applauded the recommendations; the Oregon Journal reprinted thousands of copies; and the respected City Club issued a favorable evaluation. Bowes wrote Moses that there was "a real disposition on the part of the agencies to make full use of all the recommendations." Bowes and the Postwar Development Committee worked to coordinate the response of the agencies that had sponsored the report. The result in May 1944 was overwhelming approval of $19 million in bonds for new sewers, roads, and docks and a special $5 million school levy.[58]

During the debate on the Moses plan and the several bond issues, the Planning Commission found itself treated more as a tool than as an independent agency. Subcommittees of the commission developed detailed critiques of the highway and park proposals in Portland Improvement, but Bowes and other politicians wanted a broad endorsement rather than careful analysis of strengths and weaknesses. The Portland leadership made it clear that the May bond election was to be a general referendum on the idea of a public works program and dismissed specific objections as irrelevant.[59]

Unlike the hit-or-miss situation in Portland, postwar planning north of the Columbia took place within an impressive statewide structure developed by the Washington State Planning Council (WSPC). As early as 1941, the WSPC adopted "post-victory employment" as its major task for the biennium. Preliminary studies by its small staff showed that postwar job demand would be 40 to 50 percent above the 1940 employment total, while permanent jobs were likely to grow by only 15 percent. The council's response was a 53-member State Committee for Post-Victory Employment, intended to help local governments and corporations develop programs "to provide employment opportunities . . . in private business for just as many servicemen and present employees as it is economically possible after Victory comes."[60]

The core of the state effort was the promotion of local citizens' committees with members nominated by local organizations. Roderic Olzendam, the energetic chairman of the Weyerhauser Timber

Company, led the statewide campaign as head of the public relations committee of the Committee for Post-Victory Employment. Olzendam, Governor Langlie, and a field agent funded by the State Defense Council put in long hours at luncheons and evening meetings to sell the scheme, reaching 430 audiences by the summer of 1944. The WSPC distributed 15,000 copies of a pamphlet on "The New Washington State" in August 1943 and followed with a second pamphlet in January 1944. Arthur Langlie wrote every Washington mayor on January 5, 1944, to ask what they had done to set up local citizens' groups. [61]

The results were impressive in the aggregate. The WSPC counted 27 committees in March 1944, 60 in August, and 65 in October. They covered 130 communities and 85 percent of the state's population. More than 1,300 Washingtonians served on the local or statewide organizations. Another 5,000 had participated in community surveys of postwar job opportunities, consumer spending, and business investment plans. In the Seattle area, committees operated in Renton, Kent, Everett, Auburn, Enumclaw, Issaquah, Bremerton, and Port Orchard. Some industrial and consumer surveys became community enterprises involving the American Legion, the Parent-Teacher Association, or service clubs and introduced residents to the concept of systematic planning data. In others the appointment of a postwar planning committee bogged down in local politics. Mayor "Hum" Kean of Bremerton told Governor Langlie in no uncertain terms that he could handle his own city's postwar planning needs without advice from Olympia. At the opposite extreme, a single speech by Olzendam inspired the citizens of Everett to organize two citizens' committees, one under the auspices of the Everett and Snohomish County Chambers of Commerce and the other identified with the Snohomish County Public Utility District. It took careful diplomacy to merge ideological opponents into a single committee. [62]

The WSPC approach faced stiff competition in Seattle, where journalists thought that everybody had a postwar plan. [63] The Seattle Chamber of Commerce began to study postwar markets in 1942 "in order that Seattle will become a larger and greater city." Within the year, chamber officials were urging the WSPC to undertake similar studies elsewhere in the state, and the Post-Victory Employment Committee was in part a response to the pressure from Seattle. To protect the interests of the metropolis, Ben Ehrlichman, already chair of the chamber's Post-War Economic Development Committee, agreed to serve as vice-chair of the state committee in July 1943. [64]

Despite Ehrlichman's involvement, the Citizens' Committee of the Seattle Area did not appear until February 1944. William Devin provided the impetus after Langlie's prodding but complained indirectly that another committee was scarcely needed. Devin's charge to the 33-member group at its first meeting was to find jobs for all of Seattle's citizens and to make the city "a better place in which to live" by examining needs for schools, housing, libraries, parks, and public works.[65] The new group was essentially a council of representatives from the city's wide-range of private organizations engaged in postwar planning, and it relied on studies of economic opportunities conducted by the Seattle Municipal League, the Advertising and Sales Club, the Building Owners and Managers Association, and the Committee for Economic Development (CED). Organized as part of a national network of businessmen under the guidance of the U.S. Department of Commerce, Seattle's CED was effectively an offshoot of the chamber of commerce. It continued the chamber's industrial planning work under the direction of Ehrlichman. During the spring and summer of 1944, the local CED carried out a survey of Seattle manufacturers and presented the results at the first public meeting of the Citizen's Committee of the Seattle Area in September.[66]

The same meeting heard from a separate Post-War Public Works Advisory Committee established by city council. Mayor Devin described the city group as a "committee of action" to prepare specific public works plans and financing proposals. Much in the style of Portland's Post-War Development Committee, it ran its proposals past the Planning Commission as a courtesy before announcing a $36 million construction program to meet the needs of the swollen city. The Seattle School District and King County coordinated the compilation of their own lists totaling nearly $50 million.[67]

Seattle's approach to peacetime reconversion remained under the control of private business associations from start to finish. The engagement of Robert Moses in Portland had implied at least a secondary interest in the "city planning" issues of land use and community structure. Both the WSPC and the Seattle Chamber of Commerce/CED fixed their attention directly on private employers.[68] Postwar planning, said business professor Nathaniel Engle, "differs only in emphasis from normal advance planning by business." The chair of the Seattle Citizens' Committee similarly argued that postwar planning was a business rather than a government responsibility. Walter Williams told the September 1944 meeting that members "should encourage each of our citizens not to wait on a plan from some 'planning commission,' but to strike out boldly with initiatives, creative ideas, and positive, courageous and determined action of his own."[69] The legislature summarized the prevailing attitude the next year when it merged the WSPC into a Division of Progress and Industrial Development.

CONCLUSION

Despite the excitement and prosperity of the boom years, mobilization brought little lasting change to the economy of the Northwest cities. As it had in 1919, shipbuilding business evaporated quickly after victory in the Pacific. Portland and Seattle both attracted new factories to serve an enlarged regional market, but Boeing's new Stratocruiser failed as a domestic airliner. Manufacturing employment by the end of the 1940s had increased only slightly faster than population in both cities.[70] They left the 1940s as they had entered— regional wholesaling and financial centers.[71]

The same can be said for city planning as a local government function. The Seattle and Portland planning commissions emerged from the war with agendas unchanged from the 1920s—the relief of traffic congestion, the location of civic centers, and the revision of overgenerous zoning codes. The two organizations did enjoy larger budgets and expanded staffs after 1945, but their work soon bogged down in the sort of detail that had previously reduced their effectiveness. With no records of accomplishment from the war years to boost their credibility, they found themselves again on the outside of major development decisions.[72]

The experiences of Portland and Seattle during the war itself had clearly refuted the early optimism of the planning profession. Only in 1940 and 1941 were the Portland Planning Commission and the Housing Authority of Seattle able to guide professionally "proper" decisions about land development. Sand Point Homes in Seattle and Columbia Villa in Portland both were permanent low-rent public housing designed with careful attention to landscaping, pedestrian circulation, and low-density "suburban" architecture in the approved planning style of the late 1930s.[73] By 1942 and 1943, political and civic leaders ignored both city planning commissions and the Puget Sound Regional Planning Commission when faced with hard problems. They preferred that choices about defense housing, transportation, and postwar reconversion be made and ratified by ad hoc committees.

Improvised decision making had practical advantages. Special committees and new organizations were better able than established agencies to cope with exogenous variables in the form of federal officials, Boeing, and the Kaiser empire. Outside bureaucrats and businessmen could not be directly represented in the city's formal institutions, but they could be drawn into informal organizations without causing embarrassment to local officials. More generally, ad hoc planning kept hard decisions firmly in the hands of commercial-civic elites. Earl Riley and William Devin preferred defense housing built and operated by local authorities to direct construction by the federal government.[74] The membership of Portland's Post-War

Economic Development Committee was a who's who of downtown businessmen and executives of home-based corporations, who used their positions to influence patterns of postwar land use. Overlapping memberships on the Defense Housing Committee, the Housing Authority, and the Planning Commission ensured that the same set of businessmen with orientations to the local market would make direct planning decisions.[75] Prominent businessmen in Seattle participated in ad hoc planning through the chamber of commerce. A study of Seattle politics 15 years after the war found that the city's "big ten" still included Nat S. Rogers, who served on the board of the wartime Housing Authority and chaired the chamber's Housing Division, and Ben Ehrlichman, who linked statewide postwar planning, the Citizen's Committee of the Seattle Area, the chamber of commerce, and the CED.[76]

Reliance on special committees and new organizations excluded liberal planning activists. Each city had a core of citizens who supported housing reform, applauded the planning initiatives of the New Deal, and read the books of Lewis Mumford, Clarence Perry, and Catherine Bauer. Portland's planning advocates had worked for years to gain influence on the Housing Code and Planning commissions only to find themselves cut out of the action when key decisions were moved to other organizations. Planning enthusiasts in Seattle had great expectations when Earl Millikin appointed a new set of planning commissioners in 1941, but a few months left them mired in zoning cases.[77] The evolution of the two housing agencies into real estate management and social service agencies was a further diversion. Both the Portland and Seattle authorities oversaw day-care workers, playground supervisors, and cleaning crews.[78] After the war Portland proceeded to dismantle its public housing inventory as soon as returning veterans could find other accommodations. A flood in 1948 completed the process by demolishing Vanport.

In larger perspective, Portland and Seattle followed the national trend by defining only short-range, temporary goals for the home front. The search for expedient solutions to immediate problems brought an end to the federal activism of the 1930s. In a single year, for example, Congress crippled the Farm Security Administration, curtailed rural electrification, and abolished the NRPB. It also rejected significant federal assistance to postwar planning efforts.[79] Leaders in Portland and Seattle were equally happy to set limited tasks for planning. Both cities ignored the possibility of comprehensive planning that linked physical facilities, economic development, land-use patterns, and social services. They defined housing, postwar public works, and economic reconversion as separate issues. Wartime housing was tailored for minimum impact on the value of existing property, and postwar readjustment became a problem of industrial salesmanship. As observers of local politics might have predicted in 1940, ad hoc planning helped to ensure that Seattle and Portland ended the war with a minimum of permanent changes in land-use patterns, public services, or the people in charge.

NOTES

1. John Hancock, "Planners in the Changing American City, 1900–1940," Journal of the American Institute of Planners 33 (September 1967): 300; Robert Walker, The Planning Function in Urban Government (Chicago: University of Chicago Press, 1941), pp. 192–95; Marion Clawson, New Deal Planning: The National Resources Planning Board (Baltimore, Md.: Johns Hopkins Press, 1981), pp. 158–75.

2. Walter Blucher, "Planning and Zoning Developments in 1941," in Municipal Yearbook: 1942 (Chicago: International City Managers' Association, 1942), p. 359.

3. "City Planning Agencies," in Municipal Yearbook: 1942, p. 365.

4. Walker, Planning Function, pp. 185–86; The Planners Journal 8 (October–December 1942): 4; "City Planning Agencies," p. 365.

5. Walker, Planning Function, pp. 181, 300.

6. Mel Scott, American City Planning since 1890 (Berkeley: University of California Press, 1969), pp. 390–415; Blake McKelvey, The Emergence of Metropolitan America (New Brunswick, N.J.: Rutgers University Press, 1968), pp. 124–26; Clawson, New Deal Planning, pp. 181–83; "Report of the Committee on the War Effort," Planners Journal 8 (October–December 1942): 27.

7. Elliot Janeway, "Trials and Errors: Trouble on the Northwest Frontier," Fortune 26 (November 1942): 24, 26; "Seattle: A Boom Comes Back," Business Week, June 20, 1942, p. 26.

8. Roderick D. McKenzie, The Metropolitan Community (New York: Russell and Russell, 1967), p. 107.

9. The percentages are for employment in King and Multnomah counties.

10. Chauncy Harris, "A Functional Classification of Cities in the United States," Geographical Review 33 (January 1942): 86–99.

11. Calvin F. Schmid, Social Trends in Seattle (Seattle: University of Washington Press, 1944), pp. 302–9; Oregon Shipbuilding Corporation, Record Breakers (Portland, Oreg., 1945); The Pacific Northwest Goes to War (Seattle, Wash.: Associated Editors, 1944), pp. 19–28, 39–43.

12. U.S., Bureau of the Census, County and City Data Book (Washington, D.C.: Government Printing Office, 1947). The data on war contracts and population are based on a Seattle metropolitan area defined as King County (Seattle) and Snohomish County (Everett) and a Portland metropolitan area defined as three Oregon counties on the south side of the Columbia River—Multnomah County (Portland) plus suburban Clackamas and Washington counties. Unless noted otherwise, references to the Seattle and Portland areas use these definitions.

13. Charles Bender, Report on Politics in Seattle (Cambridge, Mass.: Harvard-MIT Joint Center for Urban Studies, 1961), pp. I-21, II-1-9; Murray Morgan, Skid Road (Sausalito, Calif.: Comstock, 1971), pp. 215-50.

14. Robert B. Dunn, "Seattle League Active in Bitter Election," National Municipal Review 31 (April 1942): 228-29; William Devin, speeches of March 7 and March 9, 1942, in William Devin Papers, University of Washington Manuscripts Collection, Seattle.

15. Bender, Politics in Seattle, p. II-8.

16. Earl Riley to Marshall Dana, May 18, October 22, 1940, to Charles Sprague, May 20, 1940, to George Baker, May 21, 1940— all in Earl Riley Papers, Oregon Historical Society, Portland; Oregon Voter, November 2, 1940; E. Kimbark MacColl, The Growth of a City: Power and Politics in Portland, Oregon, 1915-1950 (Portland, Oreg.: Georgian Press, 1979), pp. 609-14.

17. Seattle Times, January 8, February 14, March 30, September 17, 1941; Grant Buterbaugh, "Review of Business Activity in the Puget Sound Area for the Year 1941," Northwest Industry 1 (January 1942): 7; Washington State Planning Council, Fifth Biennial Report for 1940-42 (Olympia, Wash.: 1943), p. 53; Roger Sale, Seattle: Past to Present (Seattle: University of Washington Press, 1976), pp. 180-82.

18. U.S., Naval Affairs Committee, Subcommittee on Congested Areas, Hearings: Part 6, Puget Sound, Washington Area, October 25-27, 1943, p. 1301; Pacific Northwest Goes to War, p. 61.

19. Clark Kerr, "Migration to the Puget Sound Industrial Area," Northwest Industry 1 (July 1942): 2; Seattle Times, August 29, 31, 1941.

20. Schmid, Social Trends, p. 323.

21. Frederic C. Lane et al., Ships for Victory: A History of Shipbuilding under the United States Maritime Commission in World War II (Baltimore, Md.: Johns Hopkins Press, 1941), pp. 48-53, 114-15, 141-46.

22. Lane et al., Ships for Victory, pp. 248-49, 254.

23. U.S., Bureau of the Census, Sixteenth Census of the United States: 1940, Population, vol. 13, Internal Migration (Washington, D.C.: Government Printing Office, 1940), tables 10, 16; idem, Wartime Changes in Population and Family Characteristics, Portland-Vancouver Congested Production Area, Series CA-2, no. 6 and CA-3, no. 6 (Washington, D.C.: Government Printing Office, May 1944); Portland Oregon Journal, May 12, 30, June 4, 1944.

24. Louis Wirth, "The Urban Community," in American Society in Wartime, ed. W. F. Ogburn (Chicago: University of Chicago Press, 1943), p. 70; L. P. Cookingham, "The Effect of War upon Cities," in Planning: 1943 (Chicago: American Society of Planning Officials, 1943), pp. 15-26.

25. Earl Riley, radio address, May 1941, in Riley Papers; Portland City Planning Commission, Minutes, October 17, 1941, Portland Bureau of Planning Library, Portland; City Club of Portland, "Report of the Committee on Housing," City Club Bulletin, April 17, 1942, pp. 129-32.

26. William Devin, statement in U.S., Naval Affairs Committee, Hearings, p. 1320; Earl Riley, radio addresses, July 13, December , 1942, in Riley Papers; Portland Oregonian, May 11, 1944.

27. Portland City Planning Commission, Annual Reports for 1938 and 1941, Minutes for July 19, 1940, Portland Bureau of Planning Library; "Report of Special Committee on a Housing Authority for Portland," January 25, 1938, in Portland Housing Authority Papers, Oregon Historical Society. Also see Carl Abbott, Portland: Planning, Politics and Growth in a Twentieth Century City (Lincoln: University of Nebraska Press, 1983), p. 5.

28. Portland City Planning Commission, Minutes, April 11, 25, July 18, October 17, 1941.

29. Portland Oregonian, April 20, 1941.

30. Portland Housing Authority, Minutes, January 26, February 10, 11, March 19, April 13, Portland Housing Authority Office, Portland; Harry Freeman to Earl Riley, April 15, 1942, Riley to Winters Haydock, April 16, 1942, Haydock to Riley, April 1942—all in Riley Papers.

31. Portland Housing Authority, Minutes, February 10, March 27, April 13, 21, June 10, November 11, 1942; Portland City Planning Commission, Minutes, June 10, 1942.

32. Portland Housing Authority, Minutes, April 21, May 20, June 6, 1942; Harry Freeman to Earl Riley, July 11, 1942, Austin Flegel to Riley, July 23, 1942, Riley, radio address, July 11, 1942, memorandum from Portland Office, Works Progress Administration, June 29, 1942—all in Riley Papers.

33. "Minutes of Meeting Called by Housing Authority of Portland Relative to Priorities, July 2, 1942," in William Bowes Papers,

Oregon Historical Society; Portland City Council, Proceedings, July 2, 1942, Portland City Archives; Portland Oregonian, July 1942; Earl Riley to John Blanford, Jr., to Herbert Emerich, and to Emery S. Land all July 28, 1942, and Senator Charles McNary to Riley, July 29, 1942—all in Riley Papers.

34. "History of the Construction of Vanport City: Federal Public Housing Project no. Oregon 35053," looseleaf notebook, September 1, 1943, Oregon Historical Society; Lane, Ships for Victory, p. 433.

35. Portland Housing Authority, Minutes, September 21, 28, October 10, 28, 1942; Portland Housing Authority to Earl Riley, April 3, 1943, in Riley Papers; Chester Moores, quoted in Portland Oregonian, April 13, 1946; Memorandum from Information Division, Portland Housing Authority, April 1945, World War II Agencies Collection, Oregon Historical Society; Portland Oregonian, September 17, 1942.

36. Donald Nelson to Earl Riley, July 24, 1942, in Riley Papers; Portland City Planning Commission, Minutes, December 14, 1942; ibid., April 7, 1943; Portland Oregonian, September 23, 1942.

37. Mary Darling to Earl Riley, October 2, 1945, and Chester Moores to Riley, October 19, 1945—both in Riley Papers.

38. Seattle Times, September 7, 10, 1940; Housing Authority of Seattle, First Annual Report (1940) and Fourth Annual Report (1943), p. 6; Seattle Municipal News, September 28, 1940.

39. Seattle Times, September 20, 1940; ibid., January 3, June 1, 1941.

40. James A. Barnes, Comprehensive Planning in Seattle: 1911-1954 (Seattle, Wash.: 1954), p. 8; "City Planning Agencies," p. 369.

41. Louis Lear to Earl Millikin, March 22, 1941, in Millikin Papers; Seattle Times, March 20, 1940.

42. Earl Millikin to Seattle City Council, June 1941, and R. G. Tyler to Millikin, March 13, 1941—both in Millikin Papers; Seattle Municipal News, March 1, 1941.

43. William Devin, Annual Message to Seattle City Council, June 1, 1942, and radio address, September 23, 1942—both in Devin Papers; Barnes, Planning in Seattle, p. 8.

44. Joshua Vogel, "Puget Sound Regional Planning Commission," Northwest Industry 2 (December 1942): 8-14.

45. Pat Hetherton to Senator Mon Wallgren, September 30, 1942, B. H. Kizer to Charles W. Eliot II, May 29, 1943, Roy Bessey to Eliot, May 29, 1943—all in Postwar Planning Files, Washington State Planning Council Collection, Washington State Archives, Olympa; Washington State Planning Council, Fifth Biennial Report, pp. 58-59; Vogel, "Puget Sound Regional Planning Commission," p. 160.

46. Northwest Industry, 1942–45; Bureau of Business Research, University of Oregon, Oregon Economic Statistics (annual volume); Bureau of Municipal Research and Service, University of Oregon, Basic Factors Relating to the Financial Problem of the City of Portland (Eugene, Oreg., 1946), pp. 5–9.

47. U.S., Department of Labor, Bureau of Labor Statistics, Impact of War on the Seattle-Tacoma Area, Industrial Area Study no. 19 (January 1945); "Portland Stalks Postwar Spectre," Business Week, November 11, 1944, pp. 17–20.

48. Portland Oregonian, May 11, 1944; Earl Riley, campaign flyers, April–May, 1944, in Riley Papers; William Devin, statement of December 31, 1943, in Devin Papers.

49. U.S., House, Committee on Naval Affairs, A Report of the Congested Areas Subcommittee of the Committee on Naval Affairs: Investigation of Congested Areas, 78th Cong., 2d sess., pp. 2494, 2500.

50. "Workers Will Stay," Business Week, November 2, 1944, p. 102; Portland Committee on Postwar Planning, Report (Portland, Oreg., 1944). The Seattle Chamber of Commerce and the San Francisco Federal Reserve Bank polled 7,708 Seattle workers; 79 percent of the 1,602 who replied wanted postwar work in the Puget Sound area. The Kaiser Corporation interviewed 81,881 of its Portland area workers and found that 76 percent hoped to stay in the area if jobs were available.

51. Nathaniel H. Engle, "Jobs after Victory," Northwest Industry 3 (October 1943): 8; Robert Moses et al., Portland Improvement (New York: William Rudge's Sons, 1943), p. 13; Memorandum from Employment Committee of Portland Area Postwar Development Committee, July 1944, in Bowes Papers.

52. "Portland Stalks Postwar Spectre," p. 17.

53. William Bowes, radio address, spring 1943, and unsigned memorandum, Portland Area Postwar Development Committee, summer 1944—both in Bowes Papers.

54. Portland City Planning Commission, Minutes, January 15, June 25, August 23, 1943; Portland Area Postwar Development Committee, Minutes, January 3, 1944, in Bowes Papers.

55. William Bowes, statement in Portland City Planning Commission, Minutes, August 23, 1943.

56. New York Times, October 3, 1943; Portland Oregon Journal, November 9, 1943; Portland Oregonian, August 30, September 12, 26, 27, 29, 1943.

57. Moses, Portland Improvement, p. 1; William Bowes, statement in Portland City Planning Commission, Minutes, August 23, 1943.

58. William Bowes, radio address, November 15, 1943; Portland Area Postwar Development Committee, Minutes, January 3, 1944; William Bowes to Robert Moses, November 16, 1943, to Portland City Club, February 7, 1944, to Multnomah County Commission, School District no. 1, and Port of Portland—all February 9, 1944, all in Bowes Papers.

59. Portland City Planning Commission, Minutes, January 17, March 2, 1944; City Club of Portland, "Portland Improvement: A Report to the People on the Moses Plan," City Club Bulletin, January 28, 1944, pp. 81-98.

60. Washington State Planning Council, Ten Years of Progress, 1934-1944: Sixth and Final Report, pp. 85-86; Roderic Olzendam, "Citizens' Committee for Post-Victory Employment," Northwest Industry 3 (November 1943): 6-16; Washington State Planning Council, Minutes, May 29, 1943, in Washington State Planning Council Collection, Washington State Planning Council.

61. Washington State Planning Council, Ten Years of Progress, pp. 86-87; Roderic Olzendam to Arthur Langlie, December 9, 1943, in Postwar Planning File, Washington State Planning Council Collection.

62. Washington State Planning Council, Ten Years of Progress, pp. 85, 87-88; P. Hetherton to B. P. Garnett, August 22, 1944, James Neal to Fred G. Barnes, March 13, 1944, L. Kean to Arthur Langlie, January 20, 1944, Henry Arends to James P. Neal, February 14, 1944, Perry Black to Roland Dick, January 19, 1944, memorandum on Snohomish County, February 9, 1944—all in Postwar Planning File, Washington State Planning Council Collection.

63. A. G. Mezerik, "Journey in America: VII," New Republic 112 (January 1945): 14.

64. Christy Thomas, "Seattle Chamber of Commerce," Northwest Industry 1 (August 1942): 11-12; P. Hetherton, mimeographed letter draft, July 31, 1942, Hetherton to B. H. Kizer, July 30, 1943, Hetherton to Christy Thomas, October 8, 1943, William Devin to Arthur Langlie, January 5, 1944—all in Postwar Planning File, Washington State Planning Council Collection.

65. Seattle Post-Intelligencer, February 17, 1944; William Devin to Arthur Langlie, January 5, 1944, Langlie to Howard Barnes, February 10, 1944, James Neal to W. Walter Williams, February 17, 1944, and Minutes of February 24, 1944, meeting of the Citizens' Committee of the Seattle Area—all in Postwar Planning File, Washington State Planning Council Collection.

66. Seattle Star, September 14, 1944; Seattle Post-Intelligencer, March 3, 1944; Washington Post-Victory Employment Committee, Minutes, April 19, 1944, in Postwar Planning File, Washington State

Planning Council Collection; Washington Post-Victory Employment Committee, Minutes, September 26, 1944, in Langlie Papers.

67. Seattle Star, September 15, 1944; Seattle Municipal News, September 2, 1944; Barnes, Planning in Seattle, p. 9; William Devin to Arthur Langlie, January 5, 1944, in Postwar Planning File, Washington State Planning Council Collection.

68. "Seattle's Problem," Business Week, September 22, 1945, pp. 104-6; James E. Louttit, "Industrial Seattle," Pacific Northwest Industry 4 (August 1945): 164.

69. Seattle Star, September 15, 1944; Nathaniel H. Engle, "Postwar Planning Manual for Washington Business," Pacific Northwest Industry 4 (August 1945): 164.

70. Seattle area manufacturing employment increased by 46 percent, and population by 42 percent. The Portland figures were a 39 percent manufacturing employment increase and a 37 percent population increase.

71. Howard J. Nelson, "A Service Classification of American Cities," Economic Geography 31 (July 1955): 189-216; Otis D. Duncan et al., Metropolis and Region (Baltimore, Md.: Johns Hopkins Press, 1960), pp. 357-88.

72. Barnes, Planning in Seattle, p. 9; Abbott, Portland, chap. 7.

73. On Sand Point, see "Sand Point Homes," Architectural Record 91 (April 1942): 54-55. On Columbia Villa, see Portland Housing Authority, Minutes, February 10, 1942, and memorandum from Information Division, Portland Housing Authority, April 1945, in World War II Agencies Collection.

74. Earl Riley to Harry D. Capell, June 5, 1941, in Riley Papers; Riley to William Bowes, April 16, 1946, and Bowes to Riley, April 8, 1941—both in Bowes Papers.

75. MacColl, Growth of a City, pp. 584-90.

76. Bender, Politics in Seattle, p. V-8.

77. R. G. Tyler to Earl Millikin, March 3, 1941, and Margaret Thompson to Millikin, July 24, 1941—both in Millikin Papers.

78. "Vanport Grows," Business Week, December 11, 1943, p. 77; Portland Oregonian, August 22, 1943; Edgar Kaiser to Charles Gartrell, July 12, 1943, in Chester Moores Papers, Oregon Historical Society; "Vanport City Community Activities," memorandum, Information Division, Portland Housing Authority, in World War II Agencies Collection; Seattle Housing Authority, Fifth Annual Report (1944), pp. 11, 23.

79. Phillip Funigello, The Challenge to Urban Liberalism: Federal-City Relations during World War II (Knoxville: University of Tennessee Press, 1978), pp. 188-235; John M. Blum, V Was for Victory (New York: Harcourt, Brace, Jovanovich, 1976), pp. 323-32.

9

The Martial Metropolis: Housing, Planning, and Race in Cincinnati, 1940–55

Robert B. Fairbanks and Zane L. Miller

Federal government investment in war-related industries had a dramatic effect on many U.S. cities during the 1940s. The flow of defense contracts revitalized urban industrial sectors, provided jobs, stimulated business, and fostered an economic boom that affected all classes and virtually every locality within metropolitan areas. At the same time, burgeoning big-city war industries promoted the interstate migration and intrametropolitan mobility of both blacks and whites, movements that produced crowded housing conditions and social unrest. Indeed, the war presented a number of challenges to city dwellers. A particularly interesting and neglected aspect of the relation between war and urban development was the way in which civic leaders and public officials defined and responded to the city's wartime problems. Did the war fundamentally alter the way policy-makers approached the city? If so, what was the nature of that change? An examination of aspects of Cincinnati's experiences sheds some light on these and other questions.

Cincinnati benefited substantially from federal defense expenditures well before the United States entered the war. Between June 1 and November 1, 1940, the National Defense Council awarded Cincinnati industries approximately $21 million in defense contracts.[1] By March 1941, 180 local firms employing 42,069 workers held defense contracts, and in May of that year a chamber of commerce spokesman claimed that the "trend of business activity is now so definitely linked with the defense program that they are almost synonymous."[2] By that time, the federal government had signed major contracts with the Cincinnati Milling Machine Company, the Lodge and Shipley Machine Tool Company, the American Tool Works, and the Ridgewood Steel Company. But the biggest prize came in July 1940 when the

Wright Aeronautical Corporation announced that the Reconstruction Finance Corporation would finance the construction of a new, $39.4 million airplane engine plant in the Cincinnati area.[3]

The decision to build the plant stemmed from the nation's intensified commitment to defense expenditures. In a speech on May 16, 1940, President Franklin D. Roosevelt requested funds "to increase production facilities for everything needed for the Army and the Navy for national defense," including the construction of 50,000 planes per year. Shortly thereafter, the president established the National Defense Advisory Commission (NDAC) and gave it, among other duties, responsibility for aircraft production. On Memorial Day in 1940, William S. Knudsen, former president of General Motors Corporation but now chairman of the NDAC, called a number of industrial leaders to Washington to help plan a defense program. At that meeting Wright, the country's leading airplane engine manufacturer, agreed to expand its operations. Just two weeks later Wright presented to the NDAC a detailed plan for a new plant capable of manufacturing 1,000 Cyclone 14-cylinder radial air-cooled engines per month. The plant would employ some 15,000 workers on a $15 million annual payroll. Knudsen approved the proposal on June 13, although the legal and financial arrangements for the project remained unclear.[4]

Nonetheless, Wright began the search for a site. Plant officials initially preferred Philadelphia, a location close to Paterson, New Jersey, and Hartford, Connecticut, major centers in 1940 of aircraft engine production. Because of the threat of war, however, army officials wanted new plants built farther inland and stipulated that the Wright plant should be situated somewhere between the Allegheny and Rocky mountains. As a consequence, Wright concentrated its search in that broad area, looking especially for a place with good transportation connections, ample fuel, cheap power, abundant water, and an adequate industrial labor pool.[5]

Representatives of several cities, including Cincinnati, expressed an interest in securing this plum. Indeed, shortly after Roosevelt's May defense speech, the Cincinnati Chamber of Commerce launched a campaign to attract airplane plants to the Queen City area. The huge Wright plant looked especially alluring. Merely constructing Wright's 37-acre machine shop and assembly building would provide jobs for 2,500 construction hands, and the chamber estimated that the Wright factory's work force of 15,000 persons would swell the metropolitan payroll by 11 percent. Together, the chamber predicted, the construction and operation of the plant would "carry general business activity to levels beyond even 1929," a pleasant prospect made even more satisfying by assurances from company officials that the plant would continue to build engines after the war.[6]

Charmed by these possibilities, chamber officials engaged Wright in several "tense weeks of negotiations," during which the chamber anxiously responded to Wright's requests for information. Finally, on July 27, 1940, the company decided to locate the facility somewhere in the Cincinnati metropolitan area. Company officials said they liked the city's reputation for friendly labor relations and the area's abundant supply of experienced workers. But the company had also been impressed by the vocational training programs conducted by the public schools and by the willingness of school officials to make a special effort to help train the necessary labor force. As a Wright vice-president put it, Cincinnati could supply the needed manpower "better than anywhere else."[7]

During the rest of the summer of 1940, Wright officials simultaneously worked out financial arrangements for the plant with the Reconstruction Finance Corporation and looked for a plant site in the Cincinnati area. For assistance in finding a location, the company engaged the Robert A. Cline Real Estate Company, a Cincinnati firm, which took options on three parcels of land in north-central Hamilton County, each of them large enough to meet Wright's land requirements. All three lay on the outer and sparsely developed edge of the Millcreek Valley industrial and transportation corridor, an area 15 minutes from downtown Cincinnati, five miles north of the most congested of Cincinnati's late nineteenth and early twentieth century industrial suburbs, and four miles east of Greenhills, one of the three New Deal greenbelt communities built during the 1930s. Two of the three optioned sites also abutted several black subdivisions north of the small city of Lockland, subdivisions that the Cincinnati Better Housing League (BHL) and the Cincinnati Metropolitan Housing Authority (CMHA) regarded as slums suitable for clearance and redevelopment for public housing. On August 21, 1940, the company decided to take one of these latter two sites, a 219-acre parcel close to Lockland and the Big Four Railroad tracks.[8]

The factory went up in short order. Workers broke ground in October 1940[9] and began constructing the sprawling complex, designed to provide some 50 acres of floor space. The main building housed a machine shop and a 100 percent "in line" production unit, and two other edifices contained an aluminum cylinder head foundry and administrative space. In June 1941, exactly one year after federal approval plans for the plant, the central production unit opened,[10] and in the next three years Wright not only completed the other two buildings but also expanded the production unit and added another machine shop, an aluminum foundry, and a magnesium foundry. In 1944 the plant reached its peak, producing 25,860 engines.[11]

Throughout this period and beyond, local officials and civic leaders scrambled to ensure the smooth operation of the new Wright plant and to handle other problems related to its construction. Many of these problems, such as manpower training, transportation, and water, were resolved quickly through the close cooperation of metropolitan officials and agencies. Others, including housing and race relations, proved more difficult.

The problem of providing manpower training, though complicated, was resolved with the least difficulty. Wright needed approximately 10,000 skilled and semiskilled workers, but the region's pool of such people had been depleted by the labor demand in other defense industries. To overcome this shortage, the area's school boards agreed to conduct special company-supervised training sessions in their vocational schools. Funded with federal dollars, these classes would acquaint students with basic skills such as shop mechanics, blueprint reading, shop theory, and the handling of basic tools. The Cincinnati School District's Mechanical High School opened the first of these classes in September 1940, and by October 1941 eight vocational schools throughout Hamilton County conducted similar classes.[12] In addition to these public programs, the company initiated its own four-week training school, using facilities of other industries throughout the county to instruct its employees in the specific procedures used in the Wright plant. To supplement the corps of newly trained workers, the company also brought in 300 executives and skilled workers from its Paterson, New Jersey, plant. The entire program produced quick results; by February 1942 the new plant employed over 10,000 workers.[13]

Resolving the transportation problem in ways satisfactory to local and federal officials was more complicated. To deal with anticipated traffic congestion in the vicinity of the plant, County Engineer Houston Coates in January 1941 proposed the construction of a three and one-half mile, six-lane highway running north from Paddock Road, near Cincinnati's city limits, and past the Wright plant along the right of way of the old Miami and Erie Canal to the Glendale-Milford Road. Securing this route, which ran through parts of the municipalities of Cincinnati, Arlington Heights, and Lockland, as well as some unincorporated territory under county jurisdiction, rested on the cooperation of local, state, and federal officials. Although most of the money for the $1 million project came from the Works Progress Administration (WPA), the county commissioners and other local government bodies acquired the rights of way for the highway.[14]

Differences between the county commissioners and the WPA delayed the completion of the most important segment of the road, the northern stretch between the Glendale-Milford and Amity roads.

That section had been designated for completion by June 1941, when the aircraft engine plant would be in full production. But a dispute over the definition of defense needs postponed work on the road until May 1942. [15] The trouble started on September 22, 1941, when G. J. Kane, state director of the WPA, suggested to Washington officials that the highway project contained items that should not be funded by defense monies. He particularly objected to spending $47,000 for an access road for certain Lockland Road property owners, who would be left isolated by the highway. In addition, Kane argued that landscaping and relocation of water and sewer mains should not be paid for with WPA defense money. [16] Because neither the county nor the WPA had allocated funds to meet these needs, construction did not begin on the southbound lanes of the six-lane highway until May 13, 1942. [17]

The delay in highway construction meant that public transportation had to fulfill a greater role than originally expected. Soon after the start of construction on the new plant, the Valley Bus Company provided service from Cincinnati's central business district to the factory site. [18] By September 1941 passengers could also reach the plant by taking a streetcar from Cincinnati to Lockland, from where a free shuttle bus ran to the plant. As Wright continued to expand and add employees, direct bus service was opened to the plant from Price Hill in western Cincinnati. Still another route appeared when the State Public Utilities Commission authorized the Cincinnati Street Railway Company to operate bus service between Wright and Government Square, located in Cincinnati's downtown, for the duration of the war. Thus by November 22, 1942, a bus line, a crosstown bus line, and a streetcar line provided transportation to the engine plant at an average fare from downtown of 15 cents. [19]

Transporting workers to the plant proved easier than finding an adequate water supply. The Wright operation consumed 6 million gallons of 55°F water a day, a requirement neither Hamilton County nor Cincinnati could supply. And when the Wright Aeronautical Company started drilling artesian wells on its property to secure water from the Millcreek Valley water table, other industrialists expressed fear that the area's water table was falling dangerously low. As its demand for water increased to between 12 and 15 million gallons a day, Wright enlisted outside aid to acquire a waterworks in Fairfield Township in nearby Butler County. The Millcreek Water Works, as it was called, was constructed by the Federal Works Agency (FWA) in September 1942 at a cost of $2.25 million. This defense measure, which was to be operated by the Ohio Water Board, consisted of 11 wells dug into the Great Miami River Valley underground water supply and piped 13 miles to the plant. [20]

Despite the strain on local resources, and the demands on local governments resulting from the construction of the Wright engine plant, metropolitan officials willingly cooperated because of their support for the defense effort and their belief that the entire metropolitan community would benefit economically from the engine plant. As a result city, suburban, and county officials joined together and met many of the plant's needs without major disruptions.

Other problems, especially those involving race, proved more volatile.[21] From the outset, Wright's management advertised that it would hire blacks as well as whites. The company kept that pledge and soon became one of the area's major employers of blacks. In deference to the "racial preferences of the community," however, it ran segregated cafeterias and restrooms and originally intended to place blacks in menial positions and keep them out of the central machine shop. But as production demands increased and the supply of labor tightened, the company began placing blacks in skilled and semiskilled positions.[22] Then in January of 1944 the plant's Congress of Industrial Organizations (CIO) union elected a black as chairman of the Grievance Committee, an event that heightened racial tensions as some union members began to grumble about black participation and leadership in the union. At this juncture the United Mine Workers (UMW) launched a campaign to recruit Wright workers in preparation for a bargaining agent election scheduled for fall 1944.[23]

This tense situation developed at just the time the plant reached its peak production, and in June the company moved blacks into the central machine shop to fill seven vacancies. On June 5, 5,000 workers staged a wildcat strike to protest the integration of the machine shop. The CIO, Wright, and the National War Labor Board beseeched the workers to return, but on June 6, D day, 10,000 additional employees walked out. Meanwhile, UMW agents supported the strike and used the occasion to sign up between 5,000 and 7,000 disgruntled CIO members. In this context the National War Labor Board issued a back-to-work-or-be-fired ultimatum, and by June 9 the strike had ended. Thereafter whites and blacks worked amicably together, and the UMW, which had been suspected of fomenting the strike, lost its bid to become the bargaining agent.[24]

The resolution of the wildcat strike suggested that even racial conflict might be overcome under wartime conditions—and with an innovative solution (integration). But that was not the case with the issue of housing and race, a traditional problem in the Cincinnati metropolitan area exacerbated by the demand for workers at Wright and other defense industries at a time when the government restricted the use of building materials as part of the war effort. Most blacks in Cincinnati had always lived in congested and unsanitary dwellings, but their plight struck local observers in the 1930s and early 1940s as especially grim. In 1933 Stanley M. Rowe, head of the CMHA, estimated that 8 percent of all black families had doubled up, contributing to a black housing problem he characterized as "desperate." Yet by 1944 some estimates placed the black "doubling up" figure at 20 percent.[25]

Though few people thought so back then, blacks found new opportunities for better housing because of racial residential segregation. Of the city's 107 census tracts in 1935, only 16 contained more than 500 blacks. The largest number of blacks, 33,419, lived in the basin, the old walking city of the mid-nineteenth century, and 90 percent of them lived in the West End of the basin, the oldest, dirtiest, most dilapidated, and most congested of the city's residential districts. Walnut Hills, a Cincinnati neighborhood located northeast of the basin, accommodated 7,000 blacks, the second largest concentration in the city. Other black enclaves in the city could be found in Madisonville, Avondale, Cumminsville-Northside, Camp Washington, Oakley, and Sayler Park. The pattern of segregated housing, perpetuated by both local and federal policies, persisted through the 1940s, although its configuration altered slightly. Between 1940 and 1950, the city's black population jumped 50 percent, much of it absorbed by the basin, where the black population increased by 44 percent and the white population decreased by 12 percent.[26] But other neighborhoods, such as Mount Auburn, Madisonville, and South Avondale, experienced more than a 100 percent increase in their black population during this decade.[27]

These population shifts frightened many civic leaders. They feared that the combination of blacks frustrated by their inability to find housing commensurate with their wartime incomes and whites threatened by the expanding black ghettos might lead to racial conflict. That sense heightened in 1943 with the report of race riots in Detroit and other cities and peaked in 1944 with the stoning of the homes of two black families in Cincinnati neighborhoods undergoing racial transition.[28] But local housing officials and reformers regarded housing for blacks as a critical and defense-related question well before these events. That consciousness dated to the announcement of the coming of the Wright plant. It centered on the fear that the factory, located adjacent to several small, shabby black subdivisions near Lockland, would attract more "bad housing." Instead, they wanted defense subsidies for the immediate construction of appropriately designed public housing.[29]

Bad housing, and good, had a distinctive meaning then. The housing problem of the 1940s, as it had been since the 1920s, was defined as a problem of community, not merely as a problem of shelter, safety, sanitation, and family privacy.[30] According to housing experts and planners, the physical disintegration and psychological disorganization they found among so many metropolitanites resulted from their residence in a place characterized by mixed land uses, an extremely heterogeneous and mobile population, and an absence of formal social organizations. The worst of such chaotic settings produced slum dwellers: apathetic, anomic, and alienated individuals with an inhibited capacity for development as citizens. The solution was to create a city of better and stable communities, places where residents could live, shop, and interact with individuals sharing similar interests. Such a city would consist of relatively homogeneous neighborhood communities (based on race, economics, and other common ties), and such communities would instill in their residents the qualities and way of life necessary for successful urban living.[31]

This conception had both shaped the nature of public housing in Cincinnati and limited who could live in it. Having embedded the housing problem in the defective physical, social, and cultural setting, those concerned with slums had tried to combat all these deficiencies by demolishing the slum and replacing it with large-scale, low-rise community development projects and by setting admissions standards in such public housing so as to bar the hopelessly dependent poor. Laurel Homes, for example, the West End's and the city's first public housing project (1938), contained not only 1,309 units but also a shopping center, playgrounds, and a community building where the white tenants could meet, establish organizations, hold dances, read the project's newspaper, and develop "community."[32] Three more projects and an addition to Laurel Homes for blacks were under way by 1940, but these seemed far short of meeting the metropolitan area's low-income housing needs. Indeed, the two basin slum-clearance projects—Laurel Homes and Lincoln Homes (for blacks, of course)—had intensified the housing problem for blacks; the projects eliminated 1,746 dwelling units for blacks and replaced them with only 1,319 apartments open to blacks.[33] Because of this displacement, local housing officials in the late 1930s stepped up their lobbying efforts in Washington for a vacant-land public housing project for blacks north of Cincinnati near Lockland, a project they had been pursuing unsuccessfully since 1933.[34] The coming of the Wright plant gave them an additional argument. Soon after Wright decided to locate its plant near Lockland, Bleecker Marquette of the BHL and Stanley Rowe of CMHA wired Washington a request for a $2 million defense housing project for blacks, contending that the plant would attract more blacks into an area already classified as a slum.[35] That produced no immediate results; but in the winter of 1940, after passage of the Lanham Act, which outlined a specific program of defense housing, local officials journeyed to Washington to confer with C. F. Palmer, defense housing coordinator, about the procedures for securing defense housing. They were told that the Wright Aeronautical Corporation should first certify the need for a housing project near its plant and that the federal works administrator and the housing coordinator would "decide on the next step."[36]

The next step came on January 28, 1941, when Clark Foreman, assistant administrator in the FWA, inspected the area around the plant and informed the local housing authority that he would recommend a 350-unit housing project for blacks on the proposed site. Furthermore, he said, the FWA wanted CMHA to act as its agent and construct the project. Finally, Foreman requested that work begin immediately so that further housing shortages could be averted.[37] Formal approval came in early February when President Franklin Delano Roosevelt authorized the 350-unit project and allotted $1,224,290 for the defense effort. On February 11 CMHA formally agreed to build the defense housing project as the federal government's agent, thus becoming the first housing authority in the nation to do so.[38]

CMHA assigned the responsibility for developing plans and negotiating contracts for the project, which would be built on the site first chosen in 1933, to J. Stanley Raffety, manager of Laurel Homes.[39] Valley Homes, as the project was called, went up with more speed than any of the other CMHA projects. Completed in October 1941, four months after the opening of the Wright plant,[40] Valley Homes covered 46 acres and consisted of three-, four-, and five-room apartments in 53 two-story row houses, each containing between four and eight apartments. The apartments had concrete foundations and floors with wood frame walls and asbestos siding. According to the BHL, the contractors used the cheapest U.S. permanent housing construction material available.[41]

Valley Homes also lacked community facilities, despite Defense Housing Coordinator Palmer's assertion that defense housing should "create neighborhoods which contribute to decent living."[42] But CMHA did what it could to correct the shortcoming. It set up a community social program, including a Valley Homes Residents Council to teach tenants the fundamentals of self-government,[43] and arranged with the Woodlawn Board of Education, the Community Park Commission, and the Regional Planning Commission to build a day-care center for 80 children and a community building. The T-shaped, one-story community building, constructed to serve all blacks in the area, included a central meeting hall, club rooms, schoolrooms, a kitchen, and office space.[44]

Although built for blacks, many of those living in substandard and crowded accommodations elsewhere found it difficult to get into Valley Homes, which filled slowly. In the first place it was closed to all but war workers. In addition, the average rent came to $25 per

month, which meant that black tenants had to pay an average of $8
per month more than for their previous flats. And Lincoln Court,
the West End slum-clearance project for black defense workers,
charged only $14.94 per month. As late as May 1942 only 63 percent
of Valley Homes' apartments had been rented, despite the continuing
housing shortages for blacks.[45]

These high vacancy rates seemed especially bothersome because
Valley Homes had been constructed in part to relieve housing congestion among blacks in the West End. Indeed, CMHA gave top priority
to prospective tenants whose defense jobs took them beyond reason-
able commuting distance of their residences. Puzzled housing officials and reformers speculated about the explanation. Some thought
that high Valley Homes rents had something to do with it, feeling
that blacks preferred to wait in the hope of getting into the less expensive black section of Laurel Homes or Lincoln Court (these rents,
incidentally, were higher than those in white projects). In addition,
some BHL officials believed that Wright's management discouraged
black employees from living in Valley Homes because it might make
them more likely to join a labor union. At least one other opinion
was advanced at a CMHA meeting, namely, that "the majority of
Negroes would prefer to live in substandard housing with cheaper
rents than pay a higher rent at Valley Homes."[46] In any event Valley
Homes did not fill until September 1942, and then only 62 percent of
the tenants worked at Wright.[47]

Despite the completion of Valley Homes and the opening of
Lincoln Court, housing officials and reformers continued to worry
about the black housing shortage. In 1942 they noted with dismay that
the crush had pushed rents up 20 percent in "the colored West End,"
and in 1943 CMHA asked Washington to fund a white vacant-land
housing project, in part so that all of Laurel Homes could be turned
over to blacks. Rebuffed, Marquette asked federal officials to discourage black migration to Cincinnati and persuaded the BHL to
place ads in Southern newspapers advising black migrants to avoid
the Queen City.[48]

Late that same year, Cincinnati civic leaders concluded that
racial tensions stemming in part from the housing shortage might
lead to rioting. In response, Republican May James Stewart established
a Mayor's Friendly Relations Committee. Appointed in November
1943, the committee consisted of representatives of "various social,
industrial, religious and other groups" charged with "studying the
problems connected with the promotion of harmony and tolerance and
[the] working out of our community problems and as acting as an advisory committee for their solution." The committee functioned as a
peacekeeping agency rather than assuming an advocacy role for

blacks and did not attempt to devise a strategy, integrative or otherwise, for dealing with the housing problem.

Others, however, refused to let the issue rest. While continuing, unsuccessfully, to pester the federal government for more black housing, [49] local officials and housing reformers began to develop a strategy to meet the postwar housing shortage, which could be intensified, they thought, by the return of veterans. In 1942 CMHA informed the Cincinnati Planning Commission, city council, and the city manager that it planned a six-year, 3,600-unit, postwar metropolitan public housing program. This scheme rested on the Real Property Survey of Cincinnati and urbanized Hamilton County, a study carried out by the City and Hamilton County Regional Planning commissions and funded jointly by the city council, the county commissions, the Cincinnati Board of Education, and the federal government. The survey not only found 66,100 substandard or overcrowded living units but also confirmed a trend that some local observers had identified in the 1930s. The survey indicated that the city of Cincinnati was losing population to its suburbs and suggested that only the "physical redevelopment of existing blighted neighborhoods" could check the "outward flow," a notion congruent with the city's comprehensive plan of 1925, although this definition of the blight problem shifted the focus of concern from the basin to the entire central city of the metropolitan area. The CMHA's postwar planning in 1942 worked from this spirit, for it hoped to destroy substandard housing units and construct public community development housing at a rate of 600 units per year for six years after the war. [50]

The Real Property Survey did not envisage the CMHA as the prime agent for dealing with the stagnation and decline of the city, however. It assumed the city government should play that role and urged the city manager to appoint an advisory committee to review the Survey's findings and "to develop and report back to Council an adequate program looking toward the solution of the problems of shifting population and economic decadence apparent from the findings of the survey." The city manager reponded favorably to this suggestion and set up a committee in 1942. [51]

Meanwhile, Alfred Bettman, chairman of the Cincinnati City Planning Commission, and Bleecker Marquette had also identified the outward flow as a critical problem and had started to work on a different process for addressing it. Since the mid-1930s, Bettman had been seeking city funds to revise the city's comprehensive plan of 1925, and in the early 1940s he began to push for the writing of a new comprehensive master plan to guide the metropolitan area's postwar development. In addition, Bettman and CMHA head Stanley Rowe, assisted by R. R. Deupree, president of Proctor and Gamble, and Frederick Geier, president of Cincinnati Milling Machine, put together in December 1943 a businessman's committee to persuade the city to fund the planning effort.[52] "While our sons are scattered throughout the World fighting our battles and suffering great hardships," argued Rowe in one appeal, "surely we shall give freely of our time, money and effort toward laying the groundwork for making this a better locality to which they will return."[53]

The business leaders cooperated in part because they had already organized to take care of returning veterans and to promote expansion after the war, which they felt had artificially stimulated industrial activity. They acted under the impetus of the federal Committee for Economic Development, headed by Paul G. Hoffman. That group persuaded Renton K. Brodie, a vice-president for Proctor and Gamble, to head the effort in southwestern Ohio; and Brodie in turn recruited Frederick V. Geier, president of Cincinnati Milling Machine, to take the lead in Cincinnati. Rowe knew about this project. Thus when Bettman came to him for help in securing funds for the master plan, noting that its implementation would provide "plenty of work for the soldiers when they come home," Rowe approached Deupree, who liked the idea of linking comprehensive planning and public works. Indeed, Deupree induced Rowe to become the first president of the citizens group by promising him the assistance of "a young and coming fellow" at Proctor and Gamble, Neil McElroy.[54]

The citizens group organized in December 1943 to support not only planning but also "every movement of a broad nature that is for the improvement of living and business conditions in the Cincinnati area." The group incorporated on a not-for-profit basis as the Citizens Planning Association for the Development of the Cincinnati Area, making it possible for contributors to take tax deductions, and in 1944 lobbied city council and the state legislature on the planning issue, started publishing a newsletter urging public support for planning and public works projects, and raised some $100,000 to underwrite a successful bond issue campaign to raise some $41 million for capital expenditures by the city, county, and Cincinnati schools.[55]

Meanwhile, council responded favorably to the planning advocates. On February 16, 1944, council appropriated $100,000 to the Planning Commission to create a Division of City and Metropolitan Planning and to hire for it a separate staff. After a careful nationwide search, the city employed Sherwood L. Reeder, former director of the Regional Federal Public Housing Authority in Detroit, as director of the Master Planning Division. As consultants, council hired Ladislas Segoe, who had helped prepare the 1925 plan, and Tracy Augur, a planner for the Tennessee Valley Authority.[56]

While the metropolitan planners developed their scheme, the postwar housing shortage became a matter of critical concern. In

November 1945 the BHL told city council that "overcrowding is at an unprecedented peak" and that Cincinnati faces "a grave shortage of housing greater than any the city has experienced in decades." The memo also predicted that "unless emergency measures are taken now, indications are that the situation is going to be completely out of hand by Spring of 1946"; for within six months some 40,000 veterans would join the 19,000 servicemen who had already returned to Greater Cincinnati, creating an additional housing shortage of between 3,000 and 6,000 units.[57]

Council responded on January 2, 1946, by following a BHL recommendation to establish a Mayor's Commission on Housing to determine factors inhibiting the construction of homes and to find housing for veterans. The committee acted quickly, setting up on January 21, 1946, an Emergency Housing Bureau. Financed by War Chest funds, the bureau served as a depository for local housing information and publicized the need to share housing with returning veterans.[58]

That same month, council, with the endorsement of BHL, decided to construct temporary housing units in the city, a solution to the housing shortage that local authorities and housing reformers had staunchly resisted through the Great Depression and World War II on the grounds that such a remedy by definition violated sound community housing principles. Under conditions prescribed by the Mead Amendment to the Lanham Act, council secured former army barracks containing 620 units and spent approximately $1,600 per unit for grading and extending utilities in the parks and on vacant land in public housing projects where officials located the temporary housing. Blacks received 20 percent of these units on sites segregated from white housing.[59]

Managed by the CMHA, the three-, four-, and five-room temporary apartments went to "distressed veterans," which the CMHA defined as people being evicted or persons occupying substandard housing.[60] Renting for $30 per month, demand for the units ran strong. By August 1946, 2,300 veterans had applied for apartments, and the CMHA had to form a Veterans Committee to select eligible tenants, considering not only need but also length of overseas duty, disability, and other war-related factors.[61] In addition, the CMHA began in September 1945 to give veterans preference in filling vacancies in public housing projects without respect to the former requirement that tenants had to come from substandard housing units. But the CMHA, despite the shortage of housing for black veterans, persisted in excluding them from its white projects, including the "white section" of Laurel Homes.[62]

Despite the reluctant adoption of temporary housing for veterans, and the CMHA's special efforts to help this group, the housing

shortage persisted. In 1947 yet another mayor's committee, the
Cincinnati Committee to Expedite Housing (CCEH), deplored the situation. The CCEH executive secretary Charles H. Stamm complained
that "the greatest obstacle in dealing with the housing problem was
the lack of comprehensive and accurate statistical information for
the Greater Cincinnati Metropolitan Area." He also called 1947 a
"year of disappointment and frustration" and pointed to the lack of
new housing for low- and moderate-income veterans, especially
those earning a little more than the maximum income limits to qualify
for public housing. He also noted the lamentable condition in the West
End, where needy families had been denied access to public housing
by war and postwar priorities. War workers with incomes above the
normal maximum had been given admissions priority in Lincoln
Court and Winton Terrace, and the CMHA had not evicted those whose
incomes exceeded even the wartime maximum standard. Thus by the
end of 1947, 1,006 overincome families occupied 20.7 percent of all
public housing units. As late as October 1948, 871 overincome families remained in CMHA projects. [63]

In 1948, then, prospects for improving low-income housing
conditions in the Cincinnati metropolitan area seemed inauspicious,
a problem addressed by the new metropolitan master plan, completed
in October 1947 and issued in 1948. The 1948 master plan called for,
among other things, massive slum clearance and residential development, nonresidential redevelopment on the riverfront and in part of
the West End, and a new urban expressway system, the first portion
of which would go through the West End. All of these projects would
displace low-income people, especially blacks, and thus increased
the need for low-income relocation housing—a need it expected to be
met in part with public housing. And the master plan also endorsed
the homogeneous neighborhood community and racial residential
segregation principles on which planning, housing officials, and
housing reformers had operated since the 1920s. [64]

More specifically, the plan of 1948 defined a circular Cincinnati
metropolitan area consisting of Hamilton County, Ohio, and Kenton
and Campbell counties in Kentucky and emphasized the redevelopment
of the existing urban structure within this area rather than the creation of a new form. The plan described the metropolitan area as a
"mature" metropolitan community with modest prospects for economic
and population growth—but one within which the popularity of the automobile would encourage a continuing drift outward of the population.
The plan also divided the metropolitan landscape into two systems,
one for "living" (residential) and one for "making a living" (industrial
area, major transportation trunkline routes, and the central business
district). [65]

The residential strategy of the plan of 1948 defined three arenas of activity: neighborhood, community, and the metropolis. This vision and strategy rested on the conviction that "when a city expands beyond a certain size it reaches the point of diminishing returns in terms of the advantages which a city, as a social community, should provide for its inhabitants." To gain maximum advantages, and to secure a sense of community at both metropolitan and submetropolitan levels, the plan proposed to organize Cincinnati's metropolitan residential areas into "communities" of about 20,000 to 40,000 people, not self-governed but "self-contained in respect to the everyday life of their inhabitants except for such facilities and services as will continue to be located in or supplied by Cincinnati as the central city, and by institutions serving the Metropolitan Area."[66]

The conception of the metropolitan residential area as a cluster of medium-sized "cities," some inside and some outside the jurisdiction of the area's major municipality (Cincinnati), and like "real" small cities in every way except governmentally, seemed to offer several advantages according to the master plan and one of the plan's special studies entitled Communities. This volume sketched a history of Cincinnati as the growth of neighborhoods around the original settlement, the annexation of a number of them to Cincinnati, their retention of "identities," and the grouping of some of them into "communities" by virtue of the Cincinnati area's hill-and-valley topography. This circumstance the study deemed most "fortunate" because it tended "to preserve as the city grew, some of the better qualities of small town life, such as the spirit of neighborliness and the sense of attachment to a locality—qualities so easily lost in the full flood of urban expansion." Specifically, asserted the study, people in "smaller cities . . . participate to a greater extent in community activities; a larger percentage goes to the polls; a higher proportion contribute to the Community Chest; more are interested in public affairs." And "here in the Cincinnati Area, to a greater degree than in most large cities, residents enjoy the economic and cultural advantages of a metropolis while living in residential localities small enough to satisfy the urge for intimacy in home surroundings and/or a social life in scale with the average family."[67]

Unfortunately, however, history had not adequately completed the task of community building, and the plan proposed "to strengthen the present rudimentary neighborhood composition of the Metropolitan Area . . . to form an organized 'cluster' of communities, each further divided into neighborhoods." The boundaries of each community should encompass 20,000 to 40,000 people on 1,000 to 2,000 acres and be drawn with reference to "separators," such as topographic features, industrial belts, railroads, large parks, greenbelts, cemeteries, institutions, and projected expressways; and each community would be connected to the expressways by community thoroughfares, and by expressways or intercommunity thoroughfares to the central business district and the larger metropolitan community of work, entertainment, education, and social and cultural activities.[68]

The plan cited four internal elements critical to the viability of the new communities: school, business, civic, and balanced housing facilities. That is, each community should be served by a high school, or at the least by two junior high schools, and a cluster of neighborhood elementary schools. Each should possess a "community business district, a secondary business district in relation to the Metropolitan Area as a whole, but the chief center of commercial activities so far as the community is concerned." Each should contain near its business district a community civic center composed of a branch library, a recreation center, a health center, a branch post office, and, in some cases, appropriate semipublic buildings. In addition, each community should possess both single-family homes and apartments of various density levels so as to accommodate "young couples, . . . growing families and . . . elderly persons," therefore eliminating the necessity for a family "to move away from friends, neighbors, churches and other associations as it arrives at various stages of the life cycle." And while the plan expected future single-family home construction to predominate outside the central city and apartments inside, thereby dividing the metropolis spatially into homeowners and renters, the distinction made little difference to the planners, who thought of both locales simply as sites for communities, small towns exhibiting the social and civic characteristics ascribed to such small towns by the planners.[69]

The 1948 plan's communities scheme, with its emphasis on accommodating the family life cycle, presented each community as equal and in many respects as identical but also provided a way of permitting and accommodating racial, ethnic, and class heterogeneity within a community without talking in those terms about diversity—a classic example of a pluralistic taxonomic system that harmonized heterogeneity with homogeneity and that accepted racial residential segregation as normal and something to be preserved. The mechanism for doing this was the notion of neighborhood, for in forming each community the planners tried to group "traditional" and therefore segregated neighborhoods on the basis of spatial contiguity without specific reference to their class, ethnic, or racial profiles.

According to the master plan, an ideal neighborhood would contain 400 to 800 acres and a population of 4,000 to 8,000 connected to its community and the metropolis by the thoroughfare and expressway systems and bounded, but not entered, by major traffic streets.

Each neighborhood, moreover, would have all the attributes of a community except a civic center. Each neighborhood, that is, would have an elementary school with a children's playground as well as additional playgrounds where necessary, one or several "neighborhood" shopping centers, and "sometimes" additional "local" shopping centers consisting of a few stores. And each neighborhood would have some mix of single-family homes and apartments, depending on its proximity (a function of its history in the history of the development of the metropolitan core and periphery) to the metropolitan central business district, the symbolic and functional center and central cohesive element of the metropolis.[70]

The plan of 1948 recognized, of course, that it had to apply its ideal neighborhood and community treatment to a real city, not an abstraction. To adjust the ideal to reality, it returned to a historical analysis, one that pictured the metropolis roughly as a concentric circle of older and newer neighborhoods, with the older neighborhoods at the core, the middle-aged in the next ring, and the new ones toward the periphery. In this connection the plan also analyzed the life cycle of a neighborhood. Together these analyses depicted a declining core, with its poor and black residents gradually moving from old residential neighborhoods falling to nonresidential uses into declining residential neighborhoods nearby. The plan thus depicted a filter-down process of urban growth by which blacks and the poor spread from the oldest and worst neighborhoods contiguously into adjacent and declining neighborhoods.

The plan was quite specific in elaborating the stages in this process. "Each neighborhood," it said, "has a distinct 'life-cycle,' and the urban area . . . consists . . . of a vast patchwork of neighborhoods which had their origins at different points in time." Each had a period of growth, shortly after the initial subdivision, then a period of stability "during which the neighborhood tends to retain its original character." Then comes "decline . . . the sale of homes rises again, with changes in the type of population coming into the neighborhood . . . a shift from owner to tenant occupancy, accelerated perhaps by the conversion into smaller apartments of larger homes," changing land-use patterns, heavier traffic, more institutions, and the incursion of industry or heavy commercial uses.[71]

Then comes the nadir, exemplified by the Basin.

In the oldest, and hence the most centrally located neighborhoods, not only will the deterioration and obsolescence of the housing have proceeded to a marked degree, with exceptionally high vacancy, a high percentage of tenant occupancy, and very low rents, but the pattern of land use may also have changed radically from

its original character into what is familiarly known as
slums and blighted areas, or, in this report, "deteriorated areas." The best examples in Cincinnati of this
situation—neighborhoods that have already reached, or
are approaching the end of their life cycle—are found,
of course, in the Basin area. Here neighborhoods that
were in their time among the finest in the city, have
become through force of circumstance ripe for the most
complete redevelopment.[72]

The master plan then classified Cincinnati's neighborhoods by
their age groups and by the housing conditions in each age group as
a preface to the prescription of treatments for each category. This
analysis produced five categories with recommendations for handling
each. Deteriorated areas received the most drastic care: "complete
clearance and a fresh start through redevelopment for either private
or public use, in accordance with the master plan." Those areas
verging on deterioration but not yet slums (blighted) were scheduled
for "neighborhood conservation and rehabilitation," which meant
demolition of the worst structures and/or areas, reduction of heterogeneity in land-use patterns and of residential overcrowding, repair
and modernization of dwelling units, and the introduction of playgrounds and schools. Middle-aged neighborhoods fell in the "conservation" rubric, a program to be carried out for the most part by
owner occupants through organized neighborhood effort with Planning
Commission staff assistance to induce property owners to modernize
buildings, to adhere to the master plan, and to help arrange financing.
Newer neighborhoods would require only "protection" through adequate zoning and careful planning. The last category was called
"preparation for new growth," which applied to "neighborhoods which
are just beginning to develop" and involved an assessment of the
character of future development and the arrangement and ordering
of the parts of the neighborhood and community structure to meet
the size and nature of these youngest of urban places.[73]
    Thus the residential strategy of the 1948 master plan aimed to
perpetuate and perfect past patterns of urban growth and the familiar
form and structure of the metropolitan area, including its social and
racial geography and the filter-down process that facilitated residential racial segregation, a process that the plan described specifically.
It predicted and encouraged rapid population growth "in the major
peripheral communities" of the metropolitan area and modest
increases or decreases "in the built-up portions of the urban area
lying generally between the Basin and the peripheral communities."
In the "older neighborhoods" of the basin, the plan projected a
50 percent population decrease by 1970, "assuming adequate

redevelopment," and a 27 percent decrease without it. Other "middle-aged sections" within the city of Cincinnati—namely, in predominantly white Avondale, St. Bernard, Clifton, Cumminsville, Norwood, and Walnut Hills—could expect to maintain their levels of population but would experience a population change nonetheless. That change, the planners said, "will be in the composition and character of the population and in the types of residential structures, rather than in . . . size." In short, poor white and black inhabitants of the Basin would move out to the next band of neighborhoods on the north and east with the implementation of the master plan of 1948, which sought to preserve rather than to create a new urban form, structure, and social and racial geography.[74]

In this sense a "conservative" document, the master plan of 1948 nonetheless proposed drastic solutions to the problems of the metropolitan area, including residential and nonresidential redevelopment schemes and expressway construction through deteriorated areas that would displace and require the relocation of thousands of poor families, most of them black. The plan called specifically for federal subsidies to relocate these families in appropriate neighborhoods and communities and identified the sites for these activities, including three major existing black enclaves, the West End, Walnut Hills, and the recently (1946) incorporated village of Lincoln Heights, which encompassed the black subdivisions north of Lockland.[75]

Not only the plan of 1948 but also local housing officials and reformers fully expected to use federal subsidies for both residential and nonresidential redevelopment. Indeed, Alfred Bettman in the 1940s participated in writing and introducing the necessary state and federal laws, both of which passed in 1949. The federal legislation provided loans and capital grants covering up to two thirds of slum-clearance costs and permitted the sale and lease of the cleared land at a price below its market value. The state law authorized cities to adopt redevelopment plans and to use the power of eminent domain to secure property for such projects. It also required city councils to certify the existence of feasible plans for the temporary relocation of families displaced by clearance.[76]

By this time, too, Cincinnati's city council had already made arrangements for the CMHA to construct and manage relocation housing, and in 1950 council appropriated $175,000 for the first such project on Irving Street near the zoo on the edge of Avondale, a neighborhood then undergoing racial transition from white to black. This was to be a permanent public housing project to be used as temporary accommodations for people displaced by redevelopment. Construction began in April 1951 and produced 66 units renting at approximately $50 per month, a relatively high figure because this was not a federally subsidized project but one designed to earn a

return on the initial investment and pay debt service on the 40-year
3 percent bonds sold by the CMHA to finance the undertaking. The
project opened with all black tenants.[77]

Thus the Irving Street project did not meet the pressing need
for relocation housing for the poor whites and blacks expected soon
to be displaced by the city's initial West End expressway and redevelopment activities. And in 1941, Charles H. Stamm, now head of the
new Redevelopment Division of the City Planning Commission, re-
minded council of that need. It seemed especially pressing because
the Planning Commission in 1951 had selected two sites consisting
of 20 contiguous blocks west of Laurel Homes and Lincoln Court for
a housing development to be built by private enterprise and therefore
too costly for the site's inhabitants. Some 1,600 families lived in the
area, most of them black and almost all of them earning less than
$3,000 per year and unable to pay $50 per month rent. Stamm also
told council that "the great majority of people living in the project
area are colored, and are certain to be discriminated against in
their efforts to relocate in other parts of the city."[78]

Still, Stamm remained optimistic about meeting the need to
relocate blacks. Using a market survey done by the Cincinnati
Bureau of Governmental Research, Stamm claimed that some 4,000
to 5,000 of the city's blacks could afford to pay $50 or more per
month for housing. He also reported that local builders had assured
him they could build rental housing for blacks in the $40 to $70 per
month range and homes for purchase for $9,000 to $10,000, although
it would be prefabricated construction. Stamm conceded that finding
sites would be difficult because housing for blacks would stir "considerable opposition from surrounding neighborhoods." But he added
that, if necessary, outside builders could be obtained who would "not
be subject to the pressure which could be placed on a local builder."[79]

Persuaded that the black relocation housing problem could be
handled, council initiated the West End redevelopment housing scheme
by placing a $2.35 million urban redevelopment bond issue on the
ballot for November 1951. At that same session Councilman Theodore
Berry secured the passage of a redevelopment policy asserting that
no families would be displaced from a site unless suitable housing
existed for them elsewhere. It also stipulated that displaced families
should receive first preference in redevelopment projects and that
developers using cleared land could not practice racial discrimination
in their projects. But the bond issue failed, going down by big mar-
gins of 61 percent in one project site and 58 percent in the other.
BHL ascribed the failure largely to the vagueness of relocation plans.[80]

This setback, plus the postponement from 1952 until 1955 of
expressway construction, gave time for further consideration of relocation housing and public low-income housing for those earning $2,000

and under. In that period the CMHA attempted to carry out a modified public housing policy under which it would not add units to existing sites, such as Winton Terrace, which had ample vacant areas.[81] Indeed, the modified CMHA policy rejected the previous strategy of building massive, self-contained public housing communities in favor of the construction of housing projects that would use existing neighborhood and community facilities, a policy dovetailing neatly with the 1948 master plan's goal of dividing all the metropolitan area's residential sector into neighborhoods and communities. In addition, the CMHA announced that it would not build public housing on redevelopment sites, for they seemed more appropriate for private sector construction, and that it preferred vacant land sites that private developers could not afford to use but where utility costs would not be excessive.[82]

This policy modification severely inhibited the CMHA's ability to develop public housing, in part because of the difficulty in securing sites. This became clear in 1952 when the CMHA announced its plan to build 340 public units for whites and blacks on 35.8 acres of land previously operated as a dairy farm on the east side of Kirby Road about one tenth of a mile north of Frederick Avenue. People living in the area vehemently protested the project, producing petitions with 1,000 names attached, claiming that the project would decrease property values and increase crime and delinquency. BHL and CMHA also heard reports that petition circulators raised the question of race by asking potential signers if "you want Niggers in your backyard?" In any event the protestors secured a court injunction to delay the project, during which time the CMHA lost its option to buy the land. Another developer picked it up for the construction of 150 prefabricated low-cost homes to sell for between $9,000 and $13,000. The CMHA chose not to use eminent domain to acquire the property, perhaps because of the developer's intention to build low-cost housing or perhaps because of the vigorous opposition to the proposed project.[83]

Nevertheless, the CMHA managed to start one project in 1954, on the eve of the beginning of the city's massive urban redevelopment program. This was Millvale Homes, a black project completed in 1955 on a location in an isolated and depressed area not far from the Millcreek Valley railroad yards in Cincinnati. All its apartments had been rented by March 1955, the year in which construction began on the expressway system and a commercial development in a 20-block area of the West End, projects that would displace over 4,500 people, most of them black and poor. They had no alternative but to double up in the aging housing stock of the new and growing inner-city black ghetto northeast of the Basin.[84]

Thus in 1954 the CMHA still operated segregated housing projects, and future prospects for the desegregation of those projects did not look bright. To be sure, Public Housing Authority (PHA) officials had urged the CMHA to stop designating black and white quotas in some of its projects and to evaluate potential residents exclusively on the basis of emergency of need (including displacement) because of persisting vacancies for whites and a shortage of vacancies for blacks.[85] In 1954, however, all of the CMHA's PHA projects were still officially designated as segregated.[86] And the city's and the CMHA's relocation strategy for the pending urban development program acknowledged that the bulk of displaced persons would be black, that those blacks who could afford private sector housing would find places in all-black neighborhoods or in neighborhoods undergoing racial transition from white to black, and that the CMHA would take care of the rest.[87] This could only mean that public housing would, to all intents and purposes, become black housing. Thus while the city and the CMHA in 1954 talked about accepting people in public housing without respect to their race, they adopted policies that would perpetuate the CMHA's and the metropolitan area's racially segregated residential pattern.

The era of World War II, then, created a number of opportunities and challenges for metropolitan Cincinnati. Its civic leaders, moreover, approached them as metropolitan issues. The war provided the Cincinnati Chamber of Commerce an opportunity to spur industrial growth through the acquisition of the Wright Aeronautical Plant. To be sure, Wright abandoned the plant after the war. But three years later the War Assets Administration sold it to the Electric Auto-Lite Company, a transaction dubbed by the president of the chamber of commerce as "the best piece of industrial news for Cincinnati since the original announcement that the Wright plant would be built."[88] During the war, too, local officials from a variety of jurisdictions worked with the state and federal governments to handle Wright's needs for manpower training, transportation, and water. Some of these efforts left a useful legacy. The suburban municipality of Harrison purchased from the federal government the water plant built for Wright and furnished water to factories in the Millcreek Valley, which had been depending on the rapidly diminishing Millcreek water table.[89] In addition, the access road to Wright proved to be an important leg in the development of the Millcreek Expressway after the war. And during the war local officials and civic leaders overcame race problems within the Wright plant and a disruptive wildcat strike by integrating the machine shop.

Civic leaders also approached the housing problem, which in their view the war and the return of veterans intensified, as a metropolitan issue. Despite persistent and serious efforts to deal with this

question, conditions in the 1940s and 1950s worsened. The source of
that failure rested in the emphasis upon creating community, which
ruled out other approaches while stressing the necessity of immersing
individuals in homogeneous neighborhoods, including large public
housing projects. Housing officials, housing reformers, and planners
believed that only in such neighborhoods could individuals learn
through cooperation the importance of interdependence and a respect
for and tolerance of diversity at the metropolitan level.[90]

This sort of emphasis on community also helps explain the
handling of the race issue. It was that approach that sustained a
policy that sought separation of equal accommodations but that per-
sistently condemned blacks to separate and unequal public and private
housing. It was that approach that made it seem sensible to establish
a race relations agency that fostered tolerance and "peaceful" race
relations rather than the advocacy of equality and residential integration for blacks. These actions may seem strange, especially in
an era when the wartime emergency forced blacks and whites to share
the same assembly line and to get along on that assembly line. Yet it
was not actual conditions but the way in which civic leaders defined
the issues that explains both these actions and the fundamental continuity between 1920 and 1950 on the issue of race in housing and
planning. Only in the 1950s, with the emergence of a tendency to
identify the individual rather than the neighborhood or metropolis as
the fundamental unit in American urban civilization, did the issues
of black inequality and residential racial segregation become identified in Cincinnati as major problems.[91] And those problems remain
with us today, reminding us of this generation's failure to formulate
appropriate resolutions to problems first defined 30 years ago.

NOTES

1. Cincinnati Post, November 19, 1949, p. 1.

2. Cincinnati Business, May 20, 1941, p. 1. For employment
figures—and the emergence of a labor shortage, rather than unemployment, as a problem—see Form ES-270A, Negro Labor Supply,
March 15, 1941, Cincinnati Urban League Papers (hereafter cited
as UL Papers), Cincinnati Historical Society (hereafter cited as
CHS); "Unemployment in Cincinnati, May 1940," Monthly Labor Review 51 (December 1940): 1367; Cincinnati Business, April 22,
1944, p. 4.

3. By December 1941 the Cincinnati-Hamilton-Middletown area
had received $289,126,000 in defense contracts. Wright alone won
contracts totaling $129 million. Memorandum, J. Bion Philipson to
Philip Klutznick, February 27, 1942, National Housing Agency

(hereafter cited as NHA), Record Group (hereafter cited as RG) 207, National Archives (hereafter cited as NA); Cincinnati Enquirer, August 6, 1948, p. 12.

4. Wright Aeronautical Corporation, Cincinnati Plant Dedication Ceremony, pamphlet, June 12, 1941, n.p., CHS.

5. Tom Lilley et al., Problems of Accelerating Aircraft Production during World War II (Boston: Division of Research, Graduate School of Business Administration, Harvard University Press, 1947), pp. 32-33; Wright Aeronautical Corporation, Cincinnati Plant, n.p.

6. Cincinnati Post, July 27, 1940, p. 2; Cincinnati Business, August 20, 1940; Millcreek Valley News, November 15, 1940, p. 1; Guy W. Vaughan, "Sixty Planes a Day," Aviation 37 (December 1940): 62. Wright vacated the plant after the war, and it remained empty until 1948. Cincinnati Post, December 18, 1947, p. 1; Cincinnati Enquirer, August 6, 1948, p. 12.

7. Minutes, Cincinnati Chamber of Commerce Board of Directors, May 24, 1940, Chamber of Commerce Offices, Cincinnati; Cincinnati Post, July 27, 1940; Cincinnati Times-Star, July 27, 1940, p. 2; Cincinnati Enquirer, October 24, 1940, p. 12.

8. Millcreek Valley News, August 23, 1940, p. 1; Cincinnati September 24, 1940, p. 2; Interview, Richard R. Deupree, Jr., August 2, 1982, Cincinnati; Cincinnati Enquirer, October 18, 1940, p. 7. The choice of a suburban location was consistent with the policy on wartime industrial location voiced by Glenn E. McLaughlen, chief of the Industrial Location Section of the National Resources Planning Board. As he put it, "A program of suburbanization offers, among other things, a means of offsetting the costs of congestion. Where plants are large and employ great masses of workers . . . industries should be influenced to locate on the peripheries of cities." See Glenn E. McLaughlen, "Industrial Location and National Policy," Proceedings of the National Conference on Planning . . . 1941 (Chicago: American Society of Planning, 1942), p. 47.

9. The delay in the ground breaking stemmed from disagreements in Washington over how to finance defense industries. See New York Times, July 24, 1940, p. 1; Clifford J. Durr, "The Defense Corporation," in Public Administration and Policy Development, ed. Harold Stein (New York: Harcourt, Brace, 1952), pp. 292-301. See also Gerald T. White, Billions for Defense: Government Financing by the Defense Plant Corporation during World War II (Birmingham: University of Alabama Press, 1980).

10. Cincinnati Enquirer, June 13, 1941, p. 19; Cincinnati Post, October 23, 1941, p. 1. Line production was the process by which raw materials entered the plant at one end and went through a "flow through" manufacturing operation in a continuous line without backtracking. A completely fabricated unit emerged at the end of the line. Vaughan, "Sixty Planes a Day," p. 63.

11. Vaughan, "Sixty Planes a Day," p. 63; Cincinnati Enquirer, January 3, 1941, p. 4; ibid., October 10, 1944, p. 17; Lilley et al., Problems of Accelerating Aircraft Production, p. 107.

12. Cincinnati Enquirer, July 28, 1940, p. 15; ibid., September 17, 1940, p. 9; Millcreek Valley News, January 17, 1941, p. 1; ibid., October 4, 1940, p. 2; Cincinnati Times-Star, October 23, 1941, p. 12; ibid., August 12, 1940, p. 5. The War Production Training Program proved very successful. In Cincinnati alone, 12 schools participated and trained 39,381 men and women in 38 fields for the area's war industry at a cost of nearly $1.678 million. Cincinnati Public Schools, Report of the Superintendent, 1944-1945, p. 41.

13. Cincinnati Post, December 30, 1940, p. 12; ibid., August 12, 1940, p. 5; Millcreek Valley News, October 4, 1940, p. 2; Cincinnati Enquirer, November 26, 1940, p. 14; Minutes, Better Housing League (hereafter cited as BHL) Board of Directors, February 2, 1942, BHL Papers, Urban Studies Collection, Archival Collections of the University of Cincinnati (hereafter cited as UC).

14. Cincinnati Enquirer, January 20, 1941, pp. 1, 5; ibid., January 30, 1941, p. 1.

15. Ibid., January 20, 1941, p. 1; Cincinnati Times-Star, September 22, 1941, p. 19.

16. Cincinnati Times-Star, September 22, 1941, p. 19; Cincinnati Enquirer, September 23, 1941, p. 12; ibid., January 11, 1942, p. 29.

17. Cincinnati Enquirer, May 14, 1942, p. 5. The southern section of the road, from Hartwell Avenue to Paddock Road, was not completed until after World War II. Cincinnati City Planning Commission, The Cincinnati Metropolitan Master Plan, 1948 (Cincinnati, Ohio: City Planning Commission, 1948), p. 84.

18. Cincinnati Enquirer, May 24, 1941, p. 24.

19. Ibid., July 12, 1942, p. 38; ibid., November 3, 1942, p. 6.

20. Ibid., January 17, 1941, p. 3; ibid., January 24, 1941, p. 24; ibid., September 1, 1942, p. 16; ibid., September 17, 1942, p. 10; ibid., May 27, 1943, p. 12.

21. Local observers tended to ascribe the area's racial problems to the influx of white Appalachians, who allegedly brought their racial prejudices with them. See, for example, Cincinnati Community Chest, Division of Negro Welfare, Bulletin, August 1943, p. 2.

22. J. Harvey Kearns to Edward Dooley, August 14, 1941, UL Papers, CHS; Edward Dooley to J. Harvey Kearns, August 18, 1941, UL Papers, CHS; Cincinnati Call Post, June 3, 1944, scrapbook collection, UL Papers, CHS.

23. Cincinnati Enquirer, January 27, 1944, p. 1.

24. Ibid., June 6, 1944, p. 1; ibid., June 8, 1944, pp. 1, 7; ibid., June 9, 1944, pp. 1, 5; ibid., June 10, 1944, p. 1; "Industrial

Disputes," Monthly Labor Review 55 (August 1944): 357; Cincinnati Post, June 8, 1944, p. 2.

25. Tenth Annual Report of the CMHA, 1943, n.p.; Stanley M. Rowe to H. A. Gray, February 5, 1937, Cincinnati Metropolitan Housing Papers (hereafter cited as CMHA), CHS; Sun, July 14, 1944, p. 1; "City Manager's Annual Report," Cincinnati Yearbook, 1912, p. 43.

26. James A. Quinn, Earle Eubank, and Lois E. Elliot, Cincinnati Population Characteristics by Census Tracts, 1930 and 1935 (Columbus: Bureau of Business Research, Ohio State University, 1940), pp. 35, 43-45.

27. Benjamin P. Groves, "Growth of Non-White Population and Number of Occupied Dwelling Units in Selected Neighborhoods in Cincinnati and Hamilton County" (Urban Redevelopment Division, Cincinnati Planning Department, June 25, 1953), p. 7.

28. Cincinnati Post, June 6, 1944, p. 1; Minutes, Executive Board of the Mayor's Friendly Relations Committee, July 13, 1944, Cincinnati Human Relations Committee (hereafter cited as CHR), UC.

29. Henry Louis Taylor, Jr., "The Building of a Black Industrial Suburb: The Lincoln Heights, Ohio Story" (Ph.D. diss., State University of New York at Buffalo, 1979), pp. 190-94.

30. Robert B. Fairbanks, "Better Housing Movements and the City: Definitions of and Responses to Cincinnati's Low Cost Housing Problems, 1910-1954" (Ph.D. diss., University of Cincinnati, 1981), pp. 71-127.

31. For more on this approach see Manuel C. Elmer, "Social Service for the Slum: What Constitutes a Slum," in Slums, Large Scale Housing and Decentralization (Washington, D.C.: President's Conference on Home Building and Home Ownership, 1931), pp. 32-33. See Harvey Warren Zorbaugh, Gold Coast and the Slum: A Sociological Study of Chicago's Near North Side (Chicago: University of Chicago, 1929), pp. 260-74, for more on the dangers of heterogeneity.

32. Fifth Annual Report of the CMHA, 1938, pp. 3-5.

33. Memorandum, Bleecker Marquette to the Housing Division of the Public Works Administration, August 31, 1935, Public Works Administration (hereafter cited as PWA), RG 196, NA; Tenth Annual Report of the CMHA, 1943, n.p.; Minutes, CMHA, April 16, 1940, CMHA Building, Cincinnati.

34. Minutes, Citizens' Committee on Slum Clearance and Low Cost Housing (CCSC), February 21, 1941, BHL Papers, UC.

35. Minutes, CHMA, November 19, 1940, CMHA Building

36. Samuel E. Trotter, "A Study of Public Housing in the United States" (Ph.D. diss., University of Alabama, 1956), pp. 170-73; Minutes, CMHA, December 10, 1940, CMHA Building.

37. Minutes, CMHA, January 28, 1941, CMHA Building.

38. Cincinnati Enquirer, February 12, 1941, p. 1; Millcreek Valley News, February 7, 1941, p. 1; Eighth Annual Report of the CMHA, 1941, p. 8.

39. Cincinnati Enquirer, March 3, 1941, pp. 8-9; ibid., March 27, 1941, p. 1; City Constructor, August 5, 1943, pp. 1, 306.

40. Tenth Annual Report of the CMHA, 1943, table 1; Eighth Annual Report of the CMHA, 1941, pp. 8-9.

41. Eighth Annual Report of the CMHA, 1941, pp. 8-9; Cincinnati Enquirer, March 27, 1941, p. 2; Minutes, BHL Board of Directors, October 28, 1948, BHL Papers, UC.

42. George Herbert Gray, Housing and Citizenship: A Study of Low-Cost Housing (New York: Reinhold, 1946), p. 240.

43. Ninth Annual Report of the CMHA, 1942, p. 5; Millcreek Valley News, November 7, 1941, p. 1; ibid., June 16, 1944, p. 1.

44. Minutes, Hamilton County Regional Planning Commission, November 11, 1942, Ohio Network, UC; Millcreek Valley News, June 16, 1944, p. 1.

45. Ninth Annual Report of the CMHA, 1942, p. 5; CMHA, May 5, 1942, CMHA Building.

46. Minutes, BHL Board of Directors, February 2, 1942, BHL Papers, UC; ibid., March 25, 1943; Ninth Annual Report of the CMHA, 1942, p. 5.

47. Minutes, CMHA, February 10, 1942, CMHA Building.

48. Ninth Annual Report of the CMHA, 1942, p. 9; Minutes, CMHA, May 9, 1938, CMHA Building; Minutes, BHL Board of Directors, January 8, 1942, BHL Papers, UC; Cincinnati Enquirer, November 1, 1942, sec. 2, p. 1; Minutes, BHL Board of Directors, September 23, 1943, BHL Papers, UC; ibid., May 18, 1944.

49. Cincinnati, Mayor's Friendly Relations Committee, "The First Five Years of the Mayor's Friendly Relations Committee," n.p., CHR Papers, UC; Minutes, Meeting to Form Organization Interested in Racial Amity, October 7, 1943, UL Papers, CHS; Memorandum, Negro Organization Interesting in Racial Amity and Good City Government to Mayor Stewart's Committee, October 7, 1943, UL Papers, CHS; Memorandum, William Castellini to Mr. Johnson, January 3, 1944, CHR Papers, UC.

50. Fairbanks, "Better Housing Movements," pp. 366-67.

51. Ibid., p. 368.

52. Richard High, "The Planning Process in a Twentieth Century City: The Case of Cincinnati, 1935-1948" (Senior thesis, University of Cincinnati, Archival Collections, 1974), p. 9; George Stimson, "They Cared: A Citizens' Planning Association, 1944-1948; The Citizens' Development Committee, 1948-1968," unpublished manuscript, n.d., pp. 11, 13, Cincinnati Community Development

Committee (hereafter cited as CDC) Papers, CHS; Fairbanks, "Better Housing Movements," pp. 368-70.

53. Statement by Rowe, December 21, 1943, p. 3, CDC Papers, CHS.

54. Stimson, "They Cared," pp. 4, 10-11, 13, 15.

55. Ibid., pp. 20-28. The standard general accounts by urban historians of planning and housing activities during World War II have overlooked the role of Hoffman's Committee on Economic Development and of businessmen generally, an oversight contributing to the notion that planners, "houses," and businessmen worked at cross purposes, rather than as a coalition, during this period of urban renaissance. See, for example, Mark Gelfand, A Nation of Cities: The Federal Government and Urban America, 1933-1965 (New York: Oxford University Press, 1975); and Philip J. Funigiello, The Challenge to Urban Liberalism: Federal-City Relations during World War II (Knoxville: University of Tennessee Press, 1978). Business leadership in comprehensive planning receives more attention in Stefan Lorant, Pittsburgh: The Story of an American City (Garden City, N.Y.: Doubleday, 1964), pp. 373-456; and in Roy Lubove, Twentieth Century Pittsburgh: Government, Business, and Environmental Change (New York: Wiley, 1969), esp. pp. 106-41.

56. Interview, Stanley M. Rowe, December 6, 1979, Mariemont, Ohio; Stimson, "They Cared," pp. 6, 13; Interview, Ladislas Segoe, December 4, 1979, Cincinnati; "Statement Made by Stanley M. Rowe upon His Election to the Presidency of a Citizens Planning Committee to Further the Preparation nad Carrying Out of a Master Plan for the Greater Cincinnati Area, December 21, 1943," CDC Papers, CHS; Cincinnati City Planning Commission, The Master Plan. Report on Program and Progress (March 1946), pp. 1-2; Sherwood L. Reeder, "Revamping the Master Plan," Journal of the American Institute of Planners (Summer-Fall 1946): 14. On the search see High, "Planning Process," pp. 41-61.

57. Memorandum, BHL and the Citizens' Committee on Slum Clearance and Low Cost Housing to City Council, November 20, 1945, p. 1, BHL Papers, UC.

58. "Report of the Mayor's Committee on Housing," January 2, 1946, Rowe Office.

59. Cincinnati Enquirer, August 6, 1946, p. 18; Minutes, CMHA, March 5, 1946, CMHA Building. Two housing organizations recommended the use of temporary dwelling units but apologized for the step as "justifiable only as an extreme measure" to meet the crisis. Memorandum, BHL and the Citizens' Committee on Slum Clearance to City Council, November 20, 1945, p. 1, BHL Papers, UC.

60. Minutes, BHL Board of Directors, June 27, 1946, BHL Papers, UC; Cincinnati Enquirer, January 15, 1946; ibid., April 24, 1946, p. 7.

61. Cincinnati Enquirer, August 6, 1946, p. 18; Minutes, BHL Board of Directors, June 22, 1947, BHL Papers, UC.

62. Cincinnati Enquirer, August 23, 1947, p. 1; ibid., September 28, 1948, p. 6; Minutes, BHL Board of Directors, May 22, 1947, October 28, 1948, BHL Papers, UC; Minutes, CMHA, June 25, 1946, CMHA Building.

63. Fairbanks, "Better Housing Movements," pp. 364-66. Over-income tenants paid higher rents, which helped the CMHA to pay operating costs and debt services, but their presence compromised the CMHA's prime mission of finding neighborhood housing for low-income families. For a detailed account of attempts to meet the postwar housing emergency, see Fairbanks, "Better Housing Movements," pp. 352-66.

64. Cincinnati City Planning Commission, Cincinnati Metropolitan Master Plan 1948, pp. 31-32, 69-70, 79-104. The plan discussed the central business district only in connection with other focal points and issues and did not call for redevelopment of any sort within the central business district. The plan did address the central riverfront as a problem, however, treating it as a separate and discrete locale and suggesting that it should be redeveloped—that is, cleared and filled with expressway connectors, new bridge approaches, a baseball stadium, a heliport, a convention center, government office buildings, a historical memorial, a natural history museum, five high-rise apartment buildings, parking lots, parks and recreation facilities, and light industry. Cincinnati City Planning Commission, Cincinnati Metropolitan Master Plan 1948, pp. 141-49. In Cincinnati, downtown redevelopment planning began in the mid-1950s. See Zane L. Miller and Geoffrey Giglierano, "Downtown Housing: Changing Plans and Perspectives, 1948-1980," Cincinnati Historical Society Bulletin 40, no. 3 (Fall 1982): 177-88. In short, central business district interests did not use the war, the postwar housing emergency, or the 1948 plan as an opportunity to secure subsidies for the redesign and reconstruction of the central business district. The plan of 1948 was exactly what the title indicated, a metropolitan master plan, and its key conceptual element was the residential community notion, which occupied the central place and was explicated first (after introductory material) in the plan.

65. Cincinnati City Planning Commission, The Economy of the Cincinnati Metropolitan Area (Cincinnati, Ohio: City Planning Commission, 1946); Cincinnati City Planning Commission, Cincinnati Metropolitan Master Plan 1948, p. 10. The industrial policy of the

plan stressed that population and economic growth could only come through competition with other cities and by capitalizing on the area's current assets. The policy called for industrial development "on a selective, quality basis." The planners evaluated 109 areas of industrial activity from the perspective of their "possible contribution to the economy of the Area" and rated most highly "service activities," such as utilities, finance, insurance, real estate, communications, and government. The policy viewed the area's economy as an "integrated" unit, using as an analogue a single firm under one ownership and management that controlled all the operations involved in processing raw materials to the final product. Thus the plan aimed not so much on attracting entirely new industrial activities, such as defense firms not established in the area, as on attracting manufacturers of goods already in high demand by other local industries (it cited glass containers and paper cups as examples) or on using the area's "craftsman heritage" to develop additional producers of "precision and scientific instruments," many of which "are now represented in the Area." Cincinnati City Planning Commission, Cincinnati Metropolitan Master Plan 1948, pp. 17-21. This policy, of course, fit neatly into the plan's emphasis on the metropolis as the unit of concern and on the plan's commitment to redevelopment rather than reconstruction of the area. The planners contended that each metropolitan area possessed distinctive locational advantages—they stressed Cincinnati's role as "Gateway between the North and South"—and a distinctive industrial structure, which together defined the economic activities it might attract in the metropolitan sweepstakes under the "integrated opportunities" concept. Cincinnati Planning Commission, Economy of the Cincinnati Metropolitan Area, pp. 63, 69-71. This kind of thinking, in general, had a tendency to predetermine which areas would be most likely to pursue defense industries (and which kind) and which would not. Finally, the planners asked if growth were desirable, answered yes, and plugged for encouraging growth in those sectors of the economy promoting higher incomes and stable employment—those sectors, that is, least accessible to untrained and poorly educated workers such as blacks. Ibid., pp. 63-65.

66. Cincinnati City Planning Commission, Cincinnati Metropolitan Master Plan 1948, pp. 11, 27-34, figure 17; idem, Residential Areas: An Analysis of Land Requirements for Residential Development, 1945-1970 (Cincinnati, Ohio: City Planning Commission, 1946), figure 2.

67. Cincinnati City Planning Commission, Communities (Cincinnati, Ohio: City Planning Commission, 1947), pp. 2-6.

68. Ibid., pp. 6, 21-22.

69. Ibid., pp. 21-22.

70. Ibid., p. 9.

71. Cincinnati City Planning Commission, Residential Areas, pp. 17-18.

72. Ibid., p. 18.

73. Ibid., pp. 42-50.

74. Ibid., pp. 76-78.

75. Ibid., pp. 34-35, 54-55, 81. For a map of the residential and nonresidential redevelopment sites, see ibid., figure 7.

76. Fairbanks, "Better Housing Movements," pp. 379-80. Rowe played an important part in securing federal subsidies by educating Ohio's Senator Robert A. Taft, a Cincinnatian and a close friend of Rowe, on slum clearance and public housing. As early as 1943 Taft pushed for federal subsidies for public housing, a cause he supported through the passage of the federal legislation of 1949. See James T. Patterson, Mr. Republican: A Biography of Robert A. Taft (Boston: Houghton Mifflin, 1972), pp. 187, 315-30, 391, 420, 433-34.

77. Minutes, CMHA, May 23, June 27, 1950, CMHA Building; ibid., June 24, 1952.

78. Cincinnati Urban Redevelopment Division, "Preliminary Report on Relocation and Rehousing," August 8, 1951, Charles P. Taft, II Papers, Cincinnati Historical Society.

79. Ibid.

80. Fairbanks, "Better Housing Movements," pp. 395-96.

81. Ibid., p. 398; Minutes, BHL Board of Directors, October 25, 1951, BHL Papers, UC; Cincinnati Enquirer, June 16, 1952, p. 4.

82. Fairbanks, "Better Housing Movements," pp. 397-99.

83. Minutes, BHL Board of Directors, March 27, June 19, 1952, BHL Papers, UC; Minutes, CMHA, February 26, April 22, 1952, CMHA Building; Cincinnati Enquirer, November 23, 1952, p. 1.

84. Fairbanks, "Better Housing Movements," pp. 403-4.

85. Howard L. Chaney to Theodore A. Vienstra, Office Memorandum, March 11, 1952, Public Housing Authority (hereafter cited as PHA), Chicago Field Office, CMHA Building; Howard L. Chaney to N. P. Dotson, Jr., Office Memorandum, March 10, 1952, PHA, Chicago Field Office, CMHA Building; PHA, Chicago Regional Office, "Second Annual Management Review of the . . . CMHA," typescript, March 30, 1955, CMHA Building.

86. O. A. Cornilius, "Report on Operations of the Cincinnati Metropolitan Housing Authority affecting Rental and Occupancy," typescript, August 4, 1954, CMHA Building.

87. Office of the City Manager, Division of Slum Clearance and Urban Redevelopment, "Relocation Plans: A Manual for Family Relocation Services," typescript, 1953, CMHA Building. The Cincinnati Community Development Corporation, which was organized on the urging of the city to help handle relocation problems, under-

took segregated projects for both races during the early and mid-1950s. See ibid.; Zane Miller, Suburb: Neighborhood and Community in Forest Park, Ohio, 1935-1976 (Knoxville: University of Tennessee Press, 1981), chap. 1, esp. pp. 19-27.

88. Cincinnati Post, December 18, 1947, p. 1; ibid., December 19, 1947, p. 1; Cincinnati Enquirer, August 6, 1948, p. 12.

89. Cincinnati Enquirer, June 3, 1947, p. 6A; ibid., November 22, 1947, p. 1; ibid., August 6, 1948, p. 12.

90. Other approaches were available and suggested. See, for example, Fairbanks, "Better Housing Movements," pp. 208-12.

91. For additional discussion of the shift from the community emphasis to the new preoccupation with the individual, see Zane L. Miller, "History and the Politics of Community Change in Cincinnati," Public Historian, in press; Miller, Suburb, pp. xvii-xix, 28-29, 227-41.

10

Conclusion:
The Martial Metropolis

Roger W. Lotchin

For many years urbanists have been engaged in the task of classifying cities. Many new terms have arisen to characterize these specialized urban forms—industrial city, commercial city, maritime city, bureaucratic-commercial city, postindustrial metropolis, and the private city. More recently, David Goldfield has added another singular type of city, the Southern city, dominated not by the usual urban culture but rather by its rural past.[1] From the topics covered in this book it should be obvious that a new type of specialized urban entity has emerged in twentieth century United States—the martial metropolis. Not every city represented in this study would qualify for that description, at least in its purest sense. New York spurned the chase for military riches and, seemingly, so did Cincinnati. In the view of historian Alan Clive, so did post-World War II Detroit.[2] Many others, however, joined the competition and in doing so transformed themselves and the U.S. pattern of urbanization.

If an industrial metropolis is one that is shaped by its partnership with industry, a martial metropolis is one molded by its alliance with the U.S. fighting services. Perhaps by 1941 San Antonio was not yet hyperdependent on its military partnership, but certainly Nassau County, Charleston, Norfolk, Los Angeles County, and Junction City were. Nor would it tax the imagination to think of several more. San Diego, San Francisco Bay, Seattle, and St. Louis come to mind readily, and they would by no means exhaust the list of possibilities. This interface between the city and the sword was so close that, for example, by the 1970s, 42.7 percent of all manufacturing employment in Los Angeles and Orange counties was dependent on aerospace contracts, which represented only a part of the military expenditures in Southern California. Even as early as the 1930s, one

223

third of San Diego's payroll derived from a single employer—the U.S. Navy.

A city whose economic base is predominantly military, whose morphology is determined in part by its military ties, whose formal and informal governmental institutions like chambers of commerce and city councils are dedicated to nurturing their ties to the services, whose congressional representatives are experts in the business of securing military resources, and whose mayors' days begin with a phone call to Washington, D.C., can accurately be labeled a martial metropolis. Neither bureaucracy, commerce, nor industry influenced earlier U.S. cities any more thoroughly than militarization has shaped the U.S. cities represented in this study and others as well. The Charlestonians' classic warning—that "if another military installation is put into the Charleston area, it will sink"—would apply to lots of other places equally well. Of course, not every U.S. city would qualify as a martial metropolis, but neither would every city qualify as a bureaucratic-commercial metropolis, an industrial city, a maritime city, or an agrarian-dominated city. It will require further research to determine how many martial metropolises there are in the United States and their relative importance in the larger urban pattern. However, at this stage it is warranted to hypothesize that the martial metropolis is a distinct form of city and that—unlike the bureaucratic, agrarian-dominated, industrial, and other specialized urban forms—the martial metropolis is new to the U.S. urban experience.

Although recent and unique, the martial metropolis does add to our understanding of the broader forces of urbanization. Despite its peculiar friendship with the military, the martial metropolis has also been a part of the larger process of urbanization. These chapters make it clear that the process of suburbanization has been significantly shaped by the fact of military development. In San Antonio the placement of air bases around the city both encouraged the spread of the city outward and limited the expanse into which it could grow. In Charleston and Norfolk the economics of militarization underwrote the growth of suburbanization. The independence of suburban entities in these areas was, in part, determined by their ability to capture service resources to guarantee their own continued growth. In Nassau County the impact was more dramatic still. Although not engaged in a traditional urban rivalry, in that Long Island area, the aircraft industry transformed an already established commuter economy, based largely on its partnership with the city of New York, into a manufacturing center connected to the Pentagon instead of just to New York City. In brief, in several cities under review, there was a very direct relationship between war and defense on the one hand and urban geography and spatial relationships on the other.

The process of suburbanization has traditionally been explained as a function of America's agrarian and small-town values, the influence of the automobile, the need for more space to accommodate new manufacturing processes, the flight from unwanted neighbors, and so forth. It takes nothing away from these interpretations to insist that militarization also played a role in the development of suburbs. Militarization underwrote some suburbs, largely created others, and in both cases helped to spread the metropolis further into its peculiar U.S. form. In Los Angeles and vicinity, the ultimate suburban city, this influence was even more pronounced than in the other cities. In short, in the metropolises studied here, there is a vital connection between Mars and urban morphology.

This is another way of saying that the presence of military installations and factories also contributed to center-city decline. These activities required large amounts of space that built-up center cities could not provide. Like other enterprises that could not be accommodated in the more traditional urban form, military development often had to occur outside the city limits. Thus the center city suffered vis-à-vis its own periphery.

If the metropolitan-martial impulse undermined center cities, it has also helped reshape the national urban pattern. The term Sunbelt does not quite cover the phenomenon of shifting patterns of urbanization; but whatever we call it, there has been a reorientation of the process of urbanization away from established centers in the Midwest and Northeast. Whether the beneficiaries of this movement have been in New England, the South, the Southwest, or the Pacific Northwest, the shift has been important and metropolitan competition has been significant in producing this alteration of the process of urbanization. Metropolitan competition alone cannot explain this phenomenon; but by attracting military investment, the fact of urban rivalry helped establish the heavy dependence on defense spending that so largely undergirds Southern and Western growth.

These accomplishments have come about as a result of a kind of federal-urban partnership. Although that phrase has usually been employed in a reform sense, implying a mutually beneficial bypassing of state governmental jurisdiction, it has great developmental significance as well. The power of the federal government has frequently been exploited by cities to boost their own economies, as was certainly the case with the new martial metropolises. Whether this feat made cities more just, rational, or orderly is another question. This "other federal-urban partnership" probably has some limited reform significance, but it has undoubtedly influenced U.S. urban history.

In all of these ways then, the martial metropolis can illuminate the study of U.S. urban history in the broader sense. Yet these insights are not its greatest significance. For years historians have debated "the central meaning or significance" of the subdiscipline of urban history. While there is no written consensus on the matter, it would seem that most urbanists would agree with the judgment of Eric Lampard that urban history should strive to view the city as a dependent variable, an independent variable, and a series of consequences for society.[3] Although there is still considerable controversy over priorities in this list, the majority of urban historians would probably emphasize the second aspect—the city as an independent variable—most frequently. That is to say that they believe that urban history should strive above all to illuminate the urban difference. The consensus seems to be that urban history should emphasize the city as an independent variable, shaping the course of history instead of being molded by it. Some more recent writers are not so certain of the importance of this goal or even of the reality of the city as an independent variable, but most practitioners of the art of urban history either explicitly or implicitly accept both.

It is precisely here that the martial metropolis has most significance. However one may define the phrase process of urbanization, the art of city building must be included. City builders have a hand in initiating, sustaining, and accelerating the process of urbanization. That role may have been either greater or lesser. For example, even within a small geographic region the pattern differed. Charles Glaab found that Kansas City, Missouri, boosters benefited as much from luck as from leadership in bringing railroads to that town, while Robert Dykstra discovered that the same booster class played a crucial role in attracting that form of transportation to Wichita, Kansas.[4] Los Angeles perhaps excelled all other booster cities, not only luring the Southern Pacific Railroad into town (by a city government subsidy, voted by the taxpayers) but even providing its own water supply. In a sense every city guarantees its own continued existence by establishing waterworks that allow the city to accommodate vast populations without water shortages, continuous fires, and repeated epidemics. Without remote water supplies, urbanization could have proceeded in the humid regions of the United States, but only with the above-mentioned problems. Local, vastly polluted sources of water supported a population of over 1 million in London by the year 1811. However, in the arid West, water was simply not available even if people had been willing to undergo the discomforts of fire, plague, and filth that earlier urban populations had endured. In a semiarid region, aridity placed an absolute ceiling on the process of urbanization. Los Angeles therefore underwrote its own continued growth, again by action of the city government authorized by a public referendum.

It will perhaps be argued that cities do not compete with each
other and that supposed urban competitions are merely a surface
cover for hidden class, economic, or other agendas buried beneath
the rhetoric of community conflict. However, the idea of urban
rivalry has had a surprising vitality among urban historians. An
earlier generation accepted the idea easily, and younger scholars
have not discarded it. In fact, some of the most interesting recent
applications of the notion have occurred among those who would
undoubtedly be considered "new urban historians." For example,
Blaine Brownell found that a civic-commercial elite of urban leaders
consistently imposed an ideology of corporate-expansive boosterism
upon Southern cities in the 1920s.[5] What Brownell found in the South,
Don Harrison Doyle found in a community study of Jacksonville,
Illinois, in the nineteenth century.[6] If the booster ethos proved useful in Southern cities, it proved just as useful in building the social
order of a frontier Illinois community and city. In studying the rise
of bossism in Cincinnati, Zane L. Miller related that fact to what he
called the "relative decline" of that city, along with other matters.[7]
If Miller phrased the best description of the malaise of a losing city,
David Hammack related the idea to the most important metropolitan
consolidation in U.S. urban history—the merger of the suburbs and
city of the New York region into a Greater New York in 1898.[8] Judd
Kahn found the same impulse in San Francisco at the turn of the
nineteenth century, where the relative decline of that city produced
a competitive urge that Kahn called the "Imperial City."[9] But whether
their Darwinian urge sprang from decline or an ambition to impose
it on others, the Imperial City, in Kahn's precise and superbly appropriate phrase, has always been an American reality. Kenneth Jackson's chapter reminds us of what might happen to cities that unlearned
the lesson of competition; and other cities, particularly in the South and
West, understood well the lesson that New York City had apparently
forgotten. They organized for self-aggrandizement.

A city creating or sustaining itself in this manner meets our
definition of the city as independent variable, producing effects instead of being created by other forces such as regional economic
growth, industrial location decisions, transportation improvements,
class, race, ethnicity, and so forth. In fact, boosterism may be the
purest form of independent urban variable, since in this case city
people, representing city interests, consciously set out to manipulate
the process of urbanization. This control was certainly exercised in
several of the martial metropolises represented in this book.

Various alternative interpretations might be advanced to account
for the distribution of military resources in the United States. Southern and Western spokesmen seem to prefer to attribute their own
good fortune to the influence of climate and geography. These con-

siderations are undoubtedly important and may explain in part the overall distribution of military wealth to the South and West. For example, military technicians undoubtedly needed vast, unoccupied spaces in which to test their wares. Commanders of ground troops required the same advantages to train men and perfect equipment. The amenities of a good climate, nearby beaches, and accessible mountains probably lured corporate executives and scientists to the Pacific Southwest defense industries as many writers have insisted. Yet these requirements could have been met in a variety of Southern and Western places. It took something more to secure the allegiance of military men to certain geographic localities. And city builders could provide this added measure of attraction.

Military location decisions are very much like industrial ones. Service planners want the same kind of mix of advantages that other large operations require, and climate and geography do not exhaust the list of assets needed for military purposes. As Gregory Fontenot has demonstrated, Fort Riley planners badly needed extra land for expansion. Kansas was literally land rich, but this land was not necessarily available to Fort Riley. This asset could be gained only through the political process. Junction City leaders provided this territory in the same way that city boosters elsewhere supplied it to other industries in the form of industrial parks and urban renewal clearance land. Just as Pittsburgh city officials evicted city dwellers from their homes to accommodate and therefore retain its steel industry, Junction City leaders ousted a part of its surrounding farm population in order to hang on to the armed forces.

Securing land was only one of the many services the town provided the base. Any number of U.S. cities and towns illustrate the importance that industry attaches to a generally accommodating urban partner organized to promote the interests of its local business. Junction City certainly provided this general service and many specific ones as well. Not the least of these was the creation of a large lake for amphibious maneuvers by Fort Riley personnel. It is perhaps superfluous to point out that in this case climate and geography worked to the disadvantage of a Western location because of the aridity of the West. It is a climate of little rainfall and few lakes or large bodies of water. Many of the latter that do exist there are the products of energetic congressmen, senators, and mayors rather than God or nature.

The chapters on Charleston, Norfolk, Nassau County, and Los Angeles illustrate the same point in a different way. As George Hopkins and Christopher Silver have documented, neither Charleston nor Norfolk was regarded as a strategic location until the navy was under pressure from local boosters. Several other geographic locales would have been suitable. By the same token, the simultaneous development of a defense-dependent aircraft industry in Nassau County (Long Island) and Los Angeles County demonstrates that the aircraft industry could rise and prosper in two quite different geographic locales. The subsequent growth of the industry at Seattle, Wichita, St. Louis, and Atlanta merely reemphasizes the point. Obviously, climate and geography were hardly decisive.

Strategic considerations offer similarly little comfort. The U.S. airframe industry was more, not less, vulnerable in maritime Nassau and Los Angeles counties than it would have been in alternative and more central locations. As previously noted, Charleston and Norfolk invented much of their own strategic rationale. It would be hard to argue, for example, that Charleston was significantly more strategically located vis-à-vis our commitments in either Latin America, Africa, or Europe than Savannah or that Norfolk was markedly superior to Baltimore. Junction City might have been strategic in the days of Sitting Bull and Custer, but hardly in the twentieth century. Moreover, as the weapons of war have become more deadly and threaten from every direction, the idea of a strategic location for any place becomes harder and harder to sustain.

The impact of war certainly would better explain the placement of military resources. World War I built up Norfolk and Charleston; World War II enriched San Antonio, Los Angeles County, Nassau County, Junction City, and many other locales. However, as we have seen, the strategic alliances between the city and the sword preceded these global conflicts. War certainly enhanced the phenomenon we are looking at, but, except in the case of Junction City, it did not create it.

Corporate power, the nature of capitalism, and regional and national economic patterns explain even less. Corporate power, for example, had little to do with creating the relationships that eventuated in the martial metropolises considered here. Neither capitalist nor corporate power, nor regional economic development, nor industrialism influenced the origins of the martial metropolis except in a negative sort of way. Almost invariably, the martial metropolis was strongest where capitalism, industrialism, corporate power, and broader patterns of economic development were weakest or less mature. In fact, cities with an interest in military resources tended to be smaller and much less industrialized. The martial metropolises were created where corporate power, capitalist development, and regional economic maturity had not already produced a more modern economy. The martial metropolis was a substitute for these things, not a product of them.

San Antonio did not become a great military aviation center when some corporation kicked in money to lure the army air force; it became that when the city government came up with a subsidy.

The aircraft industries of Nassau County and Los Angeles County began as infant industries in the interwar period when real capitalists would not touch an investment in the aircraft business and when military orders were at a minimum. The development of the martial metropolis was not dependent upon the demands of the broader economy, nor did it broaden the local economy. City boosters hoped that military investment would prime the pump of economic development and eventually turn their simple economies into complex ones through the process of economic diversification. At least in the short run, this did not happen. Ironically, the investment of military monies narrowed the economic bases of the martial metropolises at the very time that it broadened their morphologies. It would be too much to label these cities as metropolitan-military monocultures, but they clearly were headed in that direction. Like Detroit's marriage to the automobile, Toledo's affair with tires, and Peoria's affection for crawler tractors, the partnership between the city and the sword produced dependence instead of independence except insofar as suburban independence from its center city was concerned.

Yet, clearly, these were affairs of the heart. No one forced cities into their partnerships—neither corporate contractors, nor scheming generals in the Pentagon, nor anyone else. U.S. cities took on these relationships knowingly and with their eyes open, and it is perhaps this aspect of the story that illuminates military as well as urban history. Certainly it is less than accurate to label what we have seen in this anthology as a military-industrial complex because the origins were urban or metropolitan or both instead of industrial. The word industrial is too imprecise to characterize these partnerships and at the same time implies a link to industrialism that obviously did not exist. Second, the urban origins of the interface between military and civilian sectors indicate the democratic nature of this tie. The marriage between the city and the sword was one involving people at the top as well as at the bottom of society. One does not have to cite the returns from Congressman Rivers's many election victories to realize that people other than merely Pentagonese, corporate executives, and those of similarly high status are creators and supporters of what President Dwight Eisenhower mistakenly called the military-industrial complex. The democratic nature of this tie also refutes the idea that the United States was uniformly moved by antimilitarism in the interwar years. That evaluation may have been true of the majority, but our research reveals an important minority who found the military quite congenial. If antimilitarism has been one of the country's central values through the years, as historians like Walter Millis have argued,[10] then the process of urbanization has had something to do with modifying those values in the twentieth century. And finally, it is obvious that whether we call the

civilian-military interface a military-industrial complex or a
metropolitan-military complex, its origins antedate World War II,
the cold war, and the rise of the supposed Communist menace abroad.
These events have been used to explain the rise of the military-
civilian link that is so influential today, but, of course, the partnership arose much earlier.

The martial metropolis, then, contributes to our knowledge
and understanding of both military and urban history. It does so
primarily through the importance of the city as an independent variable. In a sense, even the chapters that do not illustrate the theme
of the imperial city highlight that of the independent variable. Nassau
County towns did not put on an energetic campaign to secure the aviation industry, but one can scarcely explain its presence there without
reference to the various assets provided by the New York Metropolitan Region. As Geoffrey Rossano points out, the industry needed the
wide-open spaces of Long Island and the ocean in which to train, but
it also drew on the crowded spaces of the island as well. The fledgling business needed publicity, money, capital equipment and buildings, a market, financial support, and skilled labor. Aviation found
all of these assets in the city, although the market there was less of
an asset than the military one. Urban crowds, old buildings, spare
cash, a concentrated labor market, and a taste for excitement and
innovation all helped to sustain an industry devastated by the cancellation of wartime contracts in 1918. In this case, geographic advantages, government patronage, and urban assets produced a new
industry. None by itself would have been sufficient to do the job.

The experience of Cincinnati and that of the Pacific Northwest
make the same point. Cincinnati was influenced by World War II to
the extent of successfully competing to secure an aircraft factory,
taking minimal steps toward racial integration, and moving slowly
toward public housing. However, as Zane Miller and Robert Fairbanks document beyond cavil, the city builders' conception of the
metropolis, not the exigencies of war, was the controlling factor.
Cincinnati would be planned the way Cincinnati boosters wanted it
planned rather than shaped by the war, and local urban strategy
would not change until the same class of leaders gained a new perception of the metropolis. The war did not alter the local view of
city planning in Portland and Seattle either. Although World War II
created enormous interest in city planning, that art definitely took
a backseat to urban growth in both Northwest cities, as Carl Abbott
demonstrates.

In short, whether we are considering the five cities that
actively sought to become martial metropolises, or those like Nassau
County that did so willy-nilly, or New York City that let slip its own
military resources, or Cincinnati, Portland, and Seattle that accepted

the influence of war but on their own terms, the independent variable stands out. It is downright silly to argue that huge concentrations of population make no contribution to their own fate. It could hardly be otherwise in everything from communications to marketing to voter mobilization to crowd behavior. The martial metropolis allows us to see some of these contributions to several important themes of U.S. urban history.

NOTES

1. David R. Goldfield, Cotton Fields and Skyscrapers: Southern City and Region, 1607-1980 (Baton Rouge: Louisiana State University Press, 1982), pp. 1-11.

2. Letter from Alan Clive to Roger W. Lotchin, Framingham, Massachusetts, July 7, 1981.

3. Bruce M. Stave, ed., "A Conversation with Eric Lampard," in The Making of Urban History: Historiography through Oral History (Beverly Hills, Calif.: Sage Publications, 1977), pp. 253-90.

4. Robert M. Dykstra, The Cattle Towns (New York: Alfred A. Knopf, 1968), pp. 41-55.

5. Blaine A. Brownell, The Urban Ethos in the South, 1920-1930 (Baton Rouge: Louisiana State University Press, 1975), pp. xv-xxi, 1-60.

6. Don Harrison Doyle, The Social Order of a Frontier Community: Jacksonville, Illinois, 1825-1870 (Urbana: University of Illinois Press, 1978), pp. 62-91 ff.

7. Zane L. Miller, Boss Cox's Cincinnati: Urban Politics in the Progressive Era (New York: Oxford University Press, 1968), p. 73.

8. David C. Hammack, Participation in Major Decisions in New York City, 1890-1900: The Creation of Greater New York and the Centralization of the Public School System (Ann Arbor, Mich.: Xerox University Microfilms, 1975), pp. 113-312.

9. Judd Kahn, Imperial San Francisco: Politics and Planning in an American City, 1897-1906 (Lincoln: University of Nebraska Press, 1979), pp. 1-28.

10. Walter Millis, Arms and Men: A Study in American Military History (New York: G. P. Putnam's Sons, 1956), pp. 13-71 ff.

Index

237

240

241

Tunstall, Whit P., 123
Turner, George Kibbe, 4
Tuttle, William B., 90-92, 93, 95, 96, 97, 100, 103
"two-ocean navy," 14

unemployment, 145
United Eastern Airplane, 68
United Mine Workers, 196, 197
U.S. Army, 6, 37, 39, 42, 45, 73, 89, 92-93, 95-97, 98
United States Committee for Economic Development, 202
U.S. Department of Commerce, 180
U.S. Housing Authority, 15
U.S. Maritime Commission, 169, 171, 172
urban: defense subcontracts, 142; economic diversification, 230; frontier, ix; impact on military, 54 [on military strategy, 127]; liberalism, 5; media, 70; morphology, 230; redevelopment, 126
urban-rural tension, 62
urbanism, xi
urbanization, xi, 25, 90, 92, 103, 227

Valley Homes (Cincinnati), 199-200
Van Auken, Henry, 103, 104
Van Nuys (California), 141, 143
Vancouver (Washington), 166, 169, 176
Vanport (Oregon), 172, 182
veterans, 203-04
Veterans Bureau, 154
Veterans Committee of the Cincinnati Metropolitan Housing Authority, 204
Vietnam, 1, 22, 43, 53, 54
Vinson, Carl, Chairman of the House Naval Affairs Committee, 19, 22, 52
Virginian-Pilot (Norfolk), 118
Vogel, Joshua, 174
Vought, Chance, 67, 70

Wacchtler, Sol, 80
Wainwright, Jonathan "Skinny," 38
Waiting Wives Club, 43
Walker, Robert, 164
Wallace, George (N.Y. Rep.), 80
Walnut Hills (Cincinnati), 197, 209, 210
War Assets Administration, 213
War Department, 14
War Plans Division, 9
War Production Transport Commission, 174

Warwick (Virginia), 125-26
Washington, D.C., 155, 157, 224
Washington State Committee for Post-Victory Employment, 178
Washington State Defense Council, 179
Washington State Planning Council, 178, 179, 180
welfare, xi
Wertenbaker, Thomas, 116
West, the, 228
West End, Cincinnati, 197, 198, 200, 204, 205, 210, 212
West End Expressway, Cincinnati, 210
West Point, 36
Westchester County (New York), 78
Westhampton Air Base, 154
White, Walter, 16
White Sands Proving Ground, 139
Wichita (Kansas), 227, 229
Wilbur, Curtis D., Secretary of the Navy, 10
Wildcat (Grumman), 72, 73
Willamette Iron and Steel Co., 169
Willard, Charles, 66, 67
Wilson, Woodrow, President, 5, 112, 113
Wilson administration, 6
Winton Terrace (Cincinnati, Ohio), 211
Wirth, Louis, 69
Wolfe, Roger, 70
Wood, Joseph D., Major, 122, 123
Wool, Theodore J., 112, 113
Woolridge, Dean, 137, 141, 146
working class, 61
Works Progress Administration (WPA), 195
World War I, ix, x, 17, 18, 23, 38, 67, 68, 72, 75, 81, 92, 93, 96, 101, 104, 111, 113, 116, 117, 120, 122, 126, 173, 229
World War I, impact on aviation, 69, 80
World War II, ix, xi, 18, 23, 36-37, 39, 45, 62, 66, 71, 76, 79, 81, 103, 105, 111, 112, 116, 119, 123, 125, 135, 136, 153, 163, 170, 203, 229, 231
Wright Aeronautical Corporation, 192, 193, 194, 196, 197, 198, 199
Wright brothers, 92
Wydler, John, Nassau Congressman, 79

Yesler Terrace Homes, 173
Yorktown (Virginia), 21
Young Men's Business Club, 91